Peacemaking Strategies in Northern Ireland

Building Complementarity in Conflict
Management Theory

David Bloomfield

Research Fellow
Harvard University
Cambridge, Massachusetts

Published by PALGRAVE MACMILLAN
Houndmills, Basingstoke, Hampshire RG21 6XS and
175 Fifth Avenue, New York, N.Y. 10010
Companies and representatives throughout the world

PALGRAVE MACMILLAN is the global academic imprint of the Palgrave
Macmillan division of St. Martin's Press, LLC and of Palgrave Macmillan Ltd.
Macmillan® is a registered trademark in the United States, United Kingdom
and other countries. Palgrave is a registered trademark in the European
Union and other countries.

Outside North America
ISBN 0–333–67432–4

In North America
ISBN 0–312–16346–0

This book is printed on paper suitable for recycling and
made from fully managed and sustained forest sources.

A catalogue record for this book is available from the British Library.

Library of Congress Catalog Card Number: 96–39086

Transferred to digital printing 2003

Printed and bound in Great Britain by
Antony Rowe Ltd, Chippenham and Eastbourne

For my parents, David and Elisabeth

Contents

List of Tables and Figures   xi

Acknowledgements   xiii

List of Abbreviations and Acronyms   xv

Introduction   1

Northern Ireland in Academic Study   2

The Wider Context   5

1. The Northern Ireland Conflict: Issues and
    Interpretations   8

    1. Issues   9

    2. Interpretations   13

    Conclusion and Summary   22

2. Conflict Management Practice: The Structural
    Approach   24

    1. The Structural Approach   24

    2. British Initiatives, 1969–85   26

    3. The Anglo-Irish Process since 1983   38

    Conclusion and Summary   48

3. Conflict Management Practice: The Cultural
    Approach   50

    1. The Cultural Approach   50

    2. The Northern Ireland Community Relations
       Commission   51

    3. Informal Initiatives   58

    Conclusion and Summary   66

4. Complementarity in Conflict Management Theory:
    Resolution and Settlement Approaches   67

    1. Resolution and Settlement   68

	2. Two Examples: Azar and Bercovitch	71
	3. The Dichotomy in the Literature	76
	4. Towards Complementarity	79
	5. Relating Theory and Practice	84
	6. Criteria for the Model	89
	Conclusion and Summary	94
5.	The Brooke Initiative: An Examination of the Structural Approach to Conflict Management	96
	1. A Documentary Narrative	98
	2. Brooke as Intervenor	115
	Conclusion and Summary	127
6.	The Community Relations Council: An Examination of the Cultural Approach to Conflict Management	133
	1. Background	133
	2. Establishment	138
	3. In Operation, 1990–3	144
	Conclusion and Summary	165
7.	Complementarity in Practice: Northern Ireland	169
	1. The Potential for Complementarity	170
	2. The British Government and Complementarity	178
	3. The Community Relations Council and Complementarity	180
	Conclusion and Summary	190
8.	A Model of Complementarity in Conflict Management	196
	1. Complexity in Conflict: Implications for Model-building	198
	2. A Model of Complementarity in Conflict Management	203
	Conclusion and Summary	215

9. Concluding Remarks   217
    1. Complementarity   217
    2. Northern Ireland   221
    Appendix: Biographical Details of Interviewees   224
    Notes   227
    Bibliography   230
    Index   236

List of Tables and Figures

Table 4.1 The Four Escalation Stages and their Six Axes   82

Figure 8.1 A Model of Complementarity in Conflict Management   208

Acknowledgements

The research for this book was funded through a scholarship from the Geraldine and Barrow S. Cadbury Trust, and carried out under the auspices of the Department of Peace Studies at Bradford University, England. My gratitude to both institutions is deep and lasting.

Many individuals influenced the project in significantly positive ways. In particular, I owe a huge debt to Tom Woodhouse, James O'Connell and Seamus Dunn for their invaluable insight and help. Additionally, colleagues at Bradford provided vital support, among them Maeve Lankford, Michael von Tangen Page, Oliver Ramsbotham, Andrew Rigby and Kirsten Sparre.

This work would have been meaningless without the cooperation of those whom I interviewed: Peter Brooke, Joan Broder, Mari Fitzduff, Joe Hinds, David McKittrick, Martin O'Brien and Jerry Tyrrell. Their wisdom, experience and insight into affairs in Northern Ireland was a solid rock upon which to build. I have tried to reflect their words and their intentions with the accuracy they deserve. Any additional analysis is, of course, my responsibility.

Finally, the greatest thanks of all go to Kate McGuinness, for her support, her insight, her editing skills, her creative thought, her patience and understanding, and so much more that could never be expressed here.

List of Abbreviations and Acronyms

AIC	Anglo-Irish Intergovernmental Conference (instrument of Anglo-Irish Agreement 1985)
Alliance	The Alliance Party of Northern Ireland
CAJ	Committee on the Administration of Justice
CCRU	Central Community Relations Unit, NIO
CMN	Conflict and Mediation Network
CRC	Community Relations Council
CRO	Community Relations Officer (employee of Local District Council)
DENI	Department of Education (Northern Ireland)
DUP	Democratic Unionist Party
EMU	Education for Mutual Understanding
HOG	Holiday Organisations Group
INLA	Irish National Liberation Army, republican paramilitary group
IRA	Irish Republican Army, republican paramilitary group
NICRC	Northern Ireland Community Relations Commission, 1969–74
NIF	New Ireland Forum
NIO	Northern Ireland Office (British government)
NIPF	Northern Ireland Peace Forum
NIVT	Northern Ireland Voluntary Trust
PACE	Protestant And Catholic Encounter
PUP	Progressive Unionist Party
RIR	Royal Irish Regiment (previously UDR)
RUC	Royal Ulster Constabulary
SACHR	Standing Advisory Commission on Human Rights
SDLP	Social Democratic and Labour Party
Stormont	Seat of Northern Irish parliament, 1921–72, Belfast; site of NIO, 1972–
TPI	Third Party Intervention
UDA	Ulster Defence Association, loyalist paramilitary group
UDP	Ulster Democratic Party
UDR	Ulster Defence Regiment, British army 1972–92 (now RIR)

UFF	Ulster Freedom Fighters, *nom de guerre* of UDA
UUP	Ulster Unionist Party, sometimes known as Official Unionist Party (OUP)
UVF	Ulster Volunteer Force, loyalist paramilitary group
UWC	Ulster Workers' Council (strike coordinating committee, 1974)

Introduction

I have read very widely in the general literature on conflict,
hoping to pick up ideas which would help me to understand
the Northern Ireland problem more clearly.
It has been largely a waste of time.

(John Whyte 1990, p. 252)

It is not my aim here to use the tools of conflict management
theory to illuminate or explain the Northern Ireland conflict.
Both the scope of such a task and the arrogance implicit in it are
enough to persuade me otherwise. On the contrary, my central
focus in this book is an attempt to address a specific problem in
conflict management theory by reference to the realities of
Northern Ireland. In that sense, the Northern Ireland conflict
serves here to illuminate the theory, rather than the reverse. My
main question is: what can practical peacemaking strategies in
Northern Ireland teach us about conflict management theory and
about how to improve that theory? The question of what conflict
theory can offer to peacemakers in Northern Ireland or elsewhere
I will leave to braver souls.

In a sense, then, the information about Northern Ireland
contained here is offered in a supporting role to the main
theoretical discussion of Chapters 4 and 8. Nevertheless, it does
amount to six chapters of data and analysis, comprising the bulk
of the book, and I trust it can also interest and inform in its own
right.

Put simply, what follows involves an examination, through a
case-study approach to a real situation of protracted social
conflict, of the two poles of current thinking in conflict management at the theoretical level: that which favours power-bargaining, negotiation and compromise to achieve settlement over
issues, and that which promotes non-negotiated, cooperative
problem-solving to achieve deep and integrative solution. For
convenience the two approaches can be styled respectively 'settlement' and 'resolution'.

I argue that this dichotomisation of the two theoretical approaches is exaggerated, and that both approaches have a validity
and a salience which should be employed in a complementary,

rather than an oppositional, way. To this end, the argument is
made for a model of complementarity in conflict management
which embraces both approaches concurrently. In the process of
developing this central argument about complementarity, I also
perforce reflect upon the business of model-building and theorising, and so to a degree I also seek to contribute to the understanding of the methodologies of conflict research and analysis.
In particular, the case is made for the importance of an inductively informed element in theorising, and for the need to
'field-test' theories and models against the realities they try to
explain.

Throughout, I use 'conflict management' as a neutral umbrella term to cover the entire field of study, both theory and
practice. This is necessarily somewhat artificial. Like every other
available term – conflict resolution, conflict transformation, and
so on – in a literature where there is little consistency of
terminology, its use varies according to the context, the author or
the school of thought; but in the absence of a generally accepted
term for the area of study that has not been given an extra or
subsidiary meaning, 'conflict management' should be read as
denoting no particular type of practical or theoretical approach
to conflict, but merely as a general title within which I will frame
my argument.

NORTHERN IRELAND IN ACADEMIC STUDY

To those who live within it, any social conflict is far more than
an interesting problem for analysis. Their personal involvement –
which of necessity includes some degree of partiality and prescription – is integrally a part of their analysis of the conflict. But
such involvement does not of itself disqualify them from participating in the wider analytical debate about either that particular
situation or about conflict in general. At the outset, then, I
acknowledge my own stake in the conflict in Northern Ireland: I
am involved, both in the general sense that I was born in Belfast
and have lived there through the greater part of the current
Troubles, and also more specifically through my participation, in
a small way, during the 1980s in community-level mediation and
reconciliation initiatives. I would argue, however, that such
intimate familiarity with the subject matter of this study will play

a role that is positive in its detailed knowledge and sensitivity, rather than negative in its partiality.

The current phase of the Northern Ireland Troubles represents Europe's most enduring post-war armed conflict. The overt violence of the Troubles, dating from 1968 to the 1994 ceasefires, claimed the lives of around 3168 people (*Guardian*, 31 August 1994), caused injury to ten times as many more, resulted in property damage estimated in billions of pounds, and caused grave, long-term damage to the economic and social infrastructure of the region. Additionally, the protracted nature of the violence has, through a process of institutionalisation that has spanned a generation, produced profound effects in structural and societal aspects, which are less amenable to quantification; for example, the spread and normalisation of paramilitarism, the growth of intimidation as a constraint on social behaviour, the growth of the 'security industry', the decline of the economic base, and so on.

For a variety of reasons, this conflict has been the subject of a great deal of academic study from a range of disciplines. One reason is perhaps its proximity, geographically and culturally, for many Western English-speaking academic establishments; likewise, it is similarly proximate for a corresponding media; thirdly, its very endurance has appeared almost reassuringly predictable; and fourthly, there is (or was at least until the late 1980s) the peculiarity of such a protracted conflict in an otherwise generally pacified Western Europe. Perhaps – especially in First World eyes – it is simply the most accessible and stable conflict for study.

Whatever the particular reasons, academic interest, like media interest, in Northern Ireland has been intense from virtually all the social sciences (see, for example, Whyte 1990). After a long period of neglect, since the violence flared again in the late 1960s, sociologists, psychologists, political scientists, social geographers, historians and many others have been busy for over two decades, with the result that 'it is quite possible that, in proportion to size, Northern Ireland is the most heavily researched area on earth' (Whyte 1990, p. viii).

With the notable exception of those geographically within or close to Northern Ireland, conflict theorists have to some degree lagged behind the enthusiasm of their colleagues. While Northern Ireland is frequently cited by them in lists of conflicts in a somewhat summary manner, little specific attention has been paid to it *per se*, and few detailed studies of any note carried out. This is regrettable, particularly given that, since 1968, Northern Ireland has served as something of a laboratory for peacemaking experiments by actors involved in the conflict. In so far as the conflict remains unresolved, none of these attempts can be described as completely successful. But while that underscores the complexity and protracted nature of the conflict, it does not support the outright dismissal of these attempts.

At both the political level and the community level, there have been numerous initiatives between 1968 and the present aimed at furthering or achieving some kind of settlement. For example, at the political level, the British government has made several attempts since 1972 to implement some form of devolved governmental system in Northern Ireland, or at least some formal negotiation process towards that end. At the community level, there are many examples from the myriad projects which have developed since the 1970s under the banners of 'reconciliation' or 'community relations': cross-community contact schemes, ecumenical groupings and groundswell movements such as the Peace People. Not only the researchers are busy in Northern Ireland: peace groups and initiatives abound at the community level to the point where a small but significant peace-related 'industry' has become at least partly institutionalised.

In so far as the conflict remains unresolved, these attempts at conflict management have frequently been dismissed as failures. I would argue that this is as inaccurate and misguided as post-ceasefire assertions that because the violence had been halted, the conflict was 'over'. Northern Ireland was not 'at peace': under the IRA ceasefire it was relatively free from violence, which is a very different, and much less positive, thing. Likewise, with post-ceasefire hindsight, the suspicion, perhaps even the conviction, grows stronger that many of the earlier 'failed' initiatives in fact contributed significantly, if implicitly, to the removal of violence. To dismiss these efforts is not only wrong but counter-productive. The alternative view, which informs the argument to be presented here, is that these various practical attempts should be examined for their partial worth (rather than their total failure), not least in informing theory, and furthermore should be seen not as completely discrete events, but rather as component experimental parts of a continuing and dynamic process, as elements in a sequence which can – even if only with hindsight – be recognised as coherent to some degree.

THE WIDER CONTEXT

In the broader context of Europe, these experiments in peace-making over 20 years and more have a significance outside Northern Ireland itself:

> The end of the Cold War has 'unfrozen' those aspects of international, regional, and intranational conflicts which had been contained within the dynamics of East–West relations. The most important consequences of these changes and the major dilemma to be faced in the post-Cold War international system is that the management of these conflicts has become increasingly complex. (Hoffman 1992, p. 262)

Mark Hoffman argues convincingly that raising the Cold War fire-blanket has exposed a smouldering abundance of conflicts over

> the protection and attainment of . . . material interests, the preservation of the historical and cultural values of a community, and the fulfilment of the need for some form of recognised identity. (ibid., pp. 261–2)

The narrow, containment-oriented strategies of coercion and crisis-management which prevailed during the era of superpower rivalry have been exposed as virtually impotent in the face of a wave of reinvigorated ethnic or communal conflicts in Europe. The realist approach has been found crudely ineffectual and simplistic in dealing with the psychological complexities of dis-agreements over such factors as identities and cultures. There is a pressing need to broaden the general definitions, under-standings and strategies towards conflict in order to embrace a wider comprehension of the role of such explosive factors.

So it is pertinent to examine the evidence of Europe's most enduring manifest conflict for any clues about the means to address such issues. The misfortune of Northern Ireland's popu-lation is to have benefited the interested researcher with 26 years of a violent communal conflict which is amenable to study. Given the current European context of the 1990s, it behoves researchers to examine this rich source of data for any indications of how one might more quickly and more effectively reconstruct a peacemaking strategy sufficiently broad and flexible to encompass the resurgent significance of ethnic/communal conflict.

In this sense, then, Northern Ireland can be viewed as a real-world laboratory, where practical experiments in conflict management have been developed and evolved for a sustained period. Such a viewpoint permits a constructive examination of the processes involved to see what lessons can be learnt about the practical workings of conflict theories. Viewed as such, both the conflict itself and these attempts at solutions provide the basis for a case study for testing hypotheses from conflict management theory.

Most of the research on which this study is based was completed before the ceasefires of late 1994. The ceasefires, 18 months old at the time of writing and looking increasingly fragile, are the most significant dynamic for change that Northern Ireland has seen for many years. None the less, for my purposes in this book, the applications and illustrations drawn from Northern Ireland remain relevant and pertinent to the wider case that I am attempting to make in conflict-management theory. Indeed, the new context taking shape in Northern Ireland will simply provide a new and better testing ground for the ideas I promote in the pages that follow.

Finally, a few notes on the text.

In the sections of the book dealing with Northern Ireland, I refer to the two communities there by the terms Protestant and Catholic. This is not intended to imply any greater significance for the role of religion in the conflict than is attributed to it in Chapter 1. The terminology is chosen simply because (1) those are the common usage terms for the communities among the people of Northern Ireland themselves; (2) in such common usage, the terms imply an allegiance to a certain cultural heritage rather than a particular method of religious observance; and (3) these terms, while occasionally inaccurate, are both more accurate more of the time and less ungainly all of the time than the alternatives, such as majority and minority communities (with their judgemental implications), or unionists and nationalists (accurate only in the narrower political or voting senses).

The word Unionist, used with a capital letter, indicates a formal relation to either or both of the Unionist political parties.

Used without capitalisation (unionist), it refers to the broader unionist-voting community.

All quotations from written sources are referenced fully in the text; all unreferenced quotations are taken from interviews with the author. Biographical notes on interviewees can be found in the Appendix.

1 The Northern Ireland Conflict: Issues and Interpretations

My aim here is not to make yet another contribution to the already swollen numbers of academic analyses of Northern Ireland. Nor do I claim that what follows is in any way a comprehensive review of the conflict there. I wish merely to sketch an overview of those elements of the conflict which are most pertinent to the argument I want to develop in later chapters. There are many excellent analyses already in existence, and I will simply enlist the help of extant scholarly work, rather than try to replace it with further analysis.

In understanding any conflict, it is vital to grasp as precisely as possible what are the substantive issues. The issues enable us to answer the 'what?' questions about the conflict: What is the disagreement over? What is at stake? What do the protagonists want?

But they do not answer the 'why?' questions: they do not fully explain why the conflict should become violent, or widespread, or lethal. In short, while they tell us much about the *content* of the conflict, they do not fully explain the *form* which the conflict takes. For this, we need to look beyond merely the issues to identify the underlying themes, to find out how such issues are interpreted by the protagonists of the conflict, and in particular why these issues are translated by them into matters of life-and-death importance. It is not enough, for example, to explain a conflict in terms of a group of people fighting for political control of their country; we must try to discover why they should feel the need to turn it into a violent fight, why they prioritise it so, why it is so overarchingly important, why it becomes literally more important than life itself.

This chapter will first review scholarly analysis of what the conflicting issues in Northern Ireland are, and then proceed to look at the broader question of where those issues lie in the minds of the protagonists. From this latter exploration some understanding may be achieved of how and why priorities are chosen that transform what might be simply spirited political debate into bitter war. These underlying themes, concerning perception among protagonists, 'are the conditions which give rise to lively controversy [or] deadly quarrel' (Deutsch 1991, p. 27).

1. ISSUES

A consensual view on the issues of the Northern Ireland conflict is difficult to achieve in detail. In the first place, despite the volume of research to date, scholarly consensus is minimal. As Whyte says,

> Researchers appear to have reached unanimity only on the barest matters of fact. . . . Thus, after twenty years of study by hundreds of researchers, there is still only partial agreement on the nature of the problem, and none at all on the nature of the solution. (1990, pp. 244–6)

Additionally, the boundaries between impartial scholarly analysis and partial political analysis are blurred, not least because acknowledged experts on the conflict are often members of the society they study and, almost by definition as commentators in the public domain, actors in that same conflict. So in a conflict where historical themes are so significant, opposing historiographies will be well developed. Alvin Jackson comments that

> [For] the Irish, north and south . . . their historical inheritance, though different in context, shares the same form. . . . History for all the Irish is a mantra of sacred dates, an invocation of secular saints: though the enshrouding flags differ, the martyr's coffin is a shared icon. (1989, p. 58)

Some of these historiographies are blatantly polemic with political self-interest, and for purposes of serious analysis they can easily be identified and read in that context. But the indisputable integrity of many scholars who nevertheless work from particular political standpoints, for example, the nationalist historian Michael Farrell or the unionist historian A.T.Q. Stewart, precludes such treatment.

None the less, several analysts have presented summaries of the various theories of the conflict which overlap significantly. We might choose almost arbitrarily among them, including those of

Whyte (1990), Lijphart (1975), O'Leary (1985) or Hunter (1982) (although Lijphart's approach, of Northern Ireland as a case-study in comparative politics, is perhaps less readily useful to this particular discussion). All will agree that no one theory provides a full explanation, but serves to identify a particular set of factors salient to the conflict. John Hunter, for example, identifies four sets of theories, each of which highlights a different set of issues: the political, the religious, the economic and the psychological. The basis of the political theories, says Hunter, is that:

> Put crudely, Northern Ireland's one million Protestants believe the maintenance of the Northern Ireland state is the only means of securing their future. On the other hand, the half million Catholics in Northern Ireland believe they can only secure their future within a united Ireland. (1982, p. 15)

The political theory has its roots in the history of Ireland and Anglo-Irish relations over several centuries. Such an exclusively political view depends on the close way in which the religious dichotomy in Northern Ireland parallels the political divide. The religious labels serve primarily as badges of identity, rather than indicating the existence of any truly religious or doctrinal disagreement. Only for the small numbers of religious fundamentalists in both communities, however, could the conflict be said to be in any primary sense a religious conflict. James O'Connell neatly describes religion as a 'boundary factor' of the Northern Ireland conflict, rather than a causal factor: like colour in South Africa, or language in Belgium, he argues, the boundary factor 'is used both as a mark of distinguishing and as a basis of organisation' for each camp (O'Connell 1990, p. 48). Theories of a religious conflict also depend on what Hunter calls the 'symbiotic relationship which exists between political and religious institutions' (1982, p. 32). But rather than serving merely as tools for identification,

> the traditional values of the two protagonists largely flow from their different religious faiths. Thus not only do different religious principles to a large extent define the social and cultural values of the two communities, they also serve to differentiate and consolidate them. (ibid.)

One might think of two armies facing each other on a battlefield. While they wear different uniforms in order to distinguish themselves from each other, and while those uniforms may well include symbols of their differing allegiances in the broader conflict that has brought them into confrontation, they are certainly not fighting the battle over who has the better uniform. Similarly, Northern Ireland's Catholics and Protestants are not engaged in bloody conflict over the correct way to worship a Christian god. The religious labels gain their deepest salience from their references to heritage or culture, rather than religious observance, which explains why an individual could be a committed atheist while still meaningfully pledging allegiance to the Protestant or Catholic community.

Of the economic theories of the conflict, Hunter is quite dismissive. Although history again provides some support for the thesis – notably, the displacements of the Plantation, the location in the north-east of industrial development, and so on – Hunter regards any causal relationship between economic factors and violence as questionable. The economic theories tend to spring from Marxist analysis, or from theories of relative deprivation, but Hunter will concede only that economic factors may exacerbate, rather than cause, the conflict.

He argues that psychological factors are similarly more contributory than causal. Psychological theories involve analysis of the Northern Ireland communities in terms of in-groups and out-groups, by which they maintain group solidarity by comparing their own (in-group) positive qualities with the perceived inferiority of the out-group. The process involves stereotyping of the out-group(s), and may also lead to scapegoating of the other to lay the blame for imperfections outside the in-group. Psychological factors will gain much greater salience as I consider the underlying themes of the conflict; but at this point Hunter is quite correct to minimise their contribution to the creation of actual issues of contention. He sums up his review by giving primacy to political factors, 'because of their causal significance' (1982, p. 53).

Whyte (1990) uses the same four categories to list those aspects which cause the division in Northern Irish society: political aspects (different political and constitutional aspirations, different party allegiances, opposing views on security policy); religious aspects (religious segregation, differences of philosophical outlook stemming from religious thinking); economic aspects (an economic differential between Catholics and Protestants, due in part to discrimination); and psychological aspects (insecurity which produces intense concern with identity, particularly among Protestants).

But when describing the variety of interpretations of the conflict, Whyte, like Hunter, gives primacy to the political issues, and differentiates between those older models, which see the dispute as Britain–Ireland-oriented, and the more recent 'internal conflict' model, which places the conflicting communities and identities within Northern Ireland. This is an important distinction, reflecting a development of thinking which coincides with the outbreak of violence in the late 1960s, and which was perhaps demanded in order to explain the post-1960s realities of Northern Ireland.[1]

This is in turn similar to Brendan O'Leary's distinction between exogenous and endogenous explanations of the conflict:

> Exogenous explanations situate NI [sic] in the network of Anglo-Irish state relations and/or imperialism. 'Solutions' require international transformations. Endogenous explanations analyse NI as largely autonomous of exogenous influences. 'Solutions' may employ exogenous instruments but the 'problems' are endogenous. (1985, p. 36)

O'Leary's 'exogenous' category includes traditional nationalism, which identifies British imperialism and its 'artificial border' as the cause of conflict; traditional unionism, which blames irredentism in the Irish Republic for preventing a peaceful Northern Ireland state; and what O'Leary, with some humour, dismisses as respectively orange and green Marxism. The 'endogenous' category comprises those theories that are not overtly nationalist, unionist or Marxist: atavism and 'tribal' thinking; psychological theories; theories of relative deprivation (corresponding to Hunter's economic category); and the model of Northern Ireland as a pluralist society.

All these issues, then, weave together in such a way that, in Hunter's words,

> the conflict flows from and is intensified by a complex interplay of various political, social, cultural, religious, economic and psychological forces which generally operate in a single direction to drive the two communities in Northern Ireland further apart. (1982, p. 52)

In short, the issues of the conflict are interwoven from many strands, but causality gives primacy to those political/historical issues which have evolved from centuries of Anglo-Irish relations and the 70-year history of the Northern Ireland state, and are distilled into the central issue of the future sovereignty of Northern Ireland, which forms 'the problem at the root of the conflict – the future constitutional position of Northern Ireland' (Hunter 1982, p. 52).

As both British and Irish government papers on the conflict have agreed, the fundamental problem of Northern Ireland since its formation to the present has been

> disagreement not just about how Northern Ireland should be governed, but as to whether it should continue to exist at all. (Cmnd. 5259, 1973)[2]

This 'constitutional question' is one of structures, institutions, systems of government or control. The analysis so far gives us some understanding of how various political-historical elements interact around this central constitutional question. But while it describes the issues in contention – the *content* of the conflict – it does not explain the *form* of the conflict, that is to say, why these issues promote conflict to such a lethal degree. These theories are useful tools for improving our understanding of what the protagonists are talking about in the conflict, but they are limited in explaining the process of the conflict itself. Desmond Rea comments that,

> The conflict in Northern Ireland is one between different traditions, identities and allegiances. Cultural identity, religious belief, and loyalty to one's group are basic to all who live there. (1982, p. 1)

To appreciate how 'basic to all' such concepts are, and at what depth they operate to spur 'ordinary' people into the extraordinary context of lethal conflict, the interpretational themes underlying those issues must be uncovered. This involves a shift away from observing the 'objective' issues of the conflict, as this chapter has attempted to do so far, and a concentration on the more 'subjective' interpretations of the conflict by the protagonists.

2. INTERPRETATIONS

If political issues around the central constitutional question are at the heart of the conflict in Northern Ireland, then it is necessary to examine how both communities interpret these issues. And since the issues have their roots in centuries of history, both communities have had ample time to produce highly developed historiographies:

> A fundamental aspect of the Irish tragedy is that the past is continually and ritually sacrificed to a caricature of the present. Threads are plucked from both past and present, and woven into a smothering blanket of a uniform green or orange, or red, white and blue. A monochrome history deceives only a minority, but it is the few, purblind zealots who have sculpted so much of our environment. (Jackson 1989, p. 58)

At this level of analysis, one must try to understand the nature of the separate identities that have developed and been maintained by both cultural groupings, and how such cultural entities both filter the respective views of, and aspirations for, the conflict and fuel its dynamics. In other words, what must be examined is the matter of how the issues surrounding the constitutional question are both formed and interpreted by the two cultural identities.

In a very real sense, the fact or fiction of these mythologies matters far less than the degree to which they shape the present-day sense of heritage:

> What may have actually happened is of much less significance than what people believe happened. It is on the basis of the latter that the actions of people involved in the present conflict are determined. (Hunter 1982, p. 10)

Thus what is most important, irrespective of what may be historically accurate, is how the protagonists today understand their histories, what they see as the stakes in their dispute, and how they define themselves and each other. These strands of thought can be analysed as they pertain to both the Catholic and Protestant communities in Northern Ireland, in order to understand the way that these cultural identities impinge on the conflict situation; to see not only how they differentiate themselves from each other, but also how they view the possibilities for a reconciliation between them.

The Protestants

In a perceptive article, Jennifer Todd (1987) identified two traditions within Northern Ireland Protestant political culture, according to the 'imagined community' of each group. On the one hand is the Ulster loyalist culture, 'defined by its primary imagined community of Northern Protestants'; on the other, the Ulster British tradition 'is defined by its primary imagined community of Greater Britain' (1987, p. 1). A similar distinction has been noted by other researchers: Richard Rose (1971) identifies 'ultra' loyalists and moderates; Frank Wright (1973) distinguishes between extreme and liberal Protestants.

For Todd, Ulster loyalism gives primary allegiance to the Northern Ireland Protestant community, and only a secondary allegiance to Britain, which is conditional and contractarian and directed more at the symbol of the Crown rather than at any specific parliamentary or governmental entity.

With Ulster loyalism, Protestantism of the evangelical kind is important to defining self-identity, exterior threats and enemies. Indeed at its most extreme, among a small but significant minority in the population, such a religious outlook transcends the political, relegating politics to a means of waging the eternal struggle of evangelical Protestant truth over the forces of evil and darkness. A flavour of this worldview can be gained from this extract from the *New Protestant Telegraph* (edited by Ian Paisley):

> In that [evangelical Protestant] faith our fathers brought us up, in that faith many of us have found everlasting life, in that faith, please God, we shall die, and in that faith for our children we shall carry on the holding of this Province which we love and for which we will die, if necessary, rather than surrender.... [I]f we don't win this battle all is lost. It is a matter of life and death. It is a matter of Ulster or the Irish Republic. It is a matter of freedom or slavery. It is a matter of light or darkness. (*New Protestant Telegraph*, September 1995, p. 4)

Such extreme reasoning permits Protestant demands for control of their own state on the basis of a God-given right earned religiously, which transcends any democratic obligations. This kind of divinely justified self-image of evangelical Protestantism does not permit any great degree of tolerance or political flexibility. The same viewpoint of binary oppositions, however, translates more broadly into the political realm: Ulster loyalism deals in absolute positions, in dualist perceptions. Todd describes this as 'the absolutist binary structure of Ulster loyalist thought', arguing that 'the ideological structure of Ulster loyalism is such that loyalists see dominance as the only means of preserving their identity' (1987, p. 10).

Steve Bruce argues further that this kind of Protestantism is a core element of the communal identity even among secular members, because

> for Ulster Protestants, the conflict is a religious conflict, not because it is about religious or even socio-moral issues . . . but because their religion is the core of their shared identity. The more that they are threatened, the more important that identity becomes. (Bruce 1990, p. 166)

Thus is laid the foundation of what is often termed the 'siege mentality' of Northern Irish Protestants. Such a brand of self-definition thrives best under perceived threat. In the words of Gregory Campbell, a Democratic Unionist Party (DUP) councillor, 'We cherish our British identity more *because* it is under threat' (Channel 4 TV, 1992).

In secular political terms, the Ulster loyalist philosophy imbues the thinking primarily of the DUP, with its preference for devolved government and its rejection of substantive power-sharing, and the other hard-line groupings, including the paramilitaries of the Ulster Defence Association (UDA) and their associated political party the Ulster Democratic Party (UDP), and of the Ulster Volunteer Force (UVF) and their associated Progressive Unionist Party (PUP). While these and other strands might have differing shades of opinion on the merits of devolution within the United Kingdom or independence for the Northern state, to a large degree they share deep and abiding anti-British sentiments and distrust of Whitehall.

In contrast, in the Ulster British tradition, loyalty, identity and external threats are more politically, and less religiously, defined: the 'imagined community' is that of the United Kingdom, with Northern Ireland as constituent part. The influence of religion leans more towards that of the libertarian strand in Protestantism, with its elements of individualism and tolerance, than to the exclusive, elitist and sectarian nature of its absolutist strand. This tradition is exemplified in the much more numerous, more mainstream and more middle-class supporters of the Ulster Unionist Party (UUP). For Todd 'the underlying patterns of landscape, thought and political culture upon which Ulster British ideology is based, express nothing of the loyalist sense of threat and insecurity' (1987, p. 11). To this degree, Ulster British ideology is more positively constructed, drawing confidence from a centuries-long link rather than embracing insecurity from a centuries-long threat.

As Todd admits, 'many Northern Protestants . . . have a foot in each camp and share aspects of each ideology' (1987, p. 2). While the two camps differ in their prioritisation of the 'imagined communities' of Northern Protestants or of the United Kingdom, nevertheless they each utilise a blend of both.

What is most pertinent in these observations is that they are all describing the various ways in which Protestants define their identity. In short, they do so both in inclusive terms (by identifying with the greater entity of the United Kingdom, with Protestantism, with Northern Ireland) and in exclusive terms (by distinguishing themselves from Catholics, from the Irish Republic, from nationalists). And it is in the concepts surrounding identity that they describe themselves and the conflict. Whether their own identity is primarily Protestant, or Northern, or British, or a mix of all three, it is a key to their explanation of the conflict, since it is the key to their interpretation and understanding of the issues. Some examples may help.

Two Protestant academics, Fred Boal and David Livingstone, in describing Protestant reaction to the Anglo-Irish Agreement, commented that, despite intensive perusal and criticism of the Agreement's text by Protestants,

> no voice seems to have been raised about one assumption running the length and breadth [of the Agreement], namely, that Northern Ireland houses 'two communities,' 'two traditions,' each with its own distinctive 'cultural heritage'. (1986, p. 169)

Proceeding to identify a significant degree of diversity within Protestant culture, and commenting that to some extent 'what unites Ulster Protestants, it seems, is a determined sense of what they are not' (ibid., p. 174), none the less they concluded that, with regard to 'Reformation Protestantism', 'this religious core is the prime source of cultural identity even for those now on its periphery. . . . Protecting the theology demands safeguarding the geography' (ibid., p. 174).

The Belfast psychologist A.M. Gallagher carried out a study in 1982 in which representatives of the various political entities were asked: 'What would your party describe as being the Northern Ireland problem?' As quoted by Whyte, the UUP response was: 'There is a conflict between two different national identities and national aspirations' (Whyte 1990, p. 203).

While in this study the DUP spokesperson described the situation more in terms of a security problem caused by the IRA, another publication by a leading DUP member exemplifies the party's emphasis on identity and the existence of separate cultures. From the time of the Plantation of Ulster, claims Jim Allister,

> the Province of Ulster developed its own way of life, values, identity and allegiance . . . a culture and way of life which reflects its distinctly British and Protestant heritage. (Allister nd, p. 7)

Allister talks repeatedly of separate cultures, of two peoples, of the incompatibility of the Protestant and Catholic ethos, even of 'the historical fact that the people of Northern Ireland are of a different race' (ibid., p. 13).

According to Whyte, the UDA representative in Gallagher's study gave an identity-related reply very similar to that of the UUP (Whyte 1990, p. 203). The UDA has espoused the works of Ian Adamson, who contends that Northern Protestants' antecedents were the Cruthin, the original inhabitants of Ireland who sought refuge in Scotland from the invading Gaels and for whom the later Plantation was merely a homecoming. The mythical figure of Cuchúlain, hero of the Ulster mythological cycle and defender of the province against invasion, is similarly invoked as part of an Ulster cultural heritage. For all the controversy inherent in such claims, these ideas 'have resulted in a growing body of literature within loyalism', and 'produced a continuing debate within the UDA on questions concerned with identity and history' (McAuley 1991, p. 56).

Such thinking is not limited to the paramilitaries. In 1986, the Ulster Young Unionist Council, the UUP youth wing and a solid plank of the mainstream unionist community, published a discussion document entitled 'Cuchúlain, the Lost Legend; Ulster, the Lost Culture?' which used the same arguments to further awareness of a Protestant cultural identity:

Our side of the cultural argument has not been properly heard. ... It is the aim ... to discover the rich and varied cultural heritage that is our birthright. . . . Culture is everywhere and all-embracing; it is at the heart of a people's existence. If they disregard their culture they cannot expect to exist as a people. Now is the time to rediscover the rich culture that we all have. (UYUC, 1986)

What emerges from these examples is a sense that the Protestant community in Northern Ireland have come to interpret their conflict increasingly in terms of culture, heritage and identity. This is not to belittle those political/historical issues which academic research identifies as central to the conflict – nor indeed would the same Protestants deny that those are the causal issues. But without the cultural explanation, Protestants are open to the external criticism of being simply obstinate and intolerant in their refusal to negotiate over the political issues. Through a shared cultural identity, they can explain in positive terms the importance of their community, they can validate the 'siege mentality' in terms of the need to safeguard something transcendent and sacred and, perhaps above all, they can make reply to the more cohesive Irish nationalism of their opponents with something positive and worthy of their own. As John Wilson Foster puts it, it permits them to retain self-respect:

Since no-one wants to claim second-class identity, Ulster Protestants, instead of claiming Irishness, prefer to . . . claim what is first-class and incontrovertible identity: Ulsterness within or without a constitutional Britishness. (1988, p. 410)

The Catholics

When considering questions of identity and allegiance in Northern Ireland, one factor must be recognised which clouds what might otherwise be a simple and straightforward comparison between what the New Ireland Forum (NIF) Report repeatedly refers to as 'the two traditions' (New Ireland Forum 1984). This factor is nationalism. On the one hand, Northern Catholics, as Irish nationalists, have a recognised state to which they can make full allegiance, and which will in turn, at least symbolically, embrace their aspiration. In contrast, the Protestant case, as unionism, involves a much more equivocal and uneasy relationship with the state to which it pledges allegiance. In addition to Britain's own mixed attitudes towards Northern Irish Protestants, Britain, with its constituent Scottish, Welsh and English entities (to say nothing of its twentieth-century immigrant populations), is in a strong sense a multinational state and, as Lijphart says, 'it is doubtful whether it makes sense to speak of "Britishness" as a nationality' (1975, p. 86).

This essential difference between the two communities is neatly mirrored in Todd's work. Where she identifies two strands within unionism, each with its own 'imagined community' (1987), she finds only one 'imagined community' within nationalism: the Irish nation (1990, p. 32). Thus, the nationalist search for a source of identification is straightforwardly unitary. In short, when Catholics look to definition of their identity, they have the advantage of focusing on the central plank of Irish nationalism with confidence and certainty.

The links between Catholic Northern Ireland – the community in question – and the Irish Republic – the expression of the nation – are powerful:

> They include the integration of Ulster in the course of Irish history, the common geographical and historical forces which have shaped this history, and the complex structural and cultural patterns which have resulted; the Irish Roman Catholic Church and Catholic socialisation processes; the Irish language and Gaelic games; kinship, professional and business networks; a sense, reproduced in family and locality, of having been on the same side in the political and military struggles of the early twentieth century; and the political recognition of the nation in the common right to Irish citizenship and an Irish passport. (Todd 1990, pp. 32–3)

Nationalism and Catholicism had become 'indissolubly linked together in the nineteenth century' (Aughey 1989, p. 8) but in terms of the development of nationalist identity specifically in Northern Ireland, the Catholic Church had a further central role. Todd argues that nationalist political culture is based not only on the image of nation, but also on the perceived sense of community:

> In the Stormont period, the church organised the community. ... It organised religious, educational, socio-cultural and to

some extent political activity. Priests provided the central intellectual and political cadre of the community, transmitting the tenets of their own cultural nationalism. (1990, p. 34)

As the prime provider and controller of community (and therefore a bulwark of communal identity), the Catholic Church remained relevant and involved beyond its religious role: 'this society was as much cultural and social as it was religious' (Todd 1990, p. 35). It thus maintained in a very fundamental way the link between political and religious identity among Catholics. While the Church has since been significantly challenged as the provider of community in the North by the Republican movement, and with growing success, the link remains.

So it is almost a statement of the obvious to say that Northern Ireland Catholics see themselves as a distinctive and deep-rooted identity group defined by their religious allegiance (both theologically and in terms of cultural heritage) and their nationalist aspirations. The obvious nature of the statement arises simply because for Catholics the more unitary nature of their Church and, above all, the existence of a nation-state remove some of the obstacles and uncertainties involved in self- definition.

As with Protestants, Catholics will also describe the conflict in Northern Ireland as one between two identities or traditions. To return to Gallagher's study, the Social Democratic and Labour Party (SDLP) spokesperson replied with the words: 'We see the problem as being . . . a problem of identity, and . . . of conflict of identity' (Whyte 1990, p. 203).

In the joint analysis by the New Ireland Forum, involving the SDLP and the leading political parties in the Irish Republic, the conflict is repeatedly described as one between two traditions or communities, and two sets of 'legitimate rights' are identified:

- the right of nationalists to effective political, symbolic and administrative expression of their identity, and
- the right of unionists to effective political, symbolic and administrative expression of their identity, their ethos and their way of life. (New Ireland Forum, 1984, p. 23)

Brian Feeny, a Belfast SDLP councillor, uses precisely these terms to describe his sense of the denial of political rights to Catholics:

Nationalist identity isn't recognised. British identity is enforced, when there is a duality. . . . There is discrimination: Catholics are not recognised as having an Irish identity. (Channel 4 TV, 1992)

Cardinal Cahal Daly, a key mainstream thinker in the Catholic community, in a chapter headed 'The Two Traditions', writes of 'two communities, with different senses of historical identity and of national self-definition'. Specifically within Northern Ireland,

> There are two quite distinct kinds of regional Ulster loyalty . . . that of 'British Ulster' and the other of 'Irish Ulster'. There are two distinct forms of 'Ulster identity', forms that are distinct historically, culturally, socially and politically. (1991, p. 3)

In the 1990s, such acknowledgement of identity and culture as core aspects of the conflict has taken on a powerful orthodoxy, even in the political arena. From the Anglo-Irish Agreement of 1985, through the Brooke and Mayhew talks of 1991–2, to the Downing Street Declaration of 1993 and the Framework Document of 1995 (see Chapter 2), political initiatives have increasingly included a deepening recognition of the need to deal with such interpretational or subjective issues, even if they have lacked much consensus on how that might be done.

CONCLUSION AND SUMMARY

In a conflict, a distinction can be made between issues, which constitute the substance of the conflict – the 'objective' issues – and the deeper themes – the 'subjective' interpretations and perceptions of the protagonists – which further shape the form the conflict takes.

In Northern Ireland, the causal issues of conflict are political, and centre on the question of Northern Ireland's future constitutional position. There are additional contributory issues which are religious, economic and psychological.

The review above illustrates that, while an understanding of the issues, both causal and contributory, helps us to explain 'the problem at the root of the conflict – the future constitutional position of Northern Ireland' (Hunter 1982, p. 52), it is obvious that those involved in the conflict use a language far richer than the political in order to make sense of their conflict, their roles in it, and their goals. Within the terminology they employ, we can see clearly the primacy of identity, alongside other important ingredients: culture, heritage, security, nationality, recognition, participation and community. It is concepts such as these which lie at the heart of the conflict just as much as any 'objective' issue of territorial sovereignty, and which help to explain the protagonists' appreciation of it as literally a matter of life and death.

These are at once more internalised and more subjective concepts than any overt political stances over a constitutional issue, but they cannot be denied an equal reality and importance, precisely because they are, as we have seen, the very concepts used by protagonists to expound upon and explain those political positions. Thus it can be seen that, in the Northern Ireland conflict, objective and subjective factors are entwined to a fundamental degree. Recognition of this complexity has implications for any attempts to prescribe solutions to the conflict, and these implications go to the heart of the argument of the following chapters.

2 Conflict Management Practice: The Structural Approach

In the Introduction, I referred to peacemaking initiatives in Northern Ireland since 1968, both at the political and the community level. The processes involved at the two levels can be differentiated into structural and cultural processes respectively (Ruane and Todd, 1990).

Structural initiatives are those that aim at achieving progress through structural and/or institutional change. Innovations or alterations in systems of governance and societal structures, designed to respond to the circumstances which have brought about the conflict, are the tools of the structural approach to solving conflict. They are generally devised, negotiated and implemented in the political arena. In Northern Ireland, various attempts to change the institutional structures of government have been proposed since 1972.

This chapter reviews the history and development of the structural approach in Northern Ireland from 1968.

1. THE STRUCTURAL APPROACH

In Northern Ireland, the structural approach addresses itself to the problem of competing political aspirations for British or Irish sovereignty – what was identified in Chapter 1 as the core issue of the 'constitutional question' – with the hope of achieving one or other of these aspirations, or a staged programme towards one or other, or a compromise between them.

The main agent of this approach has been the British government, which has tried to implement progress through structural change by attempts to establish an altered version of the system of government carried out by the Northern Ireland parliament at Stormont until 1972. Almost immediately after the final failure of Stormont, Britain defined its policy as two-pronged. Although it has been popular for some considerable time among commentators to bemoan the lack of consistent British policy towards Northern Ireland, in fact that early policy definition has remained largely unaltered and coherent for over two decades. It is rather in the implementation of it that criticisms of incoherence can more legitimately be made, but the policy itself, as initially outlined in a British government Green Paper of 1972 and subsequent White Paper of 1973, has remained essentially intact. It aimed to design and institute a new structure for Northern Irish governance which would combine two elements: a new form of devolved government which would facilitate the participation in the process of the previously alienated Catholic community and its political representatives ('power-sharing', as the concept was and is generally referred to); and some formal means of recognising and involving the government of the Irish Republic (the 'Irish dimension', as it was termed). It was thus a double-sided policy. From the early days of direct rule onwards, power-sharing and the Irish dimension have been the two recurring themes of a pattern. But there have been shifts of emphasis and direction within the parameters of this policy. The following review of the period will illustrate both the broad coherence of policy and its refinement and alteration over time.

Prior to 1969, the Northern Ireland parliament at Stormont had largely been left to its own devices by Westminster. It was the compromise-based structural solution which seemed to best suit Britain's interests. The partition of Ireland and the consequent new governmental systems were legislated for in the 1920 Government of Ireland Act. At that time, Britain had envisaged twin governments, in Belfast and Dublin, and the Act built in several pan-Irish mechanisms and structures which would, it was assumed, allow for subsequent, and prompt, reunification. The plan unravelled almost immediately when politicians in the South were unable to agree over its terms: civil war ensued in the South, and by the time new leaders had emerged in Dublin, the Act was irrelevant to their needs and claims. However, the northern half of the equation went ahead as planned, although the North–South structures of the Act remained stillborn.

From 1922 onwards, Stormont's Unionists reigned supreme, designing or redesigning their sub-state according to their wishes, including structures and institutions which reinforced their supremacy at the expense of the Catholic population. The pro-unification ethos of the 1920 Act swiftly evaporated, and the subsequent definitive British pronouncement on the matter was made in the 1949 Ireland Act (following the South's declaration of independence as a Republic), which stated that Northern Ireland would not cease to be a part of the United Kingdom without the Stormont Parliament's consent. Given the constant Unionist majority in Stormont, this was a virtual guarantee of perpetual partition.

From the 1920s to the 1960s, the structural solution which Britain had adopted for the Irish problem was therefore straightforward. At an overall level, Westminster retained supremacy and sovereignty over the region, and paid large and growing transfers to the North's exchequer to offset its inability to achieve parity with British standards of living; but at the more practical governmental level, Westminster left well alone. For Britain, the policy of laissez-faire seemed to pay off with several decades of reasonably peaceful silence from across the Irish Sea.

2. BRITISH INITIATIVES, 1969–85

When Stormont's hegemony finally began to crack in the face of widespread civil disturbance, and British troops were called in at Stormont's request in August 1969, the British hope was to intervene only briefly to shore up those relative moderates among Unionist politicians who accepted some need for limited reform. Prime Minister Harold Wilson met the then Northern Irish Prime Minister James Chichester-Clark and some of his cabinet at Downing Street, and the joint declaration after the meeting began by repeating the 1949 Act's assurance of the constitutional position and went on to endorse and expand the ongoing reforms of government in Northern Ireland. The message of the declaration was that the current structures were sufficient, with some reform, to cope with any problems.

Almost three years later, as violence spiralled dramatically throughout Northern Ireland, that policy had clearly failed, whether because it was faulty in its assessment or merely in its application. Westminster prorogued Stormont in 1972 and, under the Northern Ireland (Temporary Provisions) Act, assumed direct responsibility for the government of Northern Ireland, largely investing in the new office of Secretary of State for Northern Ireland the previous powers of Stormont. Although the

Act's name indicates the temporary nature of the move at the time, direct rule was effectively installed on the pattern that would, with one brief interruption, continue for over 20 years.

Direct rule brought the end of British laissez-faire, as Westminster imposed its will on Northern Ireland in the most emphatic way possible. It stepped in between the local disputants who were arguing about the nature of internal government structures and simply removed power from local hands.[3] Prior to direct rule, Britain had played the role of absentee arbiter, by default allowing Stormont to proceed untrammeled, and choosing not to exercise the latent power of the role. Direct rule, however, forced Britain to a more active interpretation of that role, one which reactivated the letter of British sovereignty over the region and demanded that the arbiter actually try to impose by virtue of that sovereignty what the default position had failed to achieve.

The intention that the move be temporary was genuine. The first Secretary of State for Northern Ireland, William Whitelaw, began consultations with the local political parties almost immediately, with a view to restoring a reformed Stormont at the earliest moment. (The SDLP refused to be formally involved, in protest at Britain's continued use of the Stormont policy of detention without trial.) He chaired a three-day conference in England at Darlington, between the Ulster Unionist, Northern Ireland Labour, and Alliance Parties – boycotted by the Democratic Unionists and the SDLP – and in October he published a Green Paper, 'The Future of Northern Ireland: a paper for discussion'. The Green Paper ranged over all the submissions from Northern Irish political parties for possible structures at Stormont, and called for further discussion of its content. The clear sense of the Green Paper was that devolution – though not in the simple pre-1972 majority rule form – was Britain's favoured solution. The Green Paper suggested the creation of an elected Assembly to replace the old Parliament. That Britain reserved the right to make the final decision (to arbitrate) on such structures, despite widespread consultation, was implicit throughout the Green Paper: 'As the Government move towards a settlement, they will of course wish to take Northern Irish opinion fully into account' (HMSO 1972, p. 37).

In defining the parameters of the debate, the Green Paper explicitly delineated the two significant principles which would form the core strategies of the double-sided British structural policy in the years ahead. First, a power-sharing formula must be incorporated in any new structure to replace the Unionists' cherished Westminster-style, simple majority rule. Secondly, the Green Paper made explicit the importance of the Republic of Ireland as a player in the game, and coined the phrase 'Irish dimension' to refer to this: 'Whatever arrangements are made for the future administration of Northern Ireland must take account of the Province's relationship with the Republic of Ireland' (ibid., p. 34). Once thus established, these two elements – power-sharing and the Irish dimension – remained integral to subsequent attempts to produce an internal structural settlement.

Interestingly, Whitelaw also alluded in the Green Paper to the limits of a structural settlement:

> No scheme of government, however carefully drawn, can do more than present an opportunity for progress. It is in the hearts and minds of the people in Northern Ireland, and not just in the aims of Government or the words of Acts of Parliament, that the capacity for working and living together must flourish. (ibid., p. 37)

His wording suggested that the job of creating the atmosphere in which new structures might flourish was beyond the remit or the capacity of government and legislation. However, there was little advice forthcoming from Westminster as to how exactly that job might be tackled, beyond perhaps the implicit, and somewhat simplistic, suggestion that the two communities should cooperate. While acknowledging that there were limits to the capacity of government structures, the Green Paper implies no awareness of any other means by which to address positively what government could not.

Following parliamentary debates on the Green Paper at Westminster, and further consultation with politicians and others in Northern Ireland, Whitelaw published the finished product in March 1973. The White Paper, 'Northern Ireland Constitutional Proposals', outlined the structures he would implement (Cmnd. 5259), and set the tone for subsequent formulas over the years. The power-sharing formula comprised an elected unicameral Assembly which would organise its own structures (an executive and a committee-based legislature) and then approach the Secretary of State, who would hand over executive and legislative powers if convinced that a power-sharing framework was in place to protect the involvement of Catholic representatives in the process. 'Transferred' matters would then be handed over to Stormont; the Secretary of State would retain power over 'reserved' matters, unless Westminster agreed to allow Stormont to legislate exceptionally on particular aspects, and over 'excepted' matters, which would be precluded from Stormont's attention. Reserved and excepted matters would include security, law and order, police, judicial appointments, foreign affairs, and so on. The Irish dimension would be discussed and defined at a subsequent constitutional conference between the UK and Irish governments and the new executive.

In the White Paper, Whitelaw also developed further the remarks from the Green Paper concerning the limits of a structural settlement:

> The solution to 'the Northern Ireland problem' is not to be found in any set of political proposals or institutions alone. However skilfully and fairly framed, these can do no more than provide opportunities which the people of Northern Ireland themselves may take or fail to take. . . . Many of the steps which remain to be taken will be for new Northern Ireland institutions, and many more will be outside the field of government altogether. There cannot be a 'governmental settlement', only a 'community settlement'. (Cmnd. 5259, p. 6)

In essence, Whitelaw asserted Britain's role as arbiter at the overall level, while permitting the local parties to devise between themselves the details of the power-sharing system. For all that he claimed not to be imposing a system on Northern Ireland,

> the United Kingdom Government has refrained from seeking to impose on Northern Ireland a rigidly defined and detailed scheme for its future which could not be done at the present time without assumptions about the wishes of its people. (ibid., p. 5)

It was clearly only in the details that the local politicians would have any leeway for structure design. They had had only a consultative role in the final proposals, and the White Paper left them little option beyond the decision to cooperate or not. Their task was to work out the details of a parliamentary system together, and then to convince the Secretary of State that it would command 'widespread support' throughout Northern Ireland.

The Assembly election was held in June 1973, but immediately afterwards the DUP and other hard-line Unionist electees (including many within the rapidly fractionating UUP)[4] formed a 'loyalist coalition' which rejected the entire new system but focused its anger particularly on the Irish dimension. The SDLP electees were under pressure from all sides over the question of their participation in the Assembly, and were finally jolted into action after the Prime Minister, Edward Heath, threatened in September to realise their worst fears:

> I would favour the total integration of N. Ireland with Great Britain if the proposed Executive is not set up by March.
> (*Belfast News Letter* 18 September 1973)

In November, after seven weeks of discussions, the SDLP, UUP and Alliance announced the membership of the executive, with the UUP's Brian Faulkner in the chair, and the SDLP's Gerry Fitt as deputy. Whitelaw scheduled a tripartite conference with Dublin and the new executive for 6–9 December at Sunningdale, in England, where the executive was approved and it was agreed to institute devolution as soon as possible. However, the conference failed to finalise the detailed form of the Irish dimension. A Council of Ireland was agreed, comprising members of the Assembly and the Dáil Éireann (the Irish Parliament in Dublin), which would have various recommendatory and consultative powers, but major details, in particular extradition arrangements across the border, remained to be resolved, and until then the formal constitutional conference could not be called. The Irish dimension was emerging clearly as the sticking point. The conference was not helped by the fact that Whitelaw, the architect of the whole process, was replaced as Secretary of State by Francis Pym just three days before Sunningdale. (The move was one of several examples throughout the period under discussion when key personnel could be changed, or key decisions made, according to the priorities solely of the domestic British political agenda.)

So by 1 January 1974, when the Assembly and executive were officially installed, antagonism to the Irish dimension had become a rallying cry not only for the boycotting loyalist coalition members of the Assembly, but for a very significant proportion of

Faulkner's own UUP. When a general election was called in February, Faulkner was routed. Ironically, the SDLP's Fitt was the only pro-Sunningdale candidate to win in the 12 Westminster constituencies. (Additionally, Labour's election victory meant that Pym was replaced by Merlin Rees.) In May, the anti-Sunningdale Unionists, under the burgeoning United Ulster Unionist Council banner, together with a wide range of workplace and other groups who came together as the Ulster Workers' Council (UWC), called for a general strike to protest. As the strike took effect, the executive continued to hammer out a way to operate the Sunningdale system, effectively looking for a formula which would play down the Irish dimension. With a formula agreed, they approached the British government and urged them to negotiate with the strike leaders, but after repeated British refusals they resigned. (The new Labour government's decision reflected Harold Wilson's reluctance to set a precedent of negotiating over industrial action in the British context: again, Northern Irish policy was being implemented more as fallout from British domestic politics, rather than in its own right.) The executive was prorogued. The power-sharing structure had fallen, apparently on the stumbling-block of the Irish dimension. Britain's double-sided policy had caused its own defeat, as one element had negated the other.

The double-sided policy contained the basis of its own defeat in that the linking of both elements provided vetoes for the parties in Northern Ireland. Unionists would not consider power-sharing as long as it was linked to an Irish dimension; nationalists, in the light of British implementation of policy to date, would not consider power-sharing unless it was linked to an Irish dimension. Either camp, therefore, could effectively block progress on the linked policy since both had it in their power to prevent the necessary 'widespread acceptance' for any initiative.

Wilson saw the downfall of the executive as a failure of the arbiter's role. Reflecting later, he commented that imposition of a settlement was no longer feasible:

> The initiatives taken at Darlington and Sunningdale, the policies of the Heath government and of our own had reached a dead end. No solution could be imposed from across the water. From now on we had to throw the task clearly to the Northern Ireland people themselves. (Wilson 1979, p. 78)

His government, while retaining the essence of the double-sided policy, adopted a less explicit approach. Merlin Rees consequently mooted the idea of a Constitutional Convention, a fall-back proposal considered briefly and rejected in Whitelaw's White Paper. The Convention would be an elected consultative body, a talking-shop in which elected politicians, while having no executive or legislative power, would be able to comment on the process of direct rule, and would be charged with originating and developing among themselves a blueprint for future governance.

Initially, the Convention was designed to sit for no more than six months, by which time it could submit a report to the Secretary of State on a way forward for governing Northern Ireland. So Rees was very literally implementing Wilson's attitude that imposition was out and that the formula must come from within. In a sense, then, the Convention proposals would derogate Britain's arbiter role: 'There is no means to impose such a system upon Northern Ireland if substantial sections of its population are determined to oppose it' (Cmnd. 5675, p. 17). But in another sense, Rees was pressuring the local parties as usual. He repeated that 'widespread acceptance' would be a necessary requirement of any formula reached by the Convention (ibid., p. 16), implying – especially to anti-power-sharing Unionists – that if Britain could not impose a structure, then neither could anyone else. Further, he retained enough of the role of power-holder to include both a threat and an incentive in the White Paper.

The threat was financial, and aimed particularly at unionists, specifically in the wake of the UWC strike. Concerning the disparity in social and living standards between Northern Ireland and Britain, and the significant financial transfers from the Westminster Exchequer required – and consistently provided over the years – to subsidise the Northern Ireland economy, he reiterated Westminster's commitment to narrowing the differential, but warned that

> it has to be appreciated that events in Northern Ireland itself, not least any resumption of industrial action for political ends, could frustrate that intention. The willingness of the Westminster Parliament responsible to the United Kingdom electorate as a whole to transfer additional money to Northern Ireland and to continue to invest resources in Northern Ireland will

inevitably be affected by the progress of events there. (Cmnd. 5675, p. 13)

The incentive was aimed particularly at nationalists:

> Nothing would transform the security situation more quickly than a determination by the whole community to support the Police Service and co-operate with it. This is not happening. If it did take place, it would also have a fundamental effect on the need for Emergency Powers in Northern Ireland, including detention, the operation of which is currently being examined. . . . It would also enable the Army to make a planned, orderly and progressive reduction in its present commitment and subsequently there would be no need for the Army to become involved again in a policing role. (ibid., p. 14)

Having clearly linked law-abiding behaviour in a conditional way both to future state funding and to a diminution of the elements of security policy most offensive to Catholics, Rees ingenuously concluded by declaring that 'peace, law and order are not bargaining counters' (ibid., pp. 14–15). But clearly – whatever his ability to deliver on either the threat or the promise – he was not above using such linkage, or doing so in an official and public government document.

Elections for the Convention were held on 1 May 1975, and its opening session took place a week later. It rapidly became clear that there was little atmosphere of compromise involved, and little faith among participants that the Convention would achieve anything. In November, by a majority UUP–DUP vote, the UUP's devolution proposal was endorsed as the official Convention Report. Based largely on an executive operating by simple majority rule, the UUP knew in advance that both the SDLP and the British government would reject the proposal. The SDLP, Alliance, Northern Ireland Labour Party (NILP) and Unionist Party of Northern Ireland (UPNI, Faulkner's short-lived pro-Sunningdale UUP rump) each produced minority reports. Rees tried to find room for manoeuvre through bilateral discussion with the parties, and reconvened the Convention in February 1976. But the parties remained deadlocked. The criterion of 'widespread acceptance' once again enabled a unionist veto.

Rees formally dissolved the Convention in March, accepted that devolution initiatives had comprehensively failed, and retreated to a policy of making direct rule operate as effectively as possible. The double-sided structural policy was shelved, given that neither its imposition by Britain nor the opportunity for local politicians to devise their own versions had produced any results. His successor in October 1976, Roy Mason, spent his three years in office similarly concentrating on the mechanisms of direct rule, with a two-pronged policy aimed at improving the security situation and increasing inward investment.

Margaret Thatcher's incoming Conservative government of June 1979 replaced Mason with Humphrey Atkins. With little knowledge or understanding of Northern Ireland, Atkins was somewhat at a loss as a late replacement for Airey Neave, the Conservative Northern Ireland spokesperson, who had been killed by the Irish National Liberation Army (INLA) three months before the general election. Why he should have decided to reactivate attempts for a local initiative is unclear: it may have been simply the reaction of an incoming government distinguishing itself from its predecessor, or it may have been a strategy aimed at countering the backbench integrationists in the Conservative Party. His initiative formally resurrected only one element of the original double-sided policy, concentrating on power-sharing but largely ignoring any suggested structure for institutionalising the Irish dimension. Exactly why he should have decided to do so is unclear, for he was never going to interest nationalists as long as there was no Irish dimension included. And he was unlikely to attract unionists with either of his formulas: a re-presentation of the power-sharing model which they had already rejected, or a majority rule system offset by a minority blocking system. In the event, the only way in which he managed dialogue in any form was to hold 'parallel talks, one with the Unionists who would not attend if an Irish dimension was discussed, and one with the SDLP who would not attend unless it was discussed' (McGarry 1988, p. 248).

Once again, British policy was hoist on its own petard of the 'widespread acceptance' criterion: having failed more than once to implement both elements of the policy simultaneously, the Atkins initiative represented a failure to implement one element at a time. Given a general lack of enthusiasm among local parties at the time for any cooperative initiative, Atkins could exert little if any pressure on them to overcome their inertia. His efforts met with widespread apathy, and they were swiftly sidelined by the crisis engendered by the IRA hunger-strikes in Long Kesh prison in 1980 and 1981, which left ten prisoners dead, one Sinn Féin member elected to the Westminster Parliament, a huge increase in Sinn Féin's profile and electoral support, and a great deal of international criticism of Britain's handling of events. Atkins' term was not the Northern Ireland Office's finest hour; in Paul Arthur's words, he 'departed as he arrived . . . bewildered and bemused' (Arthur 1989, p. 119).

But events on a different axis were beginning to gather momentum, as in 1980 and 1981 Prime Minister Thatcher and the Irish Taoiseach (initially Charles Haughey and subsequently Garret FitzGerald) held the first two Anglo-Irish summits, and began to develop the intergovernmental framework which would subsequently prove very significant (see section 4 below). As this axis gathered pace, a strategy developed that would shift the Irish dimension out of the local arena and reserve it for the intergovernmental level. Thus was developed the process of delinking the two elements of the double policy, and dealing with one at a level on which the 'widespread acceptance' veto carried no power.

Although the process would not be complete until 1985, the shift of emphasis was already evident when James Prior succeeded Atkins in September 1981. In the following April, he published his own White Paper, 'Northern Ireland: A Framework For Devolution', which described his plan for 'rolling devolution' (Cmnd. 8541). While not imposing a system on Northern Ireland's politicians, Prior nevertheless declared that they had 'an inescapable responsibility to work out an acceptable scheme for themselves' (Cmnd. 8541, p. 2) and that 'the rest of the United Kingdom looks to Northern Ireland to come to terms with its political problems' (ibid., p. 4). His plan was a flexible variation on Whitelaw's original scheme, combined with some elements of Rees's Convention. But its concentration was on power-sharing, and the Irish dimension, significantly, was not directly addressed beyond acknowledging its importance in the ritual manner of previous White Papers.

An Assembly would be elected, as before. It would organise itself in a committee structure, with a committee to correspond to each government department in Whitelaw's 1973 category of 'transferred' matters. The hope was that the resulting familiarisation with practical politicking would, over time, encourage co-operation towards a second stage, where the Assembly would be able to devise its own power-sharing devolution framework, subject to the approval of the Secretary of State on the familiar criterion of 'widespread acceptance'. Depending on the level of agreement reached and the nature of the proposed framework, the process of devolving power would begin. However, the novelty of Prior's plan was that he could use his judgement to decide either to devolve all power at once, or to do so gradually (hence the name, 'rolling devolution'). The enticement of executive power was offered as the reward for compromise and cooperation: as each committee was formed along power-sharing lines to Prior's approval, the corresponding department's powers would be devolved to that committee.

Although the White Paper repeated the necessity for an Irish dimension, it would not be a matter for the Assembly to discuss. The significance of this is telling: the Irish dimension was now a matter for the two governments to consider through the Anglo-Irish Intergovernmental framework, and was no longer directly on the local agenda. The problem of double vetoes which the linkage of the two policy elements had enabled was being recognised and addressed:

> the British government's power to move the political parties in the North in the direction of an accommodation was severely curtailed. It was a zero-sum game: Anything that appeared to be acceptable to Unionists was a sufficient reason for its rejection by Nationalists, and conversely, anything that appeared to be acceptable to Nationalists was a sufficient reason for its rejection by Unionists. (O'Malley 1990, p. 5)

The new strategy was now based on the assumption that the Unionist veto might remain uninvoked in a straightforward discussion of power-sharing, while any nationalist veto might also be avoided if they knew, via Dublin, that the Irish dimension was being addressed in a different arena.

Only Alliance immediately supported Prior's initiative. The UUP insisted on either integration (which the White Paper explicitly ruled out) or, along with the DUP, devolution on the basis of the Convention Report (already unacceptable to Britain and non-Unionists.) The SDLP were at this stage not interested in any internal solutions that might be obstacles to eventual and total unity. Similarly, Prior got little support from his own colleagues at Westminster. Tory backbenchers, still following

Powell's integrationist path, fought the passage of Prior's proposals through Parliament with endless filibustering. Others in the party were either sceptical or downright disinterested; Thatcher herself thought it 'a rotten Bill' (Prior 1986, p. 199). Nevertheless, the bill was passed, the legislation was enacted, and the election held on 20 October 1982. Immediately, the UUP embarked on wrecking tactics, boycotting the Assembly for an initial three months, and then steering the Devolution Report Committee through 18 months of argument before producing a report which was as unacceptable to nationalists as that of the Convention. The SDLP fulfilled their promise to abstain from participation, and busied themselves in the proceedings of the New Ireland Forum 1983–4. Con O'Leary points out that when, in March 1984 (with the UUP again engaged on a six-month boycott), the Assembly produced a glossy brochure entitled 'Local Democracy At Work' to celebrate its 100th session, a full 45 of the 78 members were in fact absenting themselves for one reason or another (O'Leary *et al.* 1988, p. 183).

Clearly, the blunt tactics of leaving the detailed structural design to the local politicians, offering inducements of executive power as direct rewards for specific packages of power-sharing, and hoping that familiarity with a form of parliamentary process would encourage responsibility, had failed. But by 1984, the Assembly was becoming irrelevant as events on the Anglo-Irish axis speeded up.

Douglas Hurd replaced Prior in September 1984. Two months later, at an Anglo-Irish summit, Thatcher appeared to throw a large spanner into the Anglo-Irish works as she gave her infamous 'out, out, out' response to the three proposals of the New Ireland Forum Report (see below). But the appearance was deceptive. The Anglo-Irish intergovernmental process was gathering steam, motivated on the British side by the paralysis engendered by the double veto. For Britain, the Anglo-Irish process was in part a search for a means to bypass this veto.

The change of policy implementation – to address one policy element by delinking it from the other and pursuing it outside of the Northern Ireland arena – was well underway, even if Hurd was not ready to express it overtly. He told the Assembly in December that, whether or not the Assembly managed to reach agreement on devolution, it would not 'inhibit the continuation of the Anglo-Irish dialogue', which, he hinted, was ongoing on security and other matters (O'Leary *et al.* 1988, p. 187). By January 1985, he was further suggesting that mechanisms to facilitate such dialogue were under consideration, and by March he was admitting that the necessary machinery was being actively discussed. In actuality, by this juncture the text of the Anglo-Irish Agreement, to which he was alluding, and which would establish the Irish dimension in dramatic form, was in existence in draft form. The signing of the Agreement on 15 November 1985 finally rendered the Assembly irrelevant and defunct.

3. THE ANGLO-IRISH PROCESS SINCE 1983

The increased emphasis on the Anglo-Irish process reflected not simply a British decision to find a way to impose one element of its policy. More significantly, it reflected a fundamental change in the framework in which such policy would be devised and implemented. Thus the partnership between Dublin and London exemplified by the Anglo-Irish Agreement of 1985 represented the single most significant change in the parameters of British structural policy. No longer was Britain the sole arbiter of policy in Northern Ireland: it now had a formal partner in the process, even if the balance of that relationship, and the distribution of power and responsibility, were neither clear nor unproblematic.

Joint arbitration was thus institutionalised by the Agreement through a process of co-option. The partnership was the end-product of efforts to bypass the local roadblock by operating at the international or intergovernmental level.

Interestingly, the process which culminated in the Agreement was the first successful attempt by Ireland to influence British policy directly. There was a conscious strategy on the part of Garret FitzGerald's government – and, arguably, on the prior part of Hume's SDLP via Dublin – to effect such influence. The consequences changed the framework in which future British policy would be constructed and implemented, by altering the relationship with Ireland from one of confrontation to one of cooperation and partnership.

The Irish thinking behind the strategy, and even the language in which the Agreement was couched, can be traced back to the preceding New Ireland Forum of 1983–4 in Dublin, and beyond that to the influence of the SDLP – and in particular of Hume –

on Dublin. Hume's vocabulary is discernible in the text of the Agreement. Indeed, Bill Rolston asserts that the momentum for the events which culminated in the Agreement began with Hume himself, arguing that he both achieved the means to weaken the Unionist veto on progress and retrieved the SDLP's long-standing alienation from the political process by 'changing strategy and widening the arena of debate' with the Forum Report, which 'represented a coup for Hume. At one stroke he had broken out of the sterile confines of political debate in the North' (Rolston 1987, p. 61). McGarry comments:

> The statement in the preface to the agreement indicating that the British 'recognise and respect the identities of the two communities in Northern Ireland and the right of each to pursue its aspirations by peaceful and constitutional means' not only embodies the gist of numerous SDLP policy statements and the SDLP-inspired report of the New Ireland Forum, it employs virtually the same language. (McGarry 1988, p. 241)

The pressing need for Northern nationalists in 1982 was to halt the electoral inroads being made by Sinn Féin at the expense of the SDLP. On the post-hunger strike wave of support, Sinn Féin had taken more than a third of the nationalist vote in the Assembly elections of May 1982. Constitutional nationalists throughout Ireland needed to come together to redefine consensually their analysis of the situation, and agree the necessary policy, strategy and goals which would reclaim nationalism for them, thereby halting any slide towards the dangerous and destabilising Republicanism represented by Sinn Féin. Together, FitzGerald and Hume developed their plans into the New Ireland Forum (FitzGerald 1991).

FitzGerald, however, had another aim in mind for the Forum. His broader goal was to enter negotiations with the British government to reach some formal agreement over Northern Ireland. He sensed the time was right for cooperation, and from the first he wanted 'a forum that would provide me with a flexible and negotiating mandate for an Anglo-Irish agreement on Northern Ireland' (FitzGerald 1991, p. 464). His partly formed idea for such negotiations was based on the possibilities of some kind of joint sovereignty system for Northern Ireland which could be worked out between the two countries, and consequently he also needed to see this concept included as one of the possible structural solutions offered by the Forum's final Report (ibid., p. 488). To a significant degree, therefore, his agenda for the Forum was dictated by the needs of the greater goal of international negotiation. (In the Report, joint sovereignty was entitled joint authority.)

Of course, FitzGerald shared the general concern that the SDLP's grip on Northern nationalists might be slipping away to Sinn Féin, and recognised dangerous ramifications for the Republic if that happened. At the time he expressed fears for the safety of the South's political structures if Republicanism turned its attention to its deep-seated antagonism towards Irish politics. The election to Dáil Éireann in June 1981 of two IRA hunger-strikers had reinforced the view of Sinn Féin/IRA as a growing challenge to constitutional nationalism in the South. The perceived threat only increased when Sinn Féin's share of the Northern nationalist vote in the 1983 general election climbed to 43 per cent. The lasting seriousness of this threat to the Republic's stability can be questioned (especially with hindsight, given that Sinn Féin's electoral support in fact collapsed rapidly in the Republic after this brief peak), as can the degree to which FitzGerald really took it seriously. But he undoubtedly believed that it could be used to bolster his argument to London that the threat of widespread Republican-controlled disorder in the North required the British both to enter dialogue about how best to avoid such a security problem, and to do so with an understanding of the need to be supportive to the SDLP. Bew and Patterson attribute this awareness to Hume, rather than FitzGerald, suggesting that the latter was under pressure, once he began any negotiation, to produce an agreement which would win the acceptance of the SDLP, and that he could only do so by incorporating Hume's analysis of the Northern Ireland problem as one needing to be dealt with in a framework that transcended the Northern Ireland state. 'As a result', they comment, 'Hume was very successful in ensuring that his own definition of the problem was . . . influential in the framing of the Agreement' (Bew and Patterson 1987, p. 43).

O'Malley's observation is pertinent, but incomplete:

> The Forum had two goals: a political objective to contain Sinn Féin and a policy objective to set forth the common agenda of Nationalists for achieving a New Ireland that would provide a

clear and unambiguous alternative to armed struggle. (O'Malley 1990, p. 1)

A third, diplomatic, objective must be added: FitzGerald's planting of the idea of joint authority as a basis for future intergovernmental negotiation. The Forum involved primarily the four main nationalist parties on the island of Ireland: FitzGerald's Fine Gael, Charles Haughey's Fianna Fáil and Dick Spring's Labour Party from the Republic, and the SDLP from the North. Sinn Féin were excluded. A much broader range of opinion, including that of unionism, was canvassed through written and oral submissions to the Forum. The process can be fairly characterised as a negotiation between Fianna Fáil's traditional-nationalist insistence on Irish unity as the only possible structural solution, and the position of the other three parties that other models and options should be included in the final range of possibilities (including, of course, the joint authority concept so necessary for FitzGerald's diplomatic strategy towards Britain). In the end, the Forum Report, published in May 1984, offered three options: a unitary Irish state, a (con-)federal system and joint authority. But, in appeasement to Haughey, a unitary Irish state was described in preferential terms as 'the particular structure of political unity which the Forum would wish to see' (NIF 1984, p. 29).

The Forum's goal of making the clear distinction between constitutional nationalism – requiring unionist consent to any solution – and the violent Republicanism of Sinn Féin and the IRA, was achieved. In the process, the Forum was the first instance of nationalists acknowledging the unionist/Protestant identity in positive terms and granting it a legitimate place in any future Ireland. In a sense, Dublin was finally acknowledging a 'British dimension' to Irish thinking in parallel to the British recognition of an 'Irish dimension'. Such a shift worked positively in FitzGerald's favour as he approached the prospect of negotiation with the British. It cut no ice, however, with unionists, but, as Joseph Lee points out, their overwhelmingly negative response to the Report only served to reinforce FitzGerald's view that any progress with Britain 'would have to be worked out in direct discussions between [the two governments] without consultation with the Unionists. Total negativity is not a negotiating position' (Lee 1989, p. 456).

But 'meanwhile', as O'Malley comments, even during the early stages of the Forum's twelve months of discussions, 'the real dialogue was taking place out of public view' (1990, p. 4). Throughout the summer of 1983, FitzGerald put out feelers towards British civil servants concerning the possibility of discussing the Irish dimension within the newly established intergovernmental process. His initial vision for the embodiment of this dimension concerned significant Irish input on security matters in Northern Ireland, and he was quite prepared to offer changes to the Irish Constitution's territorial claim to the North -- a high card to play -- in order to strike a deal. Over the following months, Britain's, and Thatcher's, initial scepticism changed to definite interest in a 'joint responsibility' deal framed in terms of 'a "basic equation" involving on the one side an acknowledgement of the union of Great Britain with Northern Ireland and on the other [Irish] involvement in the government of Northern Ireland, with particular emphasis on security' (FitzGerald 1991, p. 495). Hume also met Thatcher to reinforce FitzGerald's analysis of the problem and the potential for progress.

Dublin made a formal approach to Britain in May 1984, shortly after publication of the Forum Report. The formal British response in July was to suggest a reduction of the scale of such an agreement, so that no constitutional changes would be required. However, Britain expressed a definite interest in aiming at a formal international treaty establishing the Irish dimension, but insisted that the essence of any agreement must include the durability of Northern Ireland's status within the UK in order to placate Unionists.

From that point onwards, the Anglo-Irish process was explicitly aimed at a treaty-based outcome on the Irish dimension; remaining negotiations needed only to hammer out the practical form and details of that dimension. The Anglo-Irish Council met no less than 30 times between November 1983 and March 1985 (O'Malley 1990, p. 6), by which time a draft text was in existence which included the elements of the Intergovernmental Conference and the Belfast-based Secretariat.

The Agreement was formally signed on 15 November 1985. Despite what Thatcher and her team believed was a sufficient guarantee of Northern Ireland's continued status within the United Kingdom (expressed in Article 1 of the Agreement in somewhat diplomatic language designed primarily to avoid any legislative clash with either the Irish position as reflected in its Constitution or the British position as expressed in previous legislation) unionist outrage was intense. Just 18 days after the signing, Thatcher told FitzGerald that the response of unionists had been 'much worse than expected', and complained, 'You've got the glory and I've got the problems' (FitzGerald 1991, pp. 569–70).

Part of the unionist reaction can be explained simply in that they had been excluded from the negotiating process. Unionist leaders may have been slightly ingenuous in claiming that they were not informed or consulted at least minimally during the process. (Molyneaux's position as a member of the British Privy Council alone would suggest that he must have had inklings of the ongoing process, and he and his colleagues were complaining of plots two months before the signing. Nevertheless, unionist public opinion, as exemplified in the editorials of unionist newspapers, appeared either to be ignorant of the entire process or to prefer to ignore its reality.) But the Anglo-Irish tactic of bypassing the local veto was obviously employed with the unionist veto specifically in mind: Unionist politicians had little, if any, real consultation and no direct involvement at all, while Hume and the SDLP were organically incorporated into the negotiating process.

However, the most profound reason for the extreme unionist reaction was the psychological implication of the Agreement. Harold McCusker of the UUP summed this up in 1989:

> It was never the practical implications of the Agreement which concerned people like myself. It was the psychological implications. It was the major concession made to Dublin that the Union was a very conditional matter. (O'Malley 1990, p. 43)

The unionist veto, for the first time, failed to halt progress on the Irish dimension, and implied that the relationship of unionism to Britain was suddenly fundamentally changed: 'the status quo which had existed from 1920 to 1985 was destroyed with two strokes of the pen, and . . . the Union as Unionists knew it was over' (O'Malley 1990a, p. 186).

The British guarantee to protect the Union, on which unionists had depended for so long, had suddenly become explicitly conditional. Even if only in the relative sense of describing the Union in less forceful terms than previous formal British pro-

nouncements (specifically, in not actually defining Northern Ireland's status), the text of the Agreement expressed what Paul
Arthur identified as a new British 'agnosticism' on the Union
(Arthur 1989a, p. 106). And, furthermore, the Irish dimension,
which unionists had managed so effectively to veto since Whitelaw's day, was now being imposed upon them in the concrete and
visible form of the Secretariat, complete with Irish civil servants,
in a Belfast suburb. This sense of being finally on the slippery
slope towards unity was pre-eminent among unionists. As one
DUP member put it: 'Dublin not only [had] its foot in the door
– the door was off its hinges' (O'Malley 1990a, p. 182).

In describing the effects on the 'unionist psyche', O'Malley
points out that the Agreement, in co-opting Dublin into responsibility for the North and in placing a tangible Dublin presence
in Belfast in the shape of the Secretariat, inferred 'an implicit
acknowledgement by Britain that the partition of Ireland, in
political and social terms, had failed', and a dramatic about-face
from official pronouncements on the Union as late as 1982 (1990,
pp. 13–14). Such an inference was, of course, an unspeakable
heresy to unionists.

O'Malley may well be correct in identifying as one intention of
the Agreement that it should be 'a catalyst which, by requiring
Unionists to redefine their relationship to Britain, will, by
necessity, require them to redefine their relationship with the rest
of Ireland' (1990a, p. 187). But Tom Wilson is closer to the
realities of unionist reaction when he suggests that

> within Ulster, the feeling of betrayal weakened still further the
> old link with Britain but did not, of course, strengthen in any
> way the support for absorption into a united Irish Republic.
> The effect was rather to intensify the feeling of isolation.
> (Wilson 1989, p. 200)

If there was a hope, implicit in the text of the Agreement, that in
some way a more moderate voice within unionism would be
empowered to come forward and challenge the old guard's
definition of its relationship with Dublin, then it was an underestimation of the strength of feeling right across the whole spectrum
of unionism.

Initial Protestant anger was expressed in huge protest rallies
and in a startling increase in rioting and paramilitary activity
within the Protestant community. Thatcher tried to woo Moly-

neaux and Paisley back into dialogue in February 1986, suggesting a roundtable conference on devolution and the enticement
that, if such a conference made progress, then 'we should need
to consider what that meant for the work of the intergovernmental conference set up under the terms of the Anglo-Irish agreement' (Kenny 1986, p. 122).

But they declared that there could be no dialogue until the
Agreement was removed and that they were 'withdrawing consent from the Government' (ibid., p. 122). The civil disobedience
campaign continued on the streets, even to the unprecedented
extent of angry Protestants turning on the RUC, traditionally
seen as the protectors of the Protestant community but now
viewed as implementers of a hated Dublin-influenced security
policy. A DUP–UUP pact was announced on joint anti-Agree-
ment strategies which included MPs' boycotting of Westminster,
local councillors' boycotting of council business, and boycotting
by both of British ministers and their departments. Whatever the
hopes of the Agreement's designers that initial negative unionist
response might be short-lived, fragmented and ultimately positive, the campaign of reaction was resoundingly negative and
comprehensive, coalescing around the ubiquitous and telling
slogan of 'Ulster Says No!'

Whatever the assessment of the Agreement in terms of achieving the goals its devisers aimed for, it had one profound effect:

It has altered the context for all future policy action. Its
enduring importance, therefore, is the fact that it was implemented in the first place. (O'Malley 1990a, p. 189)

The post-Agreement context is the one in which all political
actors now speak, and it is in terms of their relationship to that
context that they express their general positions.

The Agreement, an international treaty between the Irish and
British governments, halted, if not actually reversed, any progress
on the other policy element – power-sharing – for more than two
years, as the unionist boycott of all aspects of government held
firm. The Agreement had the important effect of practically
assuring that any devolutionary moves could henceforth be made
only within its context and therefore in consultation with the Irish
government. Such overt institutionalisation of the Irish dimension
was more than enough to guarantee prolonged unionist disen-
gagement. The British position (and by implication, given the

new framework, that of the Irish government too) was to sit out the rough weather from the unionists and to pin hope on the long-term view. The government's analysis had been one requiring necessary short-term moves to avert long-term Catholic alienation (translating into an increased Sinn Féin/IRA power-base), at the expense of Protestant alienation which, they judged, would have to soften in the long-term.

And indeed, the Protestant community became gradually frustrated with the limits of a purely negative campaign. The expected tensions between moderates and rejectionists eventually began to stimulate internal argument. Secretary of State Tom King, appointed just two months before the Agreement was signed, suffered widespread verbal – and even physical – abuse from angry unionists, and was demonised by them to a greater degree than any of his predecessors. Nevertheless, by 1988 he was able to meet Unionist leaders several times for what became known as 'talks about talks'. Although nothing was achieved in these discussions, where the Unionists demanded the removal of the Agreement as a precondition for more talks while King insisted the Agreement was immovable, it provided a slim basis for the process which King's 1989 successor Peter Brooke developed painstakingly into face-to-face negotiations in 1991. Nevertheless, it was almost a full five years from the signing of the Agreement before Unionists responded in any positive sense to Brooke's overtures.

Brooke capitalised on the mixture of Dublin support and Unionist frustration to produce a slim gap for dialogue. He achieved the first direct negotiations between Northern Ireland's politicians since Sunningdale, 18 years previously. Inconclusive as the Brooke Initiative was, it provided the first instance in recent years of the structural approach at work at an implemental level. Chapter 5 therefore constitutes a detailed case-study of the Initiative.

The agenda of what became known as the Brooke Initiative was threefold. It emerged directly from the text and ambience of the Agreement and, previously, from the SDLP–Fine Gael approach to the New Ireland Forum. It had three strands: to address the question of a new internal form of devolved government on Northern Ireland; to define the formal relationship between any such government and that of the Irish Republic; and to explore, in the light of success in the first two spheres, a new form of Irish–British treaty to replace the Anglo-Irish Agreement. All three strands had clearly structural aims, dependent on the formation of new institutional or constitutional structures.

Under Brooke, Britain was still pursuing the double structural policy. But while the power-sharing element was still to be – had to be – pursued as before through the means of local negotiation, the approach to the Irish dimension was now very different. The debate on that element was no longer about whether the Irish dimension should or should not be created: it was now couched in the fact of its existence and concerned merely with changes or refinements to it with the understanding that it was a *fait accompli*. In effect, delinking the two sides of the policy had resulted in the decision to impose the one element which was demanded by nationalists and impervious to unionist objection, in the hope that the resulting altered situation would increase the chances of achieving the other element which was still by definition dependent on 'widespread acceptance'. The Irish dimension had been achieved, and sustained, without any semblance of 'widespread acceptance' in Northern Ireland.

Although the Brooke negotiations failed to reach any conclusions before their July 1991 deadline, Brooke's successor as Secretary of State, Patrick Mayhew, was able to reconvene them a year later, essentially on the same agenda. Once again, no conclusion was reached, although the process of dialogue and mutual understanding was significantly deepened.

But the pattern had been set: after the 1985 Agreement, and despite many serious disagreements over major issues, the Irish and British governments steadily developed a more cooperative relationship than ever in the past. Increasingly, through the 1990s, after the Brooke and Mayhew talks, their efforts were at least coordinated, and at most dove-tailed. The primary, specific aim had been achieved in the Agreement: the formal establishment of the Irish dimension. The main concentration of the structural approach would now concern power-sharing, eased by the positive addition of the support of the SDLP's sponsor-government, and by hugely significant developments within the Republican movement, but hampered by the added difficulty of profound unionist disaffection with their own previous sponsor-government. Through the Hume–Adams dialogue, covert and then overt dialogue with Sinn Féin, the Downing Street Joint Declaration of December 1993, the joint publication of the

Framework Document in early 1995 in response to the paramilitary ceasefires, and the launch of the twin-track approach (preparatory political talks with Northern parties in parallel with the establishment of the International Body on Arms Decommissioning), both London and Dublin were tightly locked into a single structural policy. Despite deep differences about the best way to manage the post-1994 peace process, the relationship has weathered many storms. Few, if any, of the significant political breakthroughs after 1992 would have been conceivable under the old regime of rivalry.

CONCLUSION AND SUMMARY

Since 1968, attempts to address the intercommunal problems of the Northern Ireland conflict have developed along two lines: a structural approach, concerned with political and institutional structures, and a cultural approach, concerned with relationships between the two cultural communities.

The pattern of Britain's modern structural approach to the problem of Northern Ireland can be distinguished through several stages, in all of which the role of arbiter remains basic to the British position. The period of 1922 to the late 1960s can be characterised as one of laissez-faire, with the arbiter retaining final sovereignty over the Stormont Parliament, but developing a default position where implementation of the policy was more in the style of an 'absentee-arbiter'. Policy between 1969 and 1972 concerned itself only with a minimal intervention to ensure some reform or modification of existing structures.

Between 1972 and 1974, Britain was forced to shed its absentee role and take on direct responsibility through direct rule, assuming that such involvement would be temporary. Instead of reform, structural policy developed on a two-strategy basis aimed at building new structures. The basic double policy – power-sharing and an Irish dimension – was defined and established, and remained the basis for British policy throughout the period under review. Despite fluctuations and changes in its implementation, caused not least by the way in which British policy in Northern Ireland generally remained secondary to, and subject to the whims of, the domestic British political agenda, the pattern of policy is surprisingly consistent. But the linkage of the two elements produced a corresponding problem of a double veto among local political parties, either faction of whom could thwart the ends of this policy. Both the Assembly (1974) and the Convention (1975) foundered on this veto, as unionists prevented the necessary 'widespread acceptance' of the Irish dimension.

Faced with such failures, the double policy was effectively shelved for four years, while less ambitious efforts were concentrated on implementing the active arbitration of direct rule as effectively as possible. From 1980 onwards, the double policy was reactivated, but with a gradual shift in its implementation. Initially, the attempt was made simply to sideline the Irish dimension and reach consensus on power- sharing, but this pleased neither side in Northern Ireland. Subsequently, however, this tactic of delinking the two policy elements was developed dramatically – and more successfully – by removing the Irish dimension from the local arena and making it the preserve of the developing Anglo-Irish intergovernmental framework. The Anglo-Irish process during 1983–5 completed the delinking of the Irish dimension from power-sharing, and effectively bypassed the local vetoes to succeed in institutionalising the Irish dimension under the Anglo-Irish Agreement. Additionally, however, the Agreement heralded a fundamental shift not only in such policy achievement, but in the very framework in which future policy was to be pursued, by co-opting the Irish government into the process. In the post-Agreement era, structural policy involved the pursuit of the single outstanding element of power-sharing within the new framework, through the strategy of trying to address the internal settlement of Northern Ireland as an integral part of the overall situation, rather than as an isolated end in itself.

3 Conflict Management Practice: The Cultural Approach

In distinction to the structural approach to conflict management, whose workings in Northern Ireland were reviewed in Chapter 2, it is also possible to identify the development of a cultural approach during the same period.

Cultural initiatives are those that operate at a broad community level, aiming to further resolution by a process of reconciliation between two or more distinct communal or cultural groups. Mutual understanding and respect through relationship-building are the aims of this approach, which operates largely outside the strictly political arena, involving mostly members of society who do not wield significant official political power. In Northern Ireland, such projects are generally termed 'reconciliation' or 'community relations' work. They are usually derived from spontaneous individual or local group initiatives, and take diverse forms.

1. THE CULTURAL APPROACH

In Northern Ireland, the cultural approach addresses itself to the question of intercommunal relationships. For most of the period under analysis this approach has, unlike its structural counterpart, had no single central and recognisable agent (such as a government) to act as the main implementer. It has, until the appearance of the Community Relations Council in 1990, lacked a focal point. The history of the cultural approach from 1969 onwards is consequently difficult to assemble and analyse, and indeed to label it an approach may be to infer a degree of coherence and unity which it has largely lacked. For the purposes of analysis, though, it can still be considered as a valid and recognisable approach. Such a lack of coherence is not a fault so much as a natural quality of the approach. Essentially, the development of the cultural approach is a story of disparate, small-scale, even piecemeal, initiatives started at various times and locations by various individuals and groups, with various aims in mind. What these initiatives do have in common, however, is what links them all into a cultural approach: they have all been concerned less with politics or structures, and more with relationships on the ground, between individuals, groups and communities. The history of the cultural approach, therefore, since it is the history of a range of initiatives which largely began as reactions to manifestations of violence since 1968, is a tale of initial independence and experimentation among these initiatives, growing gradually together to share resources and experience, to produce a coherent body of projects and workers with expertise and track-records who in their latest manifestation centre around the rallying-point of the Community Relations Council.

Almost all peacegroups or reconciliation initiatives in Northern Ireland developed in reaction to the post-1968 violence. Prior to that date, only a very few such organisations existed. One was Corrymeela, started in 1965 as a Christian reconciliation centre to facilitate dialogue and understanding within a specifically Christian ethos and in particular between Protestant and Catholic religious groups. Peace-oriented or pacifist groups existed to a small degree (for example, local branches of the Fellowship of Reconciliation, Society of Friends, Pax Christi, International Voluntary Service, Campaign for Nuclear Disarmament, and so on), but their outlook was generally international and with an orientation either towards the nuclear weapons debate or towards Christian ecumenism. Post-1968, some of these groups developed a more localised element within their work. Essentially, though, the situation in the 1960s was one where little overt effort was expended on the relationship between the two communities.

2. THE NORTHERN IRELAND COMMUNITY RELATIONS COMMISSION

Among the reforms urged on Stormont by Westminster following the widespread civil disorder and the arrival of British troops in August 1969 was the establishment of a new government Ministry for Community Relations and an accompanying Northern Ireland Community Relations Commission (NICRC). Initially then, both for Stormont and Westminster, a structural approach, through government legislation and patronage, was employed: new structures within government were hastily devised to address the problem of relationships. The new entities failed within just a few years, and their failure can be traced largely to the fact that a government structure – specifically that of a Unionist government – was by definition unable to tackle a cultural problem. For its part, the NICRC could only have tried to address the problem had it been established with real independence from government. But questions of independence and resources, arising from the tension of the NICRC's relationship to the government, bedevilled the NICRC from its inception. The speed at which the new bodies were set up – less than four months from the agreement in principle to reform until their establishment *in situ* in December – belies a lack of considered planning which in turn suggests a minimal Stormont commitment to the idea of community relations. The NICRC's first chair, Maurice Hayes, reflected later:

> There was no real attempt to find a conceptual base for the work of the Commission, and legislation setting up the body was debated only in the most superficial terms. The improvement of Community Relations was seen as a fairly peripheral activity designed . . . particularly to encourage catholics to participate in the operation of the reformed system. (Hayes 1972, p. 11)

His comments encapsulate accurately the degree of cynicism within the Unionist government towards the innovations: indeed it was the burgeoning antagonism towards the whole package of reforms which eventually fractured the Unionist Party and brought Stormont down. The Unionists' spirit of commitment to community relations can be measured by the first minister's act of resigning his membership of the Orange Order (an exclusively Protestant and anti-Catholic Masonic-type organisation with organic links to the Ulster Unionist Party) in the hope that it would be interpreted as 'greatly enhancing his liberal image' (Bleakley 1972, p. 105). In its five-year life, the Ministry had five different ministers.

The Ministry's brief was to 'promote policies which would improve community relations' (Frazer and Fitzduff 1986, p. 8), but its interpretation of community relations was closer to public relations. The relations it aimed to improve were those between

Stormont and the population, in particular the Catholic community. One internal ministerial memorandum of January 1972 makes this clear:

> The Ministry aims to secure acceptance of the Government by the people. . . . The keynote of the Ministry's work is . . . to show the sympathetic side of Government to the community and to ensure that the Government receives credit for goodwill (quoted in Griffiths 1974, pp. 29–30)

Its main method of fulfilling this task was the administration of a large financial programme of social intervention, the Social Needs programme. But noticeably, the bulk of such funding was dispensed to areas of social unrest (largely Catholic areas) rather than to areas of social need (which included at that time substantial Protestant areas): in the absence of other reliable indicators, 'areas of priority were therefore defined administratively and arbitrarily by principal reference to crisis; this was usually measured in terms of riots' (Griffiths 1974, p. 18). The Ministry was thus open to the charge of 'buying off trouble and purchasing respect' (ibid., p. 26). More fundamentally, as a government agency it was caught in a trap where its policies were aimed at protecting the political system which was largely the cause of the unrest it was attempting to quell. So it was a government department engaged in a hopeless attempt to 'purchase respect' from Catholics who were rapidly losing any respect for the entire government system. It is questionable how far any department of the Stormont government – whatever its title and whatever its brief – could have convinced the Catholic community of its concern for their well-being. Additionally, it is hard to discern any genuine element of interest on the Ministry's part in improving relations between the Catholic and Protestant communities.

Where the Ministry was charged with the promotion of policies which would improve community relations, the NICRC was charged with 'the promotion of activities relevant to this field' (Frazer and Fitzduff 1986, p. 8). Little definition of what such activities might be, or of how they might be promoted, was provided to the Commission. The lack of strategy was further apparent, in that the design of the NICRC was simply a wholesale transfer of the British Community Relations Commission (formerly the British Race Relations Board), a body designed to address racial relations in Britain. Thus, institutions which had been developed to deal with quite different problems elsewhere were introduced to Northern Ireland without any real critical examination of their relevance to [that] particular situation. (Hayes 1972, p. 7)

Had the NICRC been permitted to function as independently as its commissioners originally hoped, it might have overcome the Ministry's credibility problems arising from its government status. But, although policy design was initially left to the NICRC to devise, even at the earliest stages the Ministry retained a stranglehold on the Commission's finances (Griffiths 1974, p. 9). And when the NICRC published its first Annual Report in 1971, and outlined its intended policy, it ran into immediate conflict with the Ministry. It was the view of the Commission that their role involved the non-violent advocacy of social change and the facilitation of the voices of dissent as part of that process. 'Only a body which is seen to be independent of government can perform this role. Government itself cannot do it when it is a party to the conflict' (Hayes 1972, p. 13).

The NICRC's policy, as developed from nothing during the first year, was built mainly upon community development, defined as aiming 'to improve the economic, social and cultural conditions of communities, to integrate these communities into the life of the nation, and to enable them to contribute fully to national progress' (NICRC 1971, p. 7). Surveying the 1970 situation and finding what amounted to 'a kind of voluntary apartheid' (ibid., p. 3), the Commission asserted that such segregation, and the accompanying violence and division, were 'manifestations of deeper problems and . . . the reduction or prevention of their occurrence will ultimately depend on how we tackle the underlying problems' (ibid., p. 4). Recognising that government itself could not legislate such problems away, the NICRC described them as 'essentially community problems and in the last resort it is the community itself which must resolve them' (ibid.). Consequently,

> The Commission decided to work in local communities as it found them, whether they were Catholic, Protestant or mixed, and to raise whole communities to a level of self-confidence whereby they could deal with other whole communities without a feeling of insecurity. This involved a program of community development. . . . This first stage of community

development could provide a base for further development in the field of conflict resolution at various levels in society. . . . What we were aiming at was to build strength within the community so that [parties could be] given the confidence and skills to become involved in negotiation and conciliation. (Hayes 1972, p. 15)

It was overtly a two-stage process. First, each local community, through a process of development and self-help, would increase its own self-esteem and self-confidence. Then, on the basis of this newly built confidence, it would develop the desire to look outside itself and find areas of common interest with other communities on which they could then unite across sectarian boundaries.

Community development was the core of the Commission's policy. It was implemented directly by the Commission's staff, a team of ten Community Development Officers (later expanded to 16) who operated an outreach strategy, entering local communities, liaising with the community leaders, tenants' associations and whatever other groups they found there and giving advice, or – perhaps more often – helping to develop such groups where they did not already exist.

Completely secondary to that direct role was the provision of indirect support and encouragement for existing groups carrying out community relations programs. In the NICRC's first year, there were few such groups other than Corrymeela, Women Together (formed in 1970), and Protestant And Catholic Encounter (PACE, formed in 1969). These groups – rather than the NICRC itself – in fact represented in embryo the first phase of the cultural approach. They operated as free agents at the community level and concentrated directly on actual personal relationships between two communities which were already divided and rapidly polarising. Largely, their aim was simply to facilitate meeting:

Simply getting together – being seen with the 'other side' – becomes a significant gesture in a divided community. For this reason Women Together concentrates a good deal on the rally and the group meeting . . . the cup of tea and informal chat dominate the evening. . . . The importance does not lie in what is done at such meetings. That fact that they are taking place at all is what really matters. (Bleakley 1972, pp. 84–5)

Such programmes involved in the main simple provision of contact between the communities, in the belief that contact itself was of vital importance. NICRC gave them moral and public support for their work and some financial aid. But such background support was seen as less significant than the NICRC's own direct intervention on the community development programme. The Commission viewed these agencies – with some accuracy – as 'middle-class and suburban' (Hayes 1972, p. 14).[5] It believed that they were therefore somewhat removed from the location of the greatest alienation and that they catered predominantly to those already persuaded of the need for dialogue and encounter:

> Obviously cross-cutting contact is to be encouraged. . . . While these bodies have a contribution to make in promoting intergroup awareness and mutual understanding, to have regarded this as an important, if not the main, strategy in seeking inter-communal harmony would have been open to a charge of superficiality if not cynicism. (ibid.)

Additionally, the NICRC gave funding support to ad hoc projects bringing children together from both communities: play-schemes, holiday schemes and pre-school playgroups. But the concentration of policy was on community development, as reflected in the appointment of Hywel Griffiths as the Commission's first director, a Welsh academic whose experience and expertise were concentrated in the field of community development issues and practice.

It was this policy which led directly to a conflict between the NICRC and the Ministry. The Stormont government viewed the policy with great suspicion. Having introduced, under pressure from Westminster and against increasingly fierce internal opposition, a community relations programme which was viewed as simply part of the government's strategy to quell unrest with modest reform, Stormont responded very negatively when this turned into a rather radical campaign to encourage self-confidence and solidarity among disaffected sections of the population. What the NICRC saw as a necessary precondition for addressing the inter-community relationship, Stormont saw as a threat to its control.

After the publication of the NICRC's first Annual Report in March 1971, which outlined in some detail the conceptual basis and strategy of community development, the Ministry rapidly lost faith in its creation. The widespread disorder which followed Stormont's implementation of internment (effectively, detention without trial) in August of that year polarised the situation even more, as the NICRC temporarily shelved its programme in order to provide emergency relief during the greatest population movement Europe had seen since World War II. The crisis not only painted the NICRC in the light of a radical relief agency, documenting and responding with assistance to the effects of the government's increasingly oppressive security policy (overwhelmingly aimed at the Catholic population), but also energised violent Catholic rejection of Stormont's legitimacy and undermined the atmosphere in which a community development programme might hope to have any effect.

When the NICRC presented its plan for a radical increase in community development resources and staff at the end of the year, the Ministry rejected the proposal. In February 1972, the Commission's chair resigned, complaining that his job had become almost impossible because of

(1) the effect of present security policies in alienating almost the whole Catholic community . . . (2) the failure of politicians on all sides to engage in . . . constructive political discussion . . . and (3) the lack of any real sense of urgency [on the part of government]. (NICRC 1972, p. 20)

Two months later, when a much more modest expansion plan was again rejected by Stormont, Griffiths, the NICRC director, also resigned. By this stage, the Ministry had decided to step up its own intervention activities through the Social Needs programme, in preference to the parallel but uncontrolled activities of the NICRC.

But events had already overtaken the Ministry–Commission conflict. In March 1972, Stormont was prorogued, and power assumed by Westminster. While the NICRC continued to exist, with a considerable change in personnel among both staff and commissioners, it had effectively lost momentum and commitment to both its overall task and its central policy of community development. Westminster did not provide the support so badly needed by the dispirited Commission, and 'the record of the last two years of the Commission's life is one of disillusion, demoralisation and introspective preoccupation arising from continuing uncertainty regarding its future' (Griffiths 1974, p. 56).

When the power-sharing Executive took office in 1974, and the Ministry for Community Relations was reinstated, the decision was taken to close the NICRC, since an independent body, it was argued, was no longer needed to do the work of a new government which represented catholics in a way that the old Stormont had not (Griffiths 1974, p. 1). Eight weeks later, the Executive fell and power was returned to Westminster under direct rule. The NICRC was finally dissolved, as planned, in 1975.

Certainly the Ministry/Commission strategy must be regarded as an overall failure. Within the argument and the terminology of this study, it can be described as the inevitable failure of a structural attempt to deal with what is essentially a cultural problem. In its defence, however, it must be pointed out that at the time of the NICRC's inception, there was virtually no evidence of the existence of any cultural approach.

Responsibility for community relations initiatives under the resumed direct rule was passed to a small Community Relations Division within the Department of Education for Northern Ireland (DENI). With a small budget for the purpose, DENI was charged with both formulating policies in this area and administering grant aid to agencies carrying out the work. In effect, DENI interpreted this as providing guidelines about what would qualify as valid cross-community contact projects, mostly with children and youth, and then providing funding for projects which fulfilled the criteria.

Responsibility and funding for community development was passed to Local District Councils in 1976. But by and large, the Councils interpreted the programme as directed towards the provision of community services, and the money went mainly on sport and recreation facilities and the provision and upkeep of community centres. Community relations projects received little or no support.

3. INFORMAL INITIATIVES

The NICRC represented the failure of formal structures to address the problem of communal relationships. No government body could legislate for relationships, and likewise the NICRC was refused the independence from government which might have permitted it the freedom to address those relationships. It was an attempt to address the problem through the same channels that were being used to address all the other problems of Northern Ireland – the structural, governmental channels. Only after its demise did a real separation of approaches into structural and cultural strands emerge. The role of government, as evidenced in how DENI chose to interpret its policy, became primarily that of a funding source. DENI increasingly left the development and execution of community relations activities to those informal groups which began to spring up. In so far as the cultural approach must by definition be an informal one, and not a centrally or governmentally formal one, this arrangement left the informal, spontaneously generated, community-level agencies to develop their own *modus operandi* assisted by a modicum of central funding.[6]

As mentioned above, in 1970 the number of such agencies was minimal. Partly this was because sustained and overt violence was still a relatively new phenomenon in Northern Ireland, and partly it was due to a general hope that the worst days were over, that violence had peaked and that some form of the *status quo ante* was still likely to be resumed before long. Several large-scale traumas dispelled such optimism over the ensuing four years which, played out against a background of almost continuous violent street protests and clashes with the military, persuaded people in Northern Ireland that the Troubles were not amenable to any swift or simple solution. That realisation led an increasing number of people to make their own contribution, either towards a solution or towards the provision of relief for those suffering most, by setting up voluntary organisations for a variety of purposes.

While Women Together and, particularly, PACE continued with their contact work among adults, the emphasis among most new groups was on children and youth. Several voluntary organisations sprang up between 1972 and 1975 to provide holidays for children from those urban areas of Northern Ireland which were suffering most from the effects of violence. They included Children's Community Holidays, Holiday Projects West, Harmony Community Trust and Northern Ireland Children's Holiday Schemes. Corrymeela also became involved in holiday provision. These agencies organised residential holidays for mixed Protestant and Catholic groups of children, either in their own premises or in rented sites in Northern Ireland. They had twin aims. One, the social provision aim, was the provision of holiday relief for families adversely affected by the Troubles. The other was the promotion of the 'contact hypothesis' (Hewstone and Brown 1986), that is, simply facilitating an experience of shared living for Protestant and Catholic children and the young adults who accompanied them.

DENI partly funded these projects under its Community Relations Holidays Scheme, paying a certain amount per child per day, providing that the projects fell within certain guidelines, such as a 60:40 per cent religious balance among the children, and so on. Most of the work was done by organisations like those mentioned, recruiting their clients either through community groups or schools, but a small number of such holidays were also organised by adjacent community groups themselves joining forces to organise activities. Summer activities programmes, such as playschemes, also flourished, operated either by independent voluntary groups such as the Voluntary Service Bureau in Belfast or, again, by joint initiatives between local communities.

It is fair to say that for many of these projects, the initial aim was short-term provision of relief – either giving children respite from an atmosphere of continuing street violence in the form of a holiday, or keeping them occupied and out of trouble through supervised playschemes during school vacations. However, the cross-community contact element slowly grew in significance as the life-span of the Troubles appeared increasingly long-term. As experience and expertise in these activities grew through the 1970s, more concentration was put on using the projects to develop the relationships between the two communities. Some organisations began to 'twin' adjacent Protestant and Catholic community groups on a holiday, and to repeat the holiday annually with the same 'twinned' groups. More significantly, they also began to develop 'follow-up' activities. Groups coming together for one 10-day summer holiday would be reunited for a subsequent residential reunion weekend. Later, most holiday groups developed a fuller follow-up programme of non-residential weekly or fortnightly joint activities for the twinned groups closer to their home areas, as a means of sustaining and deepening the inter-community relationships forged on the original holiday. As the contact element of their work achieved greater significance, there was a gradual shift, in the late 1970s, from the terminology of 'holiday organisations' to 'reconciliation groups'.

Additionally, such groups began to cooperate with each other, as they built up experience and expertise, and the Holiday Organisations Group (HOG), formed in the late 1970s as an informal forum for discussion, developed into a reference point for resource-sharing, for joint planning and policy formation and, significantly, for lobbying DENI on policy and resource provision. HOG also began to consider the training needs of its member agencies and to design tentative joint training initiatives for staff and volunteers. Other dialogue-oriented groups developed throughout the 1970s. PACE and Women Together continued to operate, although in less radical ways than when they had begun. Given that they were similarly based mainly on the idea of providing contact, there was a lack of developmental orientation beyond that initial provision, and given the gradual institutionalisation of violence in the Northern Irish society, non-violent street activity became more problematic. Women Together, for example, had been very active in its initial months:

'separating rival gangs in riots by using themselves as human shields . . . dispersing a gang of youths with knives who were attacking a boy from the "other side" . . . defending neighbours who were having windows broken, and going out night after night talking to [street] gangs...' With the gun on the streets in a much bigger way, many of these activities are no longer possibilities. (*Dawn* 1978, p. 22)

Corrymeela continued its inter-religious dialogue, and other groups flourished for a time. Many of them were initially formed in response to specific incidents. For example, Witness For Peace, formed by a clergyman whose son was killed in a bombing, aimed to draw attention to the horrors of violence, in particular by planting crosses in the grounds of Belfast City Hall to commemorate the dead, and by keeping a large public 'scoreboard' of fatalities in the city centre. The most famous was the Peace People (see McKeown 1984). This began as an individual response to the death of a group of children in 1976, and mushroomed dramatically into a series of huge cross-community rallies throughout Northern Ireland. It was nothing more sophisticated to begin with than a 'mass protest against violence' (*Dawn* 1978, p. 23). People in their thousands joined together to call for what was essentially a negative definition of peace – an end to violence. But when, after the initial euphoria, the momentum of the movement demanded a more positive definition of the goal of peace, the Peace People fractured over the question of political involvement. Some elements wanted peace that included various different formulas for justice and reform – essentially political positions on structural matters – while others were reluctant to advocate more than the original demand of an end to violence. Within a few years, what had been by far the highest-profile peace group to emerge from the conflict (its organisers received the Nobel Prize for Peace in 1976) settled into the role of a small, low-profile group involved mainly in contact work among children and young adults, some holiday provision, and some cross-community dialogue work.

Overall, by the late 1970s, there were several well-established 'reconciliation' organisations who were gradually amassing experience, mostly working on the contact hypothesis. But a contemporary commentator observed that

> the overall effect of peace groups has been peripheral . . . a group like the Peace People has made some difference but has in no way substantially altered the overall situation. Other groups too may have affected hundreds or even thousands of individuals, but they have not altered the overall situation in society either. (*Dawn* 1978, p. 24)

With an increasing number of groups active in various ways in the field of promoting peace, the tendency for inter-group collaboration was not limited to HOG. In 1974, the Northern Ireland Peace Forum was devised to be an umbrella group for community-level peace initiatives. But although it lasted, at least on paper, for 14 years, the Peace Forum failed to become the centre of activity that might have been hoped for. Its inception involved Corrymeela, PACE, Fellowship Of Reconciliation, Women Together, Witness for Peace and a few other ad hoc groups; by 1982, there were 18 member groups. But while it maintained a minimal role of information exchange, the umbrella organisation role was never developed. In large part, this was because of the diversity of goals and methods displayed by its members, who included groups as diverse as the East Belfast Community Council and the United Nations Association. Consequently, Forum members tended to look elsewhere to develop their own inter-agency cooperative channels more closely focused on their particular specialisation, for example political reform, educational reform, contact activities, international peace issues, etc. (*Dawn* 1988, pp. 16–17). Undoubtedly, the holiday organisations were the clearest and best developed example of this tendency towards specialised cooperation.

Otherwise, groups encountered difficulties in terms of sharing and collaborating, caused by their wide disparity of strategies and ultimate goals. They tended, in the main, to be spontaneous initiatives, often formed in reaction to a specific violent event. Further, they often started from a desire to respond positively to a negative situation, the effect of which was to produce disparate and ad hoc groupings that lacked any prior strategy, but rather developed tactics on the job. And the initial task – simply providing contact between members of divided communities – involved logistical and organisational challenges which occupied staff and volunteers fully and further handicapped the development of strategy. Workers in this new and experimental field of community relations were busy keeping their own fledgling organisations alive and their own activities programmes intact. Without the time and resources to develop their own internal strategies, it was unrealistic for a collection of such groups to address coherently a joint strategy.

But a further strategic problem for these groups arose from the fact that their very subject matter was hazy and ill-defined:

> A major and perennial difficulty for many groups working in the area of community relations has been their difficulty in adequately defining what they see as the objectives of community relations work in Northern Ireland. This confusion has frequently been reflected in their difficulties in formulating strategies to contribute effectively to this work. (Frazer and Fitzduff 1986, p. 15)

By the early 1980s, there was an increasing number of such agencies in Northern Ireland with perhaps 10 years or more of experience behind them. (By 1986, there were an estimated 45 community relations organisations, receiving £410 000 annually from DENI for contact work; ibid., p. 11.) Most of them had been launched to address community relations through the contact approach. But their experience had led them to question the approach, as they started to see the limits of simply facilitating contact. The idea of 'focused community relations work' began to be developed. This involved taking the contact hypothesis a step further and shaping it around a more direct agenda of the problem of relationships between the two communities. For example, holiday organisations had begun by simply bringing children from both communities together to share the fun of a holiday. While the goal of greater mutual understanding through building personal friendships lay behind the holiday, the whole issue of the state of community relations in Northern Ireland was addressed only indirectly by an agenda which essentially encompassed simply shared living and activities. By the early 1980s, the holiday organisations had realised the shortcomings of this 'brief encounter' programme and had developed long-term programmes of activities throughout the year for holiday groups, which improved and maintained the cross-community contact to a much more significant degree. But the activities involved, on holiday or subsequently, were simply fun activities which could be done together. With the idea of focused community relations work, activities began to include, among the games sessions and the outings, the facilitation of discussion about issues directly connected to the Troubles. Particularly for teenage and older groups, this embraced self-development work, discussion and debate on political or religious issues, and workshops on such topics as sectarianism, civil rights, prejudice reduction, and so on. There was, in sum, a shift away from concentrating simply on the similarities between the two communities and playing down differences – the basis of the early contact work – to a more conscious addressing of those differences in focused discussion, in the hope of increasing mutual understanding and tolerance.

This shift was slow. It reflected a maturing in the 1980s of the disparate and inexperienced initiatives of the 1970s. But its strength lay in its solid base of experiment and experiential learning. The organisations involved began to spend more time in mutual discussion, sharing knowledge and experience, pooling resources, and looking at their own needs – for example, for training in organisational and fundraising skills, as well as in facilitation skills. But the field of community relations was still a publicly unrecognised one. It was still, necessarily, work with a distinctly low profile and was still too easily dismissed by the public at large as peripheral do-gooding. There was a growing sense among community relations workers that they needed to change this perception, and to reflect their increasing coherence at the operational level in a publicly recognised forum.

In the mid-1980s, a period of consultation and discussion at various levels, both in the voluntary sector and within government circles (dealt with in more detail in Chapter 6), led eventually to the establishment of the Central Community Relations Unit (CCRU) within the NIO in 1987. Within a short time, the CCRU took the decision to create an independent public body for community relations. In 1990, the Community Relations Council (CRC) was established as a semi-autonomous, government-funded public agency.

In some ways these bodies mirrored the previous incarnations of the Ministry and the Commission of 1969–74, but there were equally significant differences from those precedents. The Community Relations Council (CRC), with a brief to support and develop community relations practice through the provision of skills training, management consultancy, a forum for dialogue and a public profile, represented a concrete response to many of the practitioners' expressed needs at the end of the 1980s. It was, with hindsight, the major development of the era in community relations in Northern Ireland.

The appearance of the CCRU reflected a new commitment from government to the significance of the cultural approach, just as their subsequent establishment of the CRC signalled a new phase in the development of the approach. After some 20 years of trial-and-error growth and piecemeal achievement, there now existed a corps of experienced practitioners in Northern Ireland, and a basis for a more strategic and unified approach to the work. The CRC could facilitate this development, both operational and strategic, with a degree of coherence (and of independence from – indeed with the support of – government), which the earlier NICRC had lacked. It could also form a public location at which the profile of community relations work could be raised. Thus, after two decades of disparate and sometimes idiosyncratic policies and strategies, analysis of the cultural approach could now be more coherently focused on the central point of the CRC. Its significance in these terms alone merits a study of the contemporary position of the cultural approach as evidenced in the position of the CRC since its inception; a detailed consideration of its workings thus follows in Chapter 6.

CONCLUSION AND SUMMARY

With the outbreak of violence in 1969, the problem of intercommunal relationships was initially addressed in structural terms, although from an early point the British government was careful to point out that this was a part of the problem that lay beyond the scope of government or legislation. But the demise of the NICRC demonstrated emphatically that the structural approach could not solve this problem. As time passed and the conflict showed no signs of an early end, disparate informal initiatives began to develop, aimed at improving relationships at the community level. The small but growing number of groups involved in such work concentrated mainly on the 'contact hypothesis', doing nothing more complicated than facilitating contact between members of the two alienated communities.

The groups involved tended to operate in a separate, low-profile manner. As experience, confidence, and understanding were developed by those involved, they began to cooperate more directly with each other through the late 1970s and early 1980s. First, they began to form a more coherent body of knowledge and experience, to share resources and experience, and to reflect jointly on their activities. Secondly, they began to suspect that simple contact work was not enough, and developed the idea of focused community relations work, which involved a more directly conflict-focused use of the contact time. In general, practitioners began to establish a more solid conceptual base for the work. There was an accompanying growth in the desire for a more centrally organised and publicly visible profile.

The emergence of both of these factors – an experienced and coherent corps of practitioners, and realistic strategic thinking for the implementation of their work – encouraged the British government to respond, first, by establishing its own department for community relations within its NIO, and secondly by funding the establishment of a central support agency for the practical work, in the form of the CRC.

4 Complementarity in Conflict Management Theory: Resolution and Settlement Approaches[7]

Throughout the theoretical literature on conflict management, a dichotomy is apparent. Almost every scholar, in reviewing thinking on the subject, describes a bipolar differentiation in approaches, both in descriptive and prescriptive thinking. The distinctions, and their labels, differ of course from writer to writer, but a general acceptance of two different strands of thought is recurrent.

This chapter deals with the general theory of conflict as developed and utilised by theorists. However, despite the general nature of the theory and the generalisations of context in which it is applied, two observations need to be made concerning the base from which this theory grows. First, despite the variety of social contexts in which conflict occurs and the variety of strategies which are employed for its management, much of the current theorising on conflict management is based on proposals for, or empirical observation of, third party intervention (TPI) or mediation. Further, a great proportion of this work is set in the specific context of international conflict. Nevertheless, despite the particularities of this type of conflict management in this type of context, the bases for the arguments centred on the polarity of thought depend on a broader and more fundamental differentiation on the origins and nature of conflict.

Although the dichotomy which each author produces is usually slightly different in its focus and in the terminology employed, the similarities of emphasis are striking. In general, the distinction between the two categories into which commentators group conflict management approaches is at its clearest at the prescriptive stage, that is, in terms of the types of outcome envisaged. For this reason, I find it convenient to term the two approaches 'settlement' and 'resolution'. Additionally, I use the term 'conflict

management' in a neutral sense to denote the whole field of
study. Like every other available term, its use is inconsistent
throughout the literature and is sometimes used to denote one
side of the dichotomy or one particular approach to conflict; for
my purposes here, however, I employ it as a neutral umbrella
term embracing both settlement and resolution approaches.[8]

My intention here is not simply to add another typology to the
already terminologically confusing array of differentiations. Such
a risk does exist, given that, for example,

> there is unfortunately no agreed-upon typology for classifying
> third party interventions. . . . In some contexts, terms are used
> interchangeably (e.g. conciliation and mediation) and in some
> cases, a single term, usually mediation, is used to refer to a
> wide range of different third party interventions. (Fisher and
> Keashly 1991, p. 33)

The result is a persistent semantic confusion throughout the
literature. The first step, then, is to try to clarify what is meant
by the two approaches to which I have given these labels. This
process involves a degree of simplification or generalisation; but
I shall return to address that issue later in this chapter.

1. RESOLUTION AND SETTLEMENT

Resolution

The resolution approach prescribes an outcome derived through
mutual problem-sharing between the two parties, in which they
cooperate with each other to redefine their conflict and their
relationship. In this sense, they solve the conflict themselves by
jointly finding their own integrative solution, thereby becoming
their own guarantors of the agreement. Far from compromising
or bargaining away any of their goals, they engage in a process
of information-sharing, relationship-building, joint analysis and
cooperation. For this to be possible, they must be able, as it
were, to delve below their conflict over issues to find a deeper
level on which they can base a new relationship of mutuality. And
they must find shared values which, to reverse the metaphor,
transcend the issues that caused the conflict to erupt. Thus the
role of any third party is one of facilitation without coercion or

the use of power-persuasion, and without advocacy of any specific outcome. Proponents of this approach include John Burton (1987, 1990a), Edward Azar (1990), Ronald Fisher (1972, 1983), Herbert Kelman (1991) and Adam Curle (1986, p. 9). Underlying this approach is an understanding that the roots of conflict lie in the subjective relationships between the disputants. The subjective element implies that transformation of the conflict is possible through transformation of the disputants' perceptions of the conflict, and of each other. Out of the seedbed of the relationship grow the issues that spark a conflict, which is really about something deeper: differing values or value-systems, or the pursuit of incompatible satisfiers for similar needs. Feelings and perceptions must be shared and acknowledged, and mutual trust and understanding developed. Only then can the issues be cooperatively addressed within a new relationship between partners. Resolution aims to remove not only the current manifestation of the conflict, but its underlying cause, by addressing, redesigning and reconciling the parties' relationship with each other. This inter-disputant relationship is prioritised above all others.

Criticism of the resolution approach generally focuses on its feasibility: that while it is a penetrating and fundamental means of dealing with conflict, it is equally difficult to attain in practice, not least because conflicting parties (especially in long-standing and/or violent conflict) are the least amenable to the idea of an approach so rooted in close cooperation and because the practicalities of fostering such a simultaneously broad and deep solution are immense. Bercovitch, for example, faults the 'unrealistic expectations' (1984, p. 116) of the approach for retaining certain theoretical purities – such as the neutral or impartial intervenor – which are belied by a complex and often contradictory reality. Critics also point out, as proponents will acknowledge, that objective issue-based disagreements do not necessarily disappear as positive relationships develop.

Settlement

The settlement approach, in contrast, prescribes an outcome that is built on agreement reached by the conflicting parties through negotiation and bargaining. A settlement, by this definition, means an agreement over the issue(s) of the conflict which will often involve a compromise, or some concessions from both sides. In such an outcome, neither side may achieve all their goals, but this disappointment is offset by the mutuality of the compromise. Formal negotiation and political bargaining are examples of this approach, of which Bercovitch (1984), and Zartman and Touval (1985) are eloquent proponents. If, questionable though the dictum is, politics is the art of the possible, then settlement is similarly the art of the practical.

Underlying this approach is a particular view of the nature, form and roots of conflict. Conflict is generated over objective, power-related issues. In action, it relates closely to the power capacities of each side. If power levels are close enough, coercion will not succeed in 'winning' the conflict outright for one party, and from such a stalemate the situation may become ripe for the instigation of a bargaining process (Pruitt and Rubin 1986; Zartman and Touval 1985). During such a process, however, power remains both a salient issue and a valid resource to be used. This applies similarly to any third party who becomes involved. All parties (including any intervenor) to the bargaining process approach the goal of settlement with their own interests to be promoted or safeguarded and their own agendas to be addressed. Any third party plays an active, initiating role, and can quite legitimately employ its own resources to bribe or threaten the disputing parties into agreement. Where TPI is employed, the primary relationship for a disputing party is that between it and the intervenor. The bargaining is usually carried out between the power-holders from within each party. The feelings of the parties are subordinated to the issues; their relationship likewise is addressed only in so far as it is pertinent to the bargaining process. Settlement is reached over the objective issues; it may be achieved by means of third party persuasion, and it will be guaranteed by the power of the third party.

Criticism of this approach usually centres on claims of superficiality. A settlement may be an effective immediate solution to a difficult, and possibly violent, situation, it is argued, but its efficacy is temporary and fails to deal with the negative elements of the underlying inter-disputant relationship. These remain to flare up again at a later date, either when strength of feeling produces new issues or renewed dissatisfactions about the old ones, or when the third party's guarantee runs out. Azar and Moon disparage the shallowness of this 'quick-fix' approach (1986, p. 401).

In summary, settlement prides itself on its pragmatism in aiming at the achievable, and queries the practicality of the comprehensiveness of approach demanded by the resolution school of thought. Resolution claims its approach provides long-lasting, even permanent solutions to conflict and criticises settlement for the superficial and temporary nature of its solutions.

2. TWO EXAMPLES: AZAR AND BERCOVITCH

These different theoretical approaches are, of course, far more subtle than such a sketchy summary might imply. To understand their deeper implications, it is helpful to examine two proponents of the respective approaches in more detail. Edward Azar and Jacob Bercovitch are particularly eloquent and able adherents of, respectively, the resolution and settlement schools of thought.

Azar

Azar has worked closely with John Burton, who is generally credited with laying the foundations of the resolution approach. It was Burton who formalised the terminology of the settlement/resolution dichotomy (albeit according to his own definitions, which do not correspond completely to those used here). He did much to promote the subjective relationship-based approach, and initiated the problem-solving workshop designed on such thinking. Azar continues to develop his own work out of that conceptual base pioneered by Burton. Azar has chosen to address in particular what he terms 'protracted social conflict' (PSC), by which he refers to enduring and intercommunal (that is, between ethnic or cultural groups) conflict which usually, but not always, occurs within rather than across international boundaries (Azar 1990). Lebanon, Israel/Palestine and Northern Ireland are examples of PSC.

Azar argues forcefully that the roots of conflict are to be found not in terms of surface interests, but in some underlying strata where more fundamental psychological imperatives motivate the individual and the group towards the pursuance of such interests:

> While domestic, regional and international conflicts in the world today are framed as conflicts over material interests,

such as commercial advantages or resource acquisition, empirical evidence suggests that they are not just that. More fundamentally, most contemporary conflicts are about developmental needs expressed in terms of cultural values, human rights and security. (1990, p. 2)

His concept of 'developmental needs' is a refinement of Burton's use of needs theory to explain conflict (see Bloomfield 1991). The theory proposes that identical psychological needs are shared by all human beings, that these needs are inalienable, and that their pursuit takes priority over every other motivation or goal. The individual seeks the satisfaction of such social needs through identity groups (indeed, all these human needs have an element of, or are very closely related to, the need for identity), which are formed around such elements as religion, race, culture, etc. Azar comments that such needs-pursuit is the motivation for all social interaction, from the individual up to the international level:

What is of concern are the societal needs of the individual – security, identity, recognition and others. . . . All internal and external relations between states and nations are induced by the desire to satisfy such basic needs. (Azar 1985, p. 63)

All humans share the same human needs: in this sense we are identically motivated. But the different cultures of our different identity groups define different means of satisfying them: in this sense we are in competition with other identity groups for the means to satisfy our needs. Hence, human needs are at the basis of conflict.

However, for Azar and others, human needs are also the basis for solving conflict. Identical, shared needs are the transcendant, common elements of the parties in conflict: it is by grasping a sense of shared needs that they can transform their relationship into one of cooperation over the task of jointly satisfying their needs. Needs, to change the direction of the metaphor, are the deeper stratum of commonality below the surface level of incompatible interests. They are the common ground out of which cooperative efforts towards an integrative solution can be forged. Azar's scheme proposes, on this basis of deeper-level redrawing of the conflict in terms of needs, the 'facilitation of breakthroughs to a conflict situation through problem-solving workshops' (Azar and Moon 1986, p. 401). Here is the facilitative role of the third party as envisaged by the resolution theorists: a role of providing opportunity for communication and discussion and of providing information, while allowing the conflicting parties to keep the initiative in the search for solution. In such problem-solving workshops, the third party has no effective political power to bring to bear on the conflict, beyond the provision of a needs-based understanding of the situation in the hope that cooperative attitudes will thus be fostered. The basic assumption of the problem-solving workshop, 'is that most PSCs are conflicts over human needs for security, identity and social justice rather than over interests. Conflicts over interests are negotiable, but those over identity needs are not' (Azar and Moon 1986, p. 401).

Azar and Moon, like other theorists, identify a dichotomy in approaches. On one side they locate both the 'legal-formalist' and the 'bureaucratic-management' approaches to TPI:

Both approaches tend to be primarily interested in a settlement or containment which involves a win–lose outcome or some compromise in which all or some parties are to some degree losers. . . . Their intervention tends to take place at the time of crisis situations. . . . Once . . . authorities 'agree' to comply with outcomes of negotiations (for legal-formalists) or are 'rewarded' or 'punished' (for bureaucratic-managers), then the conflict is believed to be settled. (ibid.)

They are critical of the superficiality of this approach which offers only 'a temporary settlement or control of a crisis, without tackling the deeper structural roots underlying the crisis. . . . There are no "quick fix" solutions to these problems' (ibid.). Against such a view they propose their own PSC perspective, which, while more complex and demanding more effort to achieve a solution, operates both through the problem-solving workshop to facilitate breakthroughs and through 'self-sustaining' policies designed to achieve the satisfaction of all human needs, thus replacing the mere crisis-management approach of settlement theory with 'attempts to combine short-term efforts to arrest impending crises with long-term design to transform the conflict system in its totality' (ibid.). It is this goal of 'totality' – addressing not just the manifestation of conflict behaviour, but eradicating the very cause(s) of conflict itself – which constitutes the attraction of the resolution approach.

Bercovitch

Bercovitch provides a contrast to Azar's work. In the first place, of course, Bercovitch concentrates on the context of international relations for his analysis of conflict management. Like Azar, he is interested in mediation, or TPI. Although Bercovitch's first major research (1984) was a study of the efficacy of problem-solving at the interpersonal, intergroup and international level, it is the last environment in which he generally couches his analysis, and it is there that he finds the least use for the resolution approach.

First, his whole concept of mediation sits within the context of the negotiating process, with a consequent emphasis on the parties' power resources and self-interest. Secondly, he emphasises that such resources and agendas pertain to a third party as to any other in the conflict management process, with the implication that a merely facilitatory role, as envisaged in the problem-solving workshop, is either unachievable or, if achievable, ineffective:

> My approach to the problem of TPI is to examine it not as a separate, autonomous process, but rather to consider it as an integral part of conflict management in general, and bargaining and negotiation in particular. . . . A third party is not, and cannot be, neutral. By its very presence, it affects the process or some of the conditions of conflict management interaction. (1984, pp. 15–16)

Bercovitch finds the resolution approach impractical, for the very reason that it retains certain theoretical purities which, he argues, are belied by practice. He complains that while reality shows that third parties 'in searching for information and exercising influence . . . behave in much the same way as other actors' (1984, p. 116) the theory of conflict management has often made a theoretical assumption of the neutrality and non-involvement of the third party:

> When this assumption is made, one can offer various imaginative and creative approaches to conflict management. Such approaches, however, based as they are on unrealistic expectations, can not, alas, help us to deal with real conflict situations in international relations. (ibid.)

Indeed, it is the idea of pragmatism, of realism, which fuels Bercovitch's criticisms of the resolution approach as exemplified in the problem-solving workshop. 'We have to move between the conceptual and empirical levels,' he says. 'There is no other way of answering important questions' (ibid., p. 33).

The resolution approach, for him, is a comprehensive and coherent theory which nevertheless fails to translate into realistic practice in the face of a less coherent reality of complex and sometimes contradictory conflict behaviour. Resolution, for Bercovitch, fails to make the prescriptive transition from the conceptual to the empirical, and his criticism is scathing:

> To answer the question 'what constitutes good and effective TPI?' by offering, as a basis, the specifications of the problem-solving model may amount to exploration of the parameters of human optimism. (ibid., p. 147)

On the contrary, Bercovitch argues, settlement, whatever its limitations, can actually produce results in real conflict situations. Through negotiation and bargaining, settlement can be achieved, and if it involves coercion, manipulation, power-bargaining and compromise, then that is an acceptable fact of reality on the path to success:

> Leverage or mediator's power enhance the mediator's ability to influence the outcome. The mediator's task is primarily one of persuasion, and persuasion is best achieved . . . not when a mediator is unbiased or impartial, but when he [sic] possesses resources which either or both parties value. . . . The most successful method of mediation was that of manipulation. . . . Clearly, if a mediator can bring to bear resources such as power, influence and persuasion, he can move the parties in the desired direction and achieve some success. (1986, pp. 164–5).

Bercovitch's emphasis on what might be termed the pragmatism of the settlement approach can be traced to a particular understanding of the nature of conflict management. It lies in a behaviour-based approach. He refers to Galtung's model of conflict which proposes a triangular relationship between three components: situation, attitude and behaviour (see also Mitchell 1981). For Bercovitch, the resolution approach, which, in this particular discussion he terms the 'subjective' approach to conflict (1984, p. 6), enters the conflict at the point of *attitude*: the aim is to address primarily, via the problem-solving process, the attitudes of the parties, so later to alter the situation and, eventually, to transform the behaviour (hostility or aggression) through a new relationship of cooperation.

On the other hand, Bercovitch argues, the settlement approach finds an entry-point in the *behaviour* of the parties. Settlement works primarily on the behaviour, negotiating and dealing and compromising to alter the behaviour; a different prioritisation process is at work here among the three components. His approach, with its pragmatism and empirical realism, concentrates on the issues between the parties, and their behaviour consequent on those issues, rather than on their relationship. It is primarily a behaviour-based approach. Its attraction, particularly in the face of complex and confusing conflict, lies in its pragmatic dedication to the achievable.

3. THE DICHOTOMY IN THE LITERATURE

Azar and Bercovitch suffice as examples of a general dichotomy which is clearly visible throughout the literature on conflict management. But not only do they operate as adherents of one or other side of the argument; interestingly they, like most others in the field, provide their own version of the dichotomy. For Azar, it is characterised as a methodology that prescribes either settlement or resolution (Azar and Moon 1986, p. 399), a view of politics that concentrates either on power-based competition or on collective security (Azar 1990, p. 1), or a model that locates the roots of conflict either in scarce material resources or in developmental needs (ibid., p. 2).

Bercovitch's version of the dichotomy differentiates between instrumental and process intervention. The two approaches differ in terms of their objectives, the participants, the identity and role of the third party, and the quality of the outcomes. Process interventions 'are meant to affect the entire system of interactions and generate a satisfactory resolution of the conflict. Their scope and impact is quite extensive' (1984, p. 121). They are system-inclusive, that is, all parties to the conflict are involved. They focus on the relationship, and have as their goal 'the improvement of the parties' use of their capabilities to achieve a more creative decision making and a resolution of their conflict (ibid., p. 124). However, process intervention can only operate under certain special circumstances: a conducive environment, sufficient time, a level of competency among parties, and an acceptance of collaborative values. Bercovitch characterises process intervention as rather idealised and specialised, thus limited in appropriateness: 'We should not be so overwhelmed by its creative potential to suggest it as a universal mechanism for managing social conflicts' (ibid., p. 128).

In contrast, instrumental (or content) interventions are 'more limited in scope' and characterised by 'outcomes which alter situational contingencies, but leave the general experience and boundaries of a conflict system unaffected' (ibid., p. 121). They are also system-exclusive. In such an intervention, the third party acts in a directive role as an 'outcome-advocate'. The role involves 'advocating concessions, facilitating specific concessions without loss of face, or legitimising and rewarding concessions' (ibid., p. 129).

Other writers identify the same dichotomy of approach, although their terminology differs. Burton, as already mentioned, popularised the settlement versus resolution differentiation (1987, p. 7). Paul Wehr (1986) identifies the 'competitive/hierarchical versus collaborative/network' approaches. Morton Deutsch differentiates between ' "cooperative" and "competitive" processes of conflict resolution' (1991, p. 27). Kenneth Kressel and Dean Pruitt identify 'contextual' interventions, third party attempts to 'alter the climate' of a conflict to facilitate problem-solving, and 'substantive' interventions, which address issues with a view to attaining settlement (1985, pp. 191–4). Raimo Vayrynen (1991) argues for settlement through negotiation as a superior means of eliminating violence from a conflict, contrasting it with attempts at 'conflict transformation' whose outcomes are difficult to forecast given that 'any argument that a conflict has been solved for good . . . is based on an ahistorical illusion' (1991, p. 23). Ronald Fisher and Loraleigh Keashly differentiate two third party roles. One is 'consultation', whose rationale is

> largely based in a social-psychological perspective which sees conflict at least partly and at times predominantly as a subjective social process . . . [designed to] improve communication, diagnose underlying relationship issues, and facilitate the search towards creative resolution. (1991, p. 32)

This is in contrast to 'mediation', which, at the international level,

involves interventions by credible and competent interme-
diaries who assist the parties in working toward a negotiated
settlement on substantive issues through persuasion, the control of information, the suggestion of alternatives, and, in some
cases, the application of leverage. (ibid., p. 30)

A similar definition of mediation is used by William Zartman
and Saadia Touval (1985) to denote intervention aimed at
producing negotiated settlement through compromise, where the
mediator is motivated by self-interest, is not necessarily impartial,
and its use of manipulation or leverage is legitimate as part of
'power mediation'. Elsewhere, Touval argues that resolution is
beyond the remit of TPI, since deep-rooted conflicts

> can be *resolved* only as a result of transformations in national
> values and ideologies . . . Nevertheless, by helping to conclude
> 'small' agreements *reducing* the conflict, mediators can contrib-
> ute. (1982, p. 331; original emphases)

For Hugo Prein (1984), too, 'mediation' is a strategy where the
third party 'does not hesitate to pressure the parties. . . . This
approach is less concerned with improving mutual relations and
more concerned with finding a workable, pragmatic compromise
for the specific problem', as opposed to 'consultation strategies'
which are broader and more relationship-based (1984, p. 85). For
Stephen Cohen and Harriet Arnone (1988), the terminology of
differentiation concerns 'management' and 'resolution'; their differences centre on the breadth of involvement of parties, on the
comprehensiveness of the outcome envisaged, and, most starkly,
on the concepts of 'negative' and 'positive' peace (see O'Connell
1985). Although initially 'conflict management and conflict
resolution techniques do not differ substantially in their first
efforts' (1988, p. 177) the distinction clarifies in the respective
strategies employed to produce a sustainable solution. Cohen and
Arnone

> distinguish between the typical sort of short-range conflict
> management, in which governments must engage, and the
> long-term processes of conflict resolution, which must include
> the involvement of entire societies and the replacement of
> adversarial relations with co-operative ones. . . . Conflict man-
> agement initiatives are attempts to *contain* conflict. . . . On the
> other hand, conflict resolution initiatives attempt to address

underlying inequities and . . . to change mutual perceptions, intentions and behaviour. (1988, pp. 175–7)

It is, of course, a conceptual exercise to polarise the arguments to this extent. It provides us with a useful tool for analysis based on ideal types, with which we can clarify the main themes of the arguments. Thus we arrive at a neat dichotomisation. On the one hand, is the settlement approach: active, power-based, objectively issue-based, pragmatic, directive, aiming at containment of conflict through negotiation and compromise, where a third party acts as an 'outcome advocate' (Bercovitch 1984, p. 129) and makes legitimate use of leverage and coercion to achieve, or impose if necessary, a negotiated settlement. On the other hand, is the resolution approach: reactive, needs-based, subjectively relationship-based, comprehensive, aimed at removing or transforming the roots of conflict through joint analysis and cooperative problem-solving, where a third party takes a non-directive, facilitative role to permit the conflicting parties to redraw their relationship as one of cooperation over a mutual problem and work together towards a self-sustaining integrative resolution.

4. TOWARDS COMPLEMENTARITY

But the theory is far more nuanced than this. Complexity arises from the permutations of conflict types, causes and situations, from the shifting temporal and spatial dynamics of any conflict, and from the variables involved in the complex interrelationships of the conflicting parties, the involvement and interests of external parties, and the effects of intervention. Such complexity makes our dichotomised categorisation look simplistic, which to some extent it is, at least in so far as every theory, every model, is a simplification of reality, but serves the purpose of clarifying and displaying the various conceptual strands involved. But models are at their most interesting and, arguably, their most enlightening, at the point where they fail: that is to say, it is precisely at the limits of the models' simplifications that the nuances of the debate become evident and insight begins.

Virtually all writers in the field acknowledge the dichotomy. Furthermore, while most of them opt for the superiority of one approach over the other, nevertheless they are, implicitly or explicitly, accepting some legitimacy for the inferior approach. Such recognition permits the assumption that neither one approach nor the other is totally incorrect and misguided. Resolution theorists will readily accept that negotiated settlements can be productive and, indeed, the appropriate means of management for certain contexts (for example, Azar 1990, p. 26). Likewise, even Bercovitch is far from dismissing resolution as inappropriate in all contexts.

However, some recent studies have gone beyond this grudging tolerance to examine the possibilities of utilising both approaches on equal merit. Ronald Fisher (1990) put the case for an 'eclectic' model of conflict and has developed this with Loraleigh Keashly (1991) into an argument for a 'contingency model of third party intervention', in which they view both mediation and consultation (respectively settlement and resolution approaches to, in particular, TPI) as sharing some degree of complementarity. Their contingency model promotes the use of different approaches at differing stages of a conflict 'depending on the objective–subjective mix' (Fisher and Keashly 1991, p. 34).

Logically, such arguments focus on the prescriptive elements of theories, since it is in the transition from theory to practice – the application of the prescription – that the polarity of settlement versus resolution is challenged. The conceptual purities of theory can foster absolute distinctions which the confused realities of human interaction will not tolerate. This is why Mark Hoffman argues, concerning the settlement/resolution dichotomy, that

> While this separation may make sense at the level of theory, providing useful pedagogical distinctions and the basis on which to develop 'ideal theory' necessary to the advancement of theoretical and praxiological debates, it limits our ability to understand the third-party process as it develops 'on the ground'. (1992, p. 276)

The relationship between the two approaches as worked out in practice has an unpredictable dynamic which is absent in the cool logic of the theoretical debate. It therefore seems quite justified to pose the question why, if the arguments around the dichotomy are so complicated and nuanced in their prescriptive phase, theorists retain their insistence on the dichotomy. At the prescriptive phase, the models prove too brittle to retain intact their either/or nature; at this point the two strands begin to merge and demonstrate that, in Hoffmann's words, it is a 'false dichotomy' (1992, p. 279).

It seems futile, if not mischievous, to continue in a mode of theorising, as has generally been done in the field of conflict management, which hardens the sense of two alternative and opposing approaches. This is, of course, not to undermine the significance of the distinction between them, but merely to question the mutually exclusive terms in which the distinction has traditionally been couched. A contingency model, such as that of Fisher and Keashly, goes some way to break down the divergence encouraged by this thinking. Their comments in offering the model are important:

> The overreliance on one or another method to the detriment of others needs to be re-examined. In both theoretical work and practical application, a healthy eclecticism should be encouraged . . . the contingency model provides an initial picture of such an approach based on a rationale that accepts the objective and subjective mix that underlies most conflicts. (Fisher and Keashly 1991, p. 42)

Fisher and Keashly's contingency model depends on a staged framework of escalation: conflict moves through (1) discussion, (2) polarisation, (3) segregation and (4) destruction. (A de-escalation process likewise moves in reverse through the same stages.) Each stage is characterised by changes in each of six factors: modes of communication, mutual perceptions, the nature of the relationship, emphasised issues, possible outcomes and preferred strategies (ibid., pp. 35–6). If the factors are characterised as axes, each one has four possible axis-points relating to the four escalatory stages. The relationship between stages, axes and axis-points is represented in Table 4.1.

The contingency model uses these four developmental stages of a conflict to decide which intervention strategy is appropriate at which time. Two general strategic approaches are identified: the subjective, relationship-oriented consultation approach, and the objective, issue-based mediation. Consultation involves facilitating 'creative problem-solving by improving communication and analysing the underlying issues and the relationship between the parties', while mediation involves the facilitation of 'a negotiated settlement on a set of specific, substantive issues through reasoning, persuasion, the control of information, and the suggestion of

Table 4.1 The Four Escalation Stages and their Six Axes

Four Escalation	1. Discussion	2. Polarisation	3. Segregation	4. Destuction
Six Axes				
1. Communication and interaction modes	Discussion and debate	Indirect (mis)-interpretation	Threats	Silence and violence
2. Perceptions and images	Benign and accurate	Rigid, simple stereotypes	Good v. evil	Other as non-human
3. State of relationship	Trust and respect	Other important in own right	Mistrust and disrespect	Hopeless-ness
4. Emphasised issues	Substantive interests	Relation-ship concerns	Needs and core values	Ultimate survival
5. Perceived possible outcomes	Win–win	Compromise	Win–lose	Lose–lose
6. Preferred methods of management	Joint decision-making	Negotiation	Defensive competition	Outright destruction

Source: Developed from Fisher and Keashly (1991, pp. 34–5).

alternative compromises' (Fisher and Keashly 1988, p. 382). Six specific intervention methods are enumerated in a useful, concise typology: consultation, conciliation, pure mediation, power mediation, arbitration and peacekeeping (Fisher and Keashly 1991, pp. 33–4). These interventions can be matched to the escalation stages, according to the differential emphasis they each give to objective and subjective aspects.

In the search for cues to decide which strategy is most appropriate, 'the stage of escalation and de-escalation stands out as the critical cue for the adoption of one strategy over another' (ibid., p. 34). This is, therefore, a sequential view where conflict is seen as

> a dynamic process in which objective and subjective elements interact *over time* as the conflict escalates and de-escalates. . . . Different interventions will be appropriate *at different stages* of the conflict. . . . The overall strategy of the contingency ap-

proach is to intervene with the appropriate third party method *at the appropriate time* in order to de-escalate the conflict back down through the stages. (ibid., pp. 34–6; emphases added)

Once a conflict is identified as being in a particular escalation stage, the most appropriate strategy can then be applied. Significantly, the model also permits different strategies to be 'sequenced' in the most appropriate order within one stage. A brief acknowledgement of the possibility of simultaneous usage of differing approaches remains largely undeveloped because of what the authors identify as a dearth of evidence of such usage (Keashly and Fisher 1990, pp. 439–40).

Generally, the relationship-based approach of consultation is seen as more effective (though not exclusively so) in the earlier stages of escalation, while mediation's element of negotiation over issues is posited as usually more appropriate when escalation is in its more intense stages.

Fisher and Keashly's model makes two very significant contributions. First, they demonstrate convincingly that both theoretical approaches are valid and that to set them in opposition is counterproductive. Second, they suggest a framework for restructuring the relationship between the two: rather than seeing them as mutually exclusive, we can more usefully view them as the poles of one broad spectrum. Once they are seen as constituent parts of the same theory they can be utilised as appropriate. They become complementary rather than oppositional.

This goes some way to ease the tension between the two approaches, permitting more fully a recognition of the value of both and providing a framework in which both operate to complement each other. It is, however, tied to a specifically sequential view of conflict – that it moves inexorably and consecutively from one recognisable stage of escalation to another in time – which could circumscribe the degree to which the two approaches can interact in a fully complementary manner. For example, the model implies that only one approach would be operational at any one time.

The contingency model is none the less the most hopeful avenue to date for exploration of the potential complementarity between resolution and settlement. I intend therefore to use it as a starting point to develop the concept of complementarity further.

5. RELATING THEORY AND PRACTICE

In Chapters 2 and 3, I examined practical conflict management efforts in Northern Ireland and identified two distinct approaches: the structural and the cultural. In this chapter I have considered conflict management theory and distinguished two theoretical approaches, settlement and resolution. A relationship can be construed between the respective theoretical and practical approaches, which will assist the development of the debate over complementarity.

The settlement model was defined as an issue-based, power-related, objective, behaviour-based view of conflict which prescribes a pragmatic, outcome-oriented and system-exclusive process of negotiation and bargaining to achieve agreement through compromise. Such a prescription tallies with the nature of the structural approach: operating at the political level, it involves system-exclusive negotiation aimed at reaching a compromise-based agreement over structural or institutional changes which will address the conflictual issues arising from structural imbalances or resource scarcity. In Northern Ireland since 1969, the main agents involved in attempts at settlement have been the institutions of the British and Irish governments and the established political parties there, and their main methods have involved political negotiation, legislation or the attempted imposition of new structures by the British government sanctioned by its position of power.

At the same time, initiatives at the cultural level in Northern Ireland have continued, in the form of cross-community organisations and sporadic grassroots movements. This cultural approach is relationship-based and system-inclusive (in that the initiatives seek to address relations between the two entire communities in Northern Ireland), and involves attempts to increase communication, mutual understanding, trust and respect for each others' culture, identity and heritage. This, in turn, relates to the prescription of the resolution model: a relationship-building, value-centred approach, which rejects the use of any power-based means such as coercion or leverage, but rather depends on cooperative efforts aimed at a transformation of the conflict and of the relationship. Such a prescription stems from a view of conflict as a subjective, attitude-based phenomenon whose causes are deep-rooted in the needs and values of the disputants which underlie the presenting issues.

With such a perspective, the interesting phenomenon arises that both thinking in the theoretical sphere and actions in the practice of solution-seeking in Northern Ireland share this property: in generalised terms two distinct routes towards the goal of conflict solution can be identified. The fact that both contain a parallel dichotomy begs further investigation. In particular, it is noteworthy that the two practical approaches exist simultaneously, and appear to operate in different areas of the conflict and to address different concerns, rather than alternating with each other, either on the same parts of the conflict or on the conflict as a whole. Examination of the nature of the relationship between the two approaches might suggest data about the value of shaping a complementarity model that embraces a parallel and/or concurrent usage of the two theoretical models for different purposes rather than a sequential switching between the two with the same purpose (as in the contingency model).

Such a proposal, of course, requires testing. There is an immediate difficulty. Since these are hypothetical concepts, and not realities, the proposal remains unfalsifiable and hence untestable. One cannot observe or test an academic 'view' of conflict in the way one might observe real-world behaviour in a conflict. Additionally, were conflict behaviour to be observed, it would quickly be discovered that few of the actors themselves employ clearly delineated theoretical views but rather most remain blissfully – and unsurprisingly – unaware of the theoretical debates.

However, what can be observed are the behavioural differences between the cultural and structural practical approaches. Chapters 2 and 3 have demonstrated that these approaches exist in the reality of the Northern Ireland conflict, where they can be observed, and information can be gathered concerning, for example, their strategies and targets, which aspects of the conflict they each address, and what is the nature of the dynamic, if any, between them. If these approaches mirror the settlement and resolution models, then such empirical observation can shed light on the nature of the relationship between the models and increase our ability to scrutinise the potential for complementarity.

So let me return to the earlier review of Fisher and Keashly's contingency model of intervention. I noted earlier that their model both demonstrates the counterproductiveness of setting resolution and settlement in opposition to each other, and provides a tentative framework for restructuring the relationship between the two so that they are more positively interactional.

But the contingency model suffers two descriptive weaknesses. The first arises from its assumption of a one-dimensional – that is, temporal – profile of conflict. Conflict builds through the four stages of discussion, polarisation, segregation and destruction. By implication, the conflict cannot move backwards through any of the stages without exhibiting a de-escalation, or 'jump' stages out of sequence in either direction. A further implication is that the conflict will not exhibit properties of several stages simultaneously. (Although the model allows that one stage might require more than one strategy, the application of these strategies would be 'sequenced', that is, consecutive; and although the authors acknowledge the possibility of simultaneous usage of strategies (Keashly and Fisher 1990, p. 439), this is subsequently marginalised in their presentation of the model.) This mechanistic property of the model – viewing conflict as linear – limits its application to real inter-group conflict situations, where chaos, irrationality and confusion always make a mockery of the best models. This limitation grows from the model's reliance on sequential stages. In prolonged conflict, particularly, it can be argued that factors from various escalation stages can be in evidence simultaneously, or can be observed out of sequence.

Examination of the Northern Ireland conflict supports the argument. Fisher and Keashly identify six diagnostic factors for recognising the escalatory stage of a conflict (see Table 4.1). For example, modes of communication change through the four-stage process of escalation from (1) discussion and debate, to (2) indirect (mis)interpretation, (3) threats and (4) silence and violence. A brief observation of events in Northern Ireland at almost any given point since 1968 will demonstrate many, even all, of these different modes in operation in varying sequence or simultaneously. This makes it extremely difficult to map any one of the four stages of escalation on to this particular conflict, thus preventing clear identification of which of the model's prescriptions should be employed.

A second weakness arises because the model assumes an oversimplified view of intra-party cohesion. Diagnosis of a conflict's escalation stage depends on analysis of six factors. Each factor can be manifested in one of four ways, indicating a different escalation stage. The implication is that, for each factor, disputing parties make a unanimous espousal of only one of the four possible manifestations at any one time. But a more accurate characterisation of a disputing party, especially in protracted or complex social conflict, might be a collection of constituencies. In any inter-group conflict, complete cohesion between group members is likely to be short-lived. Thus a variety of constituencies could be posited within one disputing party – such as political factions, old and young generations, gender groups, radicals, fundamentalists, peace activists, business interests, military interests, and so on – each of whom, at any one time, might differ from the others in respect of any or all of the six factors which the contingency model uses to identify the developmental stage of the conflict.

In the public arena of Northern Ireland, at any one time within either cultural grouping, community leaders may or may not be crossing communal boundaries to build relationships, while politicians may or may not refuse to negotiate, paramilitaries may or may not kill, religious leaders preach for or against ecumenism, victims of violence call for forgiveness or vengeance, and people raise funds for paramilitary martyrs or march in protests to demand an end to violence. Clearly these sub-groups are not demonstrating synonymous views concerning their preferences for communication modes, perceptions, issue definitions, strategies or solutions. Once again, this coexistence of factors from several or all of the model's four escalatory stages complicates any attempt to correlate the situation to one particular stage, thus rendering prescription problematic.

If these descriptive elements of the model are inaccurate, the linkage with the prescriptive elements based upon them becomes correspondingly weakened. The stage-based framework at the basis of the contingency model is simply too brittle to cope with the dynamic and complex nature of social conflict. If a view of conflict is posited in which attributes of more than one stage can be in evidence simultaneously, or where stages can be 'jumped' out of sequence, the result is a more complex and comprehensive description of conflict. Then there is also a need for a prescription which encourages the simultaneous usage of different conflict management approaches. This is permitted by the contingency model, but largely undervalued in the overall design. If it is rescued from the margins and given a more central role in the model, it yields just such a more flexible and sensitive prescription.

If both settlement and resolution techniques can be valuable, a model that permits their usage concurrently rather than only consecutively is less restrictive and more adaptable. Such an approach is not a sequential one, but one based on what Quincy Wright has termed 'segregation of the aspects of a conflict' (see Wright 1951). I interpret this idea of segregation to mean the process of identifying the various component elements, issues and levels of a conflict and matching them to the appropriate model/prescription. This view of conflict as a complex and multifaceted phenomenon accords in some ways with Roger Fisher's idea of 'fractionation' (Fisher 1964), which involves breaking down a large and complex conflict into smaller and simpler elements which will present varying degrees of manageability. (But there are differences: Fisher argued mainly in the context of superpower rivalry that to fractionate a conflict both reduces the risks of war and produces a series of smaller single-issue disputes which are more winnable. I argue not for such a complete fragmentation of a conflict into separate and discrete elements, but for a conscious addressing of the elements as parts of the whole.) Thus, once the sequential analysis is removed and replaced by this kind of segregation, then (1) multiple aspects of the conflict could be addressed simultaneously, and (2) the same aspect could be addressed with different approaches over time as its dynamic demands.

This does not contradict Fisher and Keashly's basic principle of varying the prescription according to the objective–subjective mix. But it represents a significant expansion of the model. It implies the delinking of contingency from its dependence on the sequential stages of the conflict, so that the mix can be used more sensitively, and less rigidly, to make prescriptions about which conflict management approach (that is, settlement or resolution tools and techniques) is best able to address which aspect.

The contingency model emphasises a sequential method of categorising a conflict into developmental stages, and the application of whichever strategy is most appropriate *at that time*. The Northern Ireland evidence, on the other hand, suggests a model where a conflict could be categorised into its component parts and these separated out for whichever strategy is most appropriate *to the nature of that part*. For example, issues of resource scarcity might be negotiated to compromise, and acceptable political structures might be bargained towards, while *at the same time* relationship issues, such as communication, tolerance and coexistence, might be dealt with in non-negotiating facilitated contexts more suitable to the exploration of such concepts. For a complementarity model to reflect adequately this concurrent implementation of the two approaches, we need to reduce the primacy of sequential stages while enhancing the centrality of concurrence. That shift of emphasis will greatly improve the model's descriptive accuracy.

6. CRITERIA FOR THE MODEL

However, the prescriptive element of the model remains problematic. It is not enough simply to assert that complementarity involves a shifting of prescription between settlement and resolution depending on the 'appropriateness' of the approach to whichever component part of the conflict is under discussion. Clearly, some set of criteria is needed on which to base the decision to adopt a particular approach, just as the contingency model aims to 'match the type of third party intervention to certain characteristics of the conflict in question' (Fisher and Keashly 1991, p. 32).

But the sequential criteria have been shown to be limited in that they lack the multi-dimensional breadth and the diversity-sensitive flexibility which any observation of complex social group interaction must incorporate. The provenance of this criticism is informative. The contingency model – a model developed primarily within a context of theoretical generalisation – is found to be descriptively weak when applied to an actual conflict. Such descriptive weakness circumscribes the effectiveness of any consequent prescription. Put simply, its aim of generalisation across a range of conflicts and contexts mitigates its applicability to specific instances of conflict. This imbalance could be redressed by finding a means of inputting some degree of context-specificity. In other words, the predominantly theory-generated model will benefit from some practice-based input. In a very real sense, then, I am arguing here not only for a more sophisticated conceptualisation of complementarity, but also for a more dynamic form of theory/practice integration.

Specifically, I am suggesting that a complementarity model of conflict management can only gain any real prescriptive validity if it is tested against practice at each stage of its development, and altered or rejected depending on the results of that testing. The model produced in this gradual fashion will only prove valid to the extent that it fulfils the descriptive requirements of (1) drawing its form inductively from empirical reality; (2) reflecting accurately the real-world situations to which it relates; and (3) remaining flexible enough to respond to the empirical evidence. Only then can it properly fulfil the fourth, prescriptive, requirement that it actually prove useful for addressing real conflict(s).

Both deductive and inductive criteria must be used to produce a balanced model that is useful both in the general and in the particular. It is necessary, therefore, to create space within the model for contextual specifics to inform the generalisations concerning the balance of prescriptive approaches. The appropriate location for this space is in the criteria upon which prescription is to be based.

The contingency model's criteria are rendered problematic because of their alliance with the sequential element of escalatory stages. Once the escalation stages are removed, the six factors (or criteria) which originally indicated the stages of the conflict are freed as a valid set of indicators for evaluating the 'subjective–objective mix'. However, the question which is asked about each criterion might usefully be rephrased. For example, in communication modes, the stage-based model asks: 'Which mode is in operation at the moment: direct discussion, indirect (mis)interpretation, threats, or silence and violence?' It then identifies one mode, and assigns the conflict a stage. A better question for a complementarity model might be: 'Which constituencies are communicating over which aspects of the conflict in each of these modes?' This permits us an answer which more accurately reflects the complexity of the situation. Reframing the question for each of the six criteria will give us a more sensitive picture of the subjective–objective mix, suggesting which elements of the conflict might be amenable to resolution and settlement approaches. Since these criteria are constructed from within the theoretical, generalisation-oriented model, they might be termed *generalised* criteria.

This more sophisticated use of the generalised criteria still entails a generalisation from theory. Of course, the main aim in constructing a model of conflict management is to achieve exactly such generalisation. But the problem with models is that they are, by definition, a simplification of reality. It should not, therefore, be a source of surprise when they show up as imperfect when applied. Any generalised model of conflict which can only offer the same blanket prescription of a complementarity of approaches for every context is immediately limited. Within such limits, it can usefully describe the approaches, and lay out the methodologies and tools provided by each. But space must be left for the practitioners in their particular contexts to produce the workings of each approach in the form of a specific strategy. This can be done by means of *embedded* criteria, that is, practice-generated criteria which arise from the context of the specific conflict in question. Such criteria, context-embedded as they are, will tell us something about the employment of approaches by those on the ground. This implies approaching the model from the other end: from practice, rather than from theory alone.

Thus, it is necessary to examine the practical dynamics of attempts to address the conflict – in the instance of Northern Ireland, the cultural and structural approaches. Practitioners involved in these initiatives have made decisions about what they can address and with which particular strategies and resources. Such decisions imply a criterion or set of criteria. But these criteria seem to be exactly that: implicit and not observable. What we can do, however, is examine empirically the actions and processes of those involved in each of the two approaches. As the processes by which they develop their strategies, utilise their resources, set their goals and define their efforts become clearer, it may become possible to discern some of the criteria employed in the practical cultural/structural segregation.

Such a practice-generated approach on its own would also bring limitations: the embedded criteria found in practical usage in any one empirical study would likely be unique to that conflict. Consequently, we would have to produce a unique model for each conflict, which would devalue entirely the modelling exercise. However, the complementary usage of embedded and generalised criteria could help to resolve this trade-off between each conflict's uniqueness and the model's goal of generality. This would have two effects. First, it would protect the model from any over-reaching theoretical aspirations to universality, by the beneficial means of keeping it responsive to specificity.

Second, in a very real sense it would add another dimension to the model, and a further connecting level between its theory and the practice of the real situations it aims to address, and thus reinforce the model's flexibility and sensitivity.

Like a mass-manufactured, off-the-peg suit, a theoretical, generalising model will at best fit most situations roughly, but none perfectly. Similarly a unique, context-specific model will – like an individually tailored suit – fit one situation perfectly and others hardly at all. Informing theory with practice, by building into the theoretical model the spaces which must be filled by context-specific elements, will improve the best elements of both approaches without necessitating compromise. Perhaps the key improvement resulting from this combination of generalised and embedded criteria is that the decision-making level (the point at which tools, methods and approaches are selected) remains with the practitioners/intervenors in their specific context. While the theoretical approaches make available the range of conflict management tools, the embedded criteria ensure that the selection of methods and tools can only be completed after consideration of the specific conflict under analysis.

In the case of Northern Ireland, we can refer back to the three previous chapters for evidence of what elements constitute the conflict and what the natures of the practical approaches are, in order, at this early stage, to speculate on what the general nature of these criteria might be.

In Northern Ireland, objective and subjective elements of conflict are intertwined to a fundamental degree. Not only is there a core issue involving a finite resource (territory or, to be more precise, the control of that territory); there exist two communities with mutually exclusive solutions to that territorial issue, who are effectively distinct cultural groups. They define their separate identities in oppositional and interdependent terms with the labels of religion (Catholic/Protestant) which embrace much larger cultural divisions of history, heritage and political tradition. Thus, at one elemental level, the root of the conflict lies in the objective political issue of territorial sovereignty. However, three factors have woven strong subjective threads around this issue. They are: (1) the history and development of the two communities as descendants of separate indigenous and settler cultures in Ireland over several centuries; (2) the fault-lines of social, political and economic discrimination institutionalised in

50 years of Unionist/Protestant legislative domination from 1922 to 1972; and (3) the polarising and alienating effects of the institutionalisation of violence as a part of the daily norm since 1969. Thus, the objective political issue is swathed inseparably in layers of subjective concern related to matters of cultural identity and cultural security in a society dominated by mutual opposition, mistrust and fear. Such complex intertwining of elements has produced post-war Europe's most enduring violent conflict. Initiatives aimed at solution or amelioration have been ongoing throughout more than two decades of manifest violent conflict.

The cultural approach appears to deal with matters related to cultural identity, to relationships, to perceptions of self and other, of threat and security, to needs related to the communal identities of groups in conflict: in the protagonists' own words, matters concerning cultural heritage, cultural identity, and the relationship between two groups caught up in a conflict over identities and aspirations. These matters are essentially perceptual or subjective.

The structural approach appears to be concerned more with matters of political arrangements, with structures for governing, with territorial control, and with needs related to community security and political participation: with essentially objective matters more directly based on the issue component of the conflict.

Such appearances reinforce Fisher and Keashly's basic point that the criteria for deciding the relevance of one approach or another might involve whether an aspect of the conflict is concerned primarily with subjective perceptions or with objective issues; and whether it is addressable by improved communication and understanding or requires direct negotiation to compromise.

In sum, then, some overall correlation can clearly be posited between the cultural/structural division within the reality of solution-seeking in Northern Ireland, and the resolution/settlement prescriptions of conflict management theory. A relationship can be construed between the respective theoretical and practical approaches, which will shed further light on the notion of complementarity.

The theoretical debate remains academic until it can be related to a context in the real world from which empirical evidence can be gathered to demonstrate the applicability or otherwise, and the sophistication or otherwise, of its prescriptions. For this reason, I now turn to considerations of the empirical observations that can be made about cultural and structural approaches to the solution of the Northern Ireland conflict. True to the observations made earlier concerning the nature of theoretical models, such empirical observations are informed particularly with the goal of seeing where this tentative model fails in its representation of reality and thus where it is at its most enlightening. Case studies of each practical approach in Northern Ireland therefore follow in the next two chapters.

CONCLUSION AND SUMMARY

The two prescriptive approaches, resolution and settlement, have their bases in differing views on the nature of conflict: the former emphasises the subjective elements of conflict, the latter emphasises its objective elements. This dichotomy can be traced through the literature, where it is recognised, implicitly or explicitly, in the work of most scholars. Fisher and Keashly have enriched the debate between approaches by positing a complementary prescription which energises the components of both approaches.

   Their contingency model, however, is limited by an over-simple descriptive element. Applying it to Northern Ireland demonstrates the limits of its generalisations: it elides differences within complex and dynamic parties, and it oversimplifies the temporal dimension of a conflict into a series of rigid, exclusive stages. In particular, the contingency model emphasises consecutive complementarity, with only one approach in operation at a time, when the reality of Northern Ireland suggests that both approaches should function concurrently. One way to retain the overall aim of developing complementarity, while reducing the problems of simplification which come with model-building, might be to use a more inductive approach whereby a space is inserted into the model in which context-specific criteria can be used to make prescriptions more precise and relevant to the conflict in question.

   In Northern Ireland, the practical business of conflict-solving includes both cultural and structural approaches, corresponding respectively to the theoretical approaches of resolution and settlement. By examining in more detail the current workings of both these practical approaches, information can be gathered to illuminate further the argument for a more sophisticated and comprehensive model of complementarity. Once that empirical information has been gathered and analysed in the following three chapters, I shall return to this theoretical discussion in Chapter 8.

5 The Brooke Initiative: An Examination of the Structural Approach to Conflict Management

Peter Brooke was appointed British Secretary of State for Northern Ireland in July 1989. After preliminary meetings with, and overtures to, the political parties, he launched in January 1990 a concerted effort to bring about negotiations between the Ulster Unionist, Democratic Unionist, Social Democratic and Labour, and Alliance Parties[9] on a devolved system of government with an Irish dimension. The process quickly came to be known as the 'Brooke Initiative'. After a further 15 months of dogged bilateral discussions with Northern parties and the Dublin government, Brooke announced a three-strand framework for negotiations in April 1991. The framework provided for initial internal Northern dialogue on devolution (Strand 1), North–South talks on the form of a subsequent Dublin–Belfast relationship (Strand 2), and talks to reshape the relationship between Britain and the Republic of Ireland (Strand 3). The first seven weeks of the allotted ten-week negotiation span were delayed by wrangling over the structures for Strand 2, and the last three weeks provided a total of eight days of internal Strand 1 negotiations which ended inconclusively in early July 1991. The subsequent months eventually produced one further Strand 1 meeting in March 1992. After the British general election in April 1992, Brooke was replaced as Secretary of State. For reasons of space, I can offer only the briefest of narrative sketches below of the Initiative in Section 1, which I hope will suffice simply to sustain the analysis that follows. (A full history of the Initiative, a fascinating story in itself, is in preparation.)

The main focus of this chapter is Brooke's own role in the Initiative and the strategies he employed in trying to enable a structural solution to the Northern Ireland conflict.

The exercise of observing intervention in real social conflict in an attempt to produce some coherent classification or evaluation of the methodologies involved is a fairly recent innovation in the literature of conflict management. Most of the studies involved have focused on the international level, and in particular on the Middle East. Further, virtually all of them have concerned structural approaches and settlement aims, observing formal negotiation processes. The most wide-ranging instance is Touval's assessment of intervenors in the Arab–Israeli conflict from the establishment of the state of Israel up to the Camp David Accords (1982). Camp David, indeed, has been a fruitful subject, producing analysis from Jacob Bercovitch (1986) and Tom Princen (1991). Other similar studies include that by Brian Mandel and Brian Tomlin (1991) on Kissinger's Middle East intervention. Not only do these studies focus on essentially structural, compromise-oriented negotiations, but their analysis is couched in the terms of the settlement school of thought prevalent in the International Relations field within which these scholars operate.

Slightly different in subject matter is the work focusing on the intervention, particularly in Ethiopia/Eritrea, by Jimmy Carter and the International Negotiation Network (INN) (Spencer and Spencer 1991; Spencer, Spencer and Yang 1992). The essential difference in these studies lies in the broader approach of the intervenor(s). The INN team in Ethiopia consciously utilised a four-path approach: bargaining, negotiation, problem-solving, and external pressure (Spencer *et al.* 1992, p. 95), suggesting some awareness of the complementarity of both settlement and resolution theory.

To an extent, these studies together constitute a small body of pioneering literature, opening the debate on the process of classifying the structural intervenor's style through case-study examination. The main body of this chapter falls coherently within the same debate.

Fisher and Keashly (1991) have significantly assisted the debate by offering a typology of intervention strategies. The typology is couched within an argument for a contingency model of intervention (see Chapter 4), and thus attempts to cover the spectrum of resolution/settlement (or, in their terminology, consultation/mediation) intervention strategies. In the process, however, *pace* variations in terminology, they have produced a typology that is, despite its simplifications, generally acceptable to all sides in the resolution/settlement debate. The six intervention types they identify are pure mediation, conciliation, consultation, power mediation (or mediation with muscle), arbitration and peace-keeping (Fisher and Keashly 1991, p. 33). Section 2 of this chapter will apply this typology in order to identify Brooke's strategies of intervention.

There are, however, constraints on the straightforward view of Brooke as an intervening third party. These stem first from the dual nature of Brooke's role: not only did he act as a third party facilitator and guarantor of inter-party dialogue in the particular context of Strand 1, but he was also the representative of the British government in the broader context and as such was the main power-wielder in a game in which he represented the interests of the major player. Secondly, further constraints and complications arise from the complex and contradictory nature of his relations with the parties involved.

Consequently, in Section 1 I shall briefly outline the political context of the Initiative, and then review Brooke's relationships with the participating parties, before documenting the events of the talks process itself.

1. A DOCUMENTARY NARRATIVE

The Context

The Initiative aimed to produce for Northern Ireland a devolved system of internal government. As such, it was simply the latest attempt to implement the favoured structural solution which had been British policy since the prorogation of Stormont in 1972: the Power-sharing Executive, the Constitutional Convention, the Assembly with 'rolling devolution', and direct rule itself, were all instances of Britain's continuing attempt to implement a structural policy (see Chapter 2). The 1985 Anglo- Irish Agreement, in particular, was a broader and more sophisticated attempt to make structural progress towards devolution,

> signed as part of a jointly designed British and Irish... master-plan to coerce unionists into accepting a power-sharing devolved government together with an Irish dimension, knowing that the intergovernmental conference could survive whatever strategy the unionists would use to undermine it. (O'Leary and McGarry 1993, p. 238)

It was the Agreement which made Brooke's Initiative different from previous ones. On the one hand, it gave him a framework – proof against unionist boycotting or wrecking tactics – within which to work, and the significant, novel addition of formal Irish support. On the other, where previous Secretaries of State had tried variously to force, threaten or entice Northern politicians to accept devolution, this new partnership role with Dublin constrained his ability so to dictate within the bounds of what Dublin would support, and required that devolution be instituted by consent only. The Agreement – specifically the Intergovernmental Conference, and the joint Secretariat based at Maryfield, Belfast – drew Gerry Collins (Irish Foreign Affairs Minister and Brooke's counterpart in the Initiative) and the Irish government inside the camp for the first time. 'The British government was anxious that the Irish government share responsibility, if not power, for the management of Northern Ireland' (O'Leary and McGarry 1993, p. 242). Brooke inherited the same structural mandate as his predecessors, and his efforts were entirely coherent with their policies; but he now shared some of the responsibility for the implementation of the mandate with Dublin. The shared responsibility significantly altered what had traditionally been a relationship of opposition between Dublin and Westminster to one of increased cooperation, and this impacted on the Initiative: while Brooke was less free to act alone in the sole interests of Britain, Dublin was also forced to moderate its oppositional brand of Irish nationalism into something more acceptable to its new partner.

It was the Agreement, above all, which laid the basis on which dialogue could be constructed. The Agreement altered the balance of the equation in Northern Ireland, moving the onus for reaction and change from nationalists to unionists. Three years after its signing, the unionist community had learnt the painful lesson that the Agreement had indeed survived the strongest protest tactics they could muster. Protest had waned, and abstentionism and a constant repetition of 'Ulster Says No!' no longer constituted a viable programme of resistance. By 1988, the senior Unionist politicians were under intense pressure both from their party memberships and from their constituencies to take a more positive approach by re-engaging in the political process: since simply ignoring the Agreement had not made it go away, a growing voice demanded that they enter dialogue to negotiate an alternative to it. On the nationalist side, the Agreement had strengthened the SDLP against Sinn Féin, brought Dublin formally into the game on the side of the nationalist community while creating a gulf of distrust between Unionism and Westminster, and encouraged the belief that dialogue might bring further nationalist rewards, but that the Agreement was a safety net for their greatest gain so far, the Irish dimension.

These significant post-Agreement changes of attitude in the two communities were the factors that gave negotiation a slim chance. From very different starting-points and with very different reasoning, both communities wanted to see their representatives involved in dialogue: as Brooke acknowledges, 'right through my set of talks, all the politicians were conscious of the pressure that was coming from the community that they should in fact come to conclusions.' His greatest initial strength was his ability to capitalise on such factors and to recognise and take advantage of the narrow window of opportunity for dialogue that could otherwise have passed unnoticed.

Brooke's Roles and Relationships

That the process of Northern Irish political dialogue between 1989 and April 1992 has come to bear the name of the British Secretary of State for Northern Ireland at the time is some measure of the personal credit widely attributed to him by participants and observers alike. As an individual, Peter Brooke exercised the greatest influence in bringing the talks into existence, bringing personal attributes – in particular a fecund mix of doggedness and patience, and a determinedly low-key approach to the management of a volatile debate – to bear on the process. In Brooke's own words, 'my preference for negotiation in a lowish voice and with a lowish profile, with a concentration on the workable' (O'Malley 1990, p. 83) was undoubtedly an approach perfectly suited to the situation. Concentrating on the workable also meant avoiding ultimate goals in order to contribute positively to the cumulative process:

> What you are looking at in Northern Ireland in terms of these negotiations are a series of waves advancing up the beach. And the important thing is that one day the wave will reach the top of the beach and you will have achieved your objective. Every

wave should get further than the last one, in other words you continue to advance but you must be patient and not frustrated if particular waves are not strong enough to get there.

As the prime mover in the talks process, Brooke presents an obvious focus on which to base an analysis of the strategies involved. As a self-styled facilitator, he wanted to be seen in the light of a outside intervenor between disputants. But there are significant limitations on this simple view of Brooke as an intervening third party. These stem first, from his role in Northern Ireland and second, from his relationships with the players. In the first place, his role had a paradoxical element. Not only did he seek to intervene between the political parties of Northern Ireland, but, as British Secretary of State for Northern Ireland, he was by definition also a major player in the game in which he intervened. A previous Secretary, James Prior, described his own feelings about the role:

> As Secretary of State for Northern Ireland I found myself performing a dual role, as a Governor-General representing the Queen and as such the enemy of every Republican in the province, but also . . . acting like a referee in a boxing ring whose authority seemed to be resented equally by both sides. I was combining two tasks kept separate until the introduction of direct rule. (Prior 1986, pp. 181–2)

Prior was aware of the uncomfortable duality of the Secretary's role even before the Agreement made the Unionist connection far more problematic. Brooke accepts his characterisation of the job as a fair one:

> You can't get away from the fact that you are the senior representative of the government on the ground. And yet . . . the fact that you are seeking to move matters forward means that you have no choice but to become an active player.

In the second place, Brooke's dual role – being both referee and player – is further highlighted in the complexity of his interrelationships with the other players in the conflict, towards each of whom he held contradictory positions arising out of his role and status as Secretary.

The twisting balance of interrelations between the various players in the Initiative illustrates that there was no one role for him to play, and encapsulates the constraints on attempts to evaluate him merely as an intervening third party.

The Irish Government

To the government of the Republic of Ireland, in the context of the Initiative, Brooke was, first, an equal partner in the process of the talks. As a newcomer to the post of Secretary, he was freer than his predecessor King to encourage cooperative attitudes with Dublin where previously there had been a rather prickly relationship. He facilitated this significantly, drawing Collins into the heart of the Initiative at an early stage, negotiating a joint formula for the talks process which simultaneously gave him a more stable base on which to build dialogue among the parties, and gave Dublin a shared interest in working towards a successful outcome.

Secondly, however, in the specific context of the Anglo-Irish Agreement, Brooke represented the British side of a different relationship with Dublin. Thatcher had commented to FitzGerald shortly after the Agreement was signed, 'You've got the glory and I've got the problems' (FitzGerald 1991, p. 570). It was a rather dramatic description of the Agreement's institutionalisation of an 'Irish dimension' in Northern Irish affairs, but not without truth: the Republic had gained a consultative role in the North's internal affairs, but it had no defined executive power. While it could now comment on and question policy in Northern Ireland – specifically at the Conference meetings – nevertheless it remained British policy, designed and executed ultimately by Westminster. In this particular context, Britain retained very firmly the senior partner status.

Thirdly, Brooke not only represented the British presence in Ireland which, in the traditional nationalist view, carried the blame for the whole conflict, but he was also seen as the traditional sponsor of unionism. In this sense, for the purposes of the talks, Dublin saw him not only as a partner in a process in which to some extent both partners were 'outside' the conflict, but also as an opponent in the wider game, both as British representative and as sponsor of unionism. While the argument can be made that the Agreement in fact weakened British sponsorship of unionism, nevertheless the traditional nationalist view in Dublin – of a struggle against British-supported unionism – remained, even heightened to some degree by the comparison with the formalisation of the Republic's own sponsor relationship with Northern nationalists. Further, with the Unionists in 'internal exile' from political engagement, Dublin had every reason to view Britain as representing the unionist interest:

> Unless Ulster unionists accepted [the Agreement] and negotiated an agreed form of devolution with the SDLP, then the British government would act as spokesperson for unionism in the intergovernmental conference. (O'Leary and McGarry 1993, p. 227)

In short, in Dublin's view Brooke was simultaneously an equal partner, the senior partner, and the opposition. Consequently, at some times he was working cooperatively with Dublin alongside as his co-sponsor in the process, while at others he was playing a brokering role between Dublin and the Unionists.

The Unionists

Brooke's relationship with the Unionist politicians was similarly problematic. First, the traditional unionist view of Britain as the benign authority, which had never quite recovered from the shock of Westminster's prorogation of Stormont in 1972, had been fundamentally challenged by the Agreement, and Britain was seen as treacherous and no longer to be trusted. Such mistrust is obvious in the comment from Peter Robinson (DUP Deputy Leader) that, unlike Dublin's role as regards the SDLP, 'the British government won't be acting on behalf of the unionist community in those talks' (*Irish Times*, 15 June 1990). Robinson was merely repeating a general post-Agreement understanding among Unionists previously expressed by Harold McCusker of the UUP:

> Part of the theory behind the Agreement is that, while the Irish government is there as a surrogate for the minority community in Northern Ireland and their representatives, the British government is there as surrogates for the majority. The British government is not a surrogate for the majority community . . . . In fact, invariably over the last twenty years, it's been hostile to everything we aspire to. (O'Malley 1990, pp. 43–4)

The same deep-seated suspicion shows in the Unionist insistence that they should be present in Strand 3 talks since they did not trust Britain to deal alone with Dublin. Effectively, whatever

Dublin thought, Unionists very clearly saw Britain as an ex-sponsor.

Secondly, however, as a member of the British government, Brooke remained, in Unionist eyes, the representative of the legitimate government in Northern Ireland: he was a Westminster MP as were many of them; and in so far as they were willing British subjects (which is very far) he was 'their' Secretary of State. While he, and the British government in recent years, might not act as Unionists would wish – particularly in doing deals with the arch-enemy of Dublin – he was nevertheless far more 'theirs' than any one else's.

And thirdly, he was a member of a specifically Conservative government. This produced tensions late in the Initiative as a British general election loomed. His government role gave way to his party responsibilities as he made party political overtures to the UUP in the shadow of a hung parliament. When he hinted in a newspaper interview that there were circumstances in which Westminster 'would have to contemplate all the things Mr Molyneaux suggests' (*Irish Times*, 27 September 1991), it was a pragmatic and overt Conservative overture to the UUP integrationists[10] which contradicted every devolution-based policy statement of recent years from Westminster. Such overtures in turn served to disrupt the already strained cohesion of the Unionist parties.

The internal Unionist divisions – the devolution/integration argument, a general inter-party rivalry and a leadership/membership tension – further exacerbated the difficulties for Brooke and the Unionists in maintaining stable relationships.

To Unionists, in short, Brooke represented both sponsor and betrayer, simultaneously on their side as British ruler and in opposition to them as partner with the enemy, a complicated view exacerbated by the internal strain of their attempts to present a united front to him. As an intervenor, therefore, he moved variously between facilitating the Unionists in dialogue with the SDLP, brokering deals between them and Dublin, and trying to pressure or threaten them into concessions from his position of power over them.

The SDLP

The SDLP had a similarly confusing relationship with Brooke. First, he was the representative of the traditional enemy, Britain; he was the controller of a security policy to which they strongly objected; and he was in effect the 'head of state' of the sub-state which they saw as the source of their grievances.

Secondly, however, he represented the same British government which had signed the Agreement and was committed to working within the framework of the Agreement (which they viewed largely as a safety net for their interests); they were happy to see him putting pressure on their Unionist opponents; and he was the equal partner, at least in some respects, with their Dublin sponsor (who urged SDLP cooperation with Brooke). And he was the Secretary of State who insisted on Britain's role in Northern Ireland as a neutral one; a public statement which they valued greatly, whatever their private feelings on the matter.

Thirdly, of course, he was also the Secretary who insisted, right at the start of his Initiative, that they nail their colours to the devolution mast. While their previous rhetoric demanded their agreement on this, it was something with which elements of the leadership remained uncomfortable throughout the process. For the SDLP, there was a running internal debate over whether devolution might actually delay the ultimate goal of Irish unity. (Indeed, while Unionist intransigence saved them from having to finally declare their position during the Brooke negotiations, it became apparent in the subsequent Mayhew talks of Autumn 1992 that their commitment to Northern Irish devolution – in preference to Irish unity – was less straightforward than their Dublin sponsors desired.)

And fourthly, his partnership with Dublin through the Conference and beyond gave him access to, and support from, their sponsor in a way that left the SDLP less free than in the past to act with Dublin's implicit support, and more likely to have to accede, at least on occasion, to Dublin's will.

So, for the SDLP, Brooke represented the traditional enemy while also being a partner of their sponsor; and an ally in pursuing their stated goals while also pressing them uncomfortably on their commitment to those goals. He was thus both the opposition in the dialogue process as well as being the facilitator of that dialogue.

The Events

Brooke was appointed Secretary of State in July 1989, replacing Tom King who had entered office in 1985. With a British general election expected within a year, consensus was that Prime Minister Thatcher had installed a cautious nightwatchman who could be relied on not to rock the boat with any novel policies.

King, as Secretary at the time of the Anglo-Irish Agreement, had been demonised by Unionist politicians, who had boycotted all official contact with government in protest at the Agreement. Nevertheless, he had managed to instigate a round of confidential opinion gathering in 1987–8 by his deputy Brian Mawhinney. This process, termed 'talks about talks', had sounded out opinion among second-tier leaders in all parties except Sinn Féin, and indicated that, especially on the Unionist side, however unclear a way forward might be, there was nevertheless much desire to end the current inertia.

Brooke inherited both the results of Mawhinney's talks about talks and a team of officials at the NIO who felt that the time was right for movement. He spent the period from July to December 1989 testing the water in his own right, and beginning to build relationships with all the relevant players. In meetings, the SDLP explained to him that they were keen to enter talks with the Unionists within the framework of the Agreement. The Alliance Party also expressed its commitment to a talks process to develop new structures for devolution in Northern Ireland. The two Unionist leaders together explained to him that their terms for talks were as they had indicated in the previous year to Mawhinney: they had proposals for a devolved structure of internal government, but they would not enter negotiations unless the Agreement was suspended. In the North he surprised politicians with his geniality and his knowledge, and in Dublin he doggedly saw the Intergovernmental Conference through some highly contentious meetings and managed to build a solid working relationship with his Irish counterpart, Minister for Foreign Affairs Gerry Collins.

By the end of the year, the Unionists had refined their demands for a suspension of the Agreement into three specific preconditions under which they would enter talks. First, both the Irish and the British governments must agree in advance that the negotiations would replace the Agreement with a completely new structure. Second, all Intergovernmental Conference meetings must be suspended for the duration of the negotiations. And third, the operations of the Secretariat of the Agreement, the Irish and British civil servants working at Maryfield, must also be suspended for the duration. Just as resolutely, the SDLP were insisting that no suspension of the Agreement could be countenanced.

By January 1990, Brooke had decided there was a possibility of movement between the various positions. He officially launched his Initiative with a speech on 9 January, in which he outlined what he saw as a consensus among the parties for devolved government in Northern Ireland, and offered his and his government's assistance in facilitating talks on that basis. He also hinted at a British willingness to consider the negotiation of a replacement to the Agreement, directly addressing the first Unionist precondition.

In late January, Taoiseach Haughey announced helpfully that Dublin would also contemplate replacing the Agreement with a new and transcendant structure through negotiation. Effectively, precondition 1 had now been met. From then until July, most of Brooke's efforts were aimed at finding a formula to satisfy the two remaining Unionist preconditions on a suspension of the workings of the Agreement – the Conference meetings and the Maryfield Secretariat – while keeping both Dublin and the SDLP on side. The parties, meanwhile, offered him their various opinions on a possible talks agenda, which he tried to work up into a consensual document.

The breakthrough came in April when, under pressure from Thatcher and Haughey, Collins and Brooke hammered out a two-part formula. First, there would be a prolonged and pre-specified gap in Conference meetings over the coming summer; and second the Secretariat staff would be reallocated from Conference duties to service the interparty talks. This, it was hoped, could be publicly interpreted by the Unionists as a *de facto* suspension of the Agreement's workings, and by the SDLP simultaneously as nothing of the kind. Talks would then be held during the summer break, involving a series of parallel and concurrent 'strands' involving various permutations of parties and governments depending on the subject matter of the particular strands.

On 11 May, Brooke met the Unionist leaders. He confirmed to them officially that both governments were prepared to consider a replacement to the Agreement (precondition 1), and specified the dates of the summer gap in Conference meetings when talks could be held (precondition 2). But reallocation of Maryfield staff was not enough to satisfy their demand on precondition 3: they insisted on a complete shutdown. Brooke consulted with Collins and reconvened the meeting with Paisley and Molyneaux two weeks later to offer them a direct quid pro quo: a slightly clearer suspension of Maryfield, in return for the involvement of Dublin in the talks at an 'appropriate' (that is, early) stage.

In the aftermath of the meeting, all Northern parties seemed confident that a formula for talks was close. Brooke and Collins met again to fill in more details: Brooke would launch a further series of bilateral meetings to finalise an agenda for the talks, which would operate on two strands, one concerning internal devolution arrangements for Northern Ireland, and one concerning a possible renegotiation of the Agreement. A scheduled Conference meeting in September would be used to announce a two-month gap, and talks would begin immediately after.

However, while substantial progress had been made in various aspects of the formula, there was still a lack of clarity over when and in which strand the Irish government would be involved. Everyone knew that meeting directly and formally with the Dublin government would constitute a huge step for both Unionist parties, who had long held the view that the internal affairs of Northern Ireland were not the business of a 'foreign government'. Equally, Dublin wanted to assert its new responsibility under the Agreement to have a say in any such internal talks.

Having by June painstakingly produced a formula which satisfied the three Unionist preconditions on suspension of the Agreement, Brooke suddenly found that it was now Dublin that was making demands. The Irish government hardened its insistence on two points regarding the talks: that it should be involved in all strands, and that it should be involved right from the start. Unionist objections on both counts were resolute. For six weeks, Brooke shuttled between the parties and the Irish government, trying to reach a compromise. His notional deadline was his desire to make the formal announcement of September talks during the House of Commons debate on Northern Ireland on 5 July. With little disagreement, the two-stranded framework was developed into three strands. Much more controversially, however, Brooke proposed the Unionist idea that Dublin would enter the talks when Strand 2 opened after 'substantial progress' had been achieved in Strand 1. But Dublin (and the SDLP) rejected the formula, afraid that it would provide the Unionists with a veto by means of blocking any progress and therefore freezing Dublin out.

Faced with the threat of a complete pull-out by both the SDLP and by Dublin, Brooke was forced to drop his plan to announce talks, and merely informed the House on 5 July that progress was still being made and that he hoped to report further before long. From July to December 1990, the process stalled effectively on the question of the timing of Dublin involvement. Over the summer and autumn, the pressure, public and private, built up on the Irish government to make some concession to put the process back on track. Brooke met variously with Collins and the Unionists without finding any means to progress. A joint subcommittee of Irish and British civil servants from the Intergovernmental Conference met repeatedly but failed to find a formula of words on Irish involvement which might break the deadlock. Finally in November, Brooke and Haughey met informally. Brooke suggested that Dublin's entry into the talks be timed at Brooke's discretion and 'after significant internal discussions', a reworking of an earlier rejected formula. It was unofficially agreed that the maximum delay on Dublin's entry would be five weeks.

At the end of December, the Unionists responded to the new rephrasing with their own proposals. As the New Year came, however, Brooke retained both the Irish and the Unionist proposals without offering them around for discussion or negotiation. Instead, he began to utter dark warnings that it might be time to 'put up the shutters' and call an end to the Initiative. Finally in March he and Collins redrafted the wording, and then passed it to the subcommittee for further work. The aim was to produce the text of an agreed statement which Brooke could deliver in the House of Commons during Northern Ireland Question Time on 14 March to announce a basis for talks.

The draft statement was circulated to all parties for comment, and then Brooke announced, on 14 March as planned, that he was offering his formula for talks, agreed by Dublin, to the four parties. He would give them two weeks to respond. Molyneaux and Paisley wrote to him requesting clarification of various aspects of the formula. Thirteen days later, the four party leaders visited Brooke separately to confirm their acceptance. On 26 March 1991, Brooke announced that a formula for talks had been agreed by all the parties, including the matter of Dublin's entry into the talks. Strand 1 talks would begin first, to be followed 'within weeks' by Strand 2 when, 'after consultation', Brooke judged the time to be right.

On 26 April, Brooke and Collins held the last Conference meeting before the negotiating gap, and announced that talks would begin on 30 April and continue until 16 July, the date of the next Conference meeting.

Consequently, on 30 April, the delegations from the four Northern parties installed themselves at Stormont, the site of the old Northern Parliament, prepared to enter the first formal negotiations since Sunningdale in 1973. Delegations comprised ten members per party, no more than seven to be in the debating chamber at one time, and no more than three at the table in direct speaking roles.

It had been envisaged that the first week of Strand 1 discussions would consist of bilateral meetings between Brooke and the four parties to decide the agenda and procedures for the plenary session which would commence in the following week. But within a day, serious differences had sprung up concerning the arrangements, not for Strand 1 plenaries, but for Strand 2. Brooke insisted that these matters be sorted out before he would allow Strand 1 plenaries to open. First of all, there was no agreement about the venue for Strand 2: while Unionists insisted that all negotiations with a 'foreign power' must be held in London, the British capital, Dublin (and the SDLP) insisted that, since part of those negotiations would concern the Irish Constitution's claim over the territory of the North, they could not be expected to negotiate their own constitution on foreign territory. The impasse deepened rapidly: only through Strand 2 negotiations could the Irish constitution be changed; only on Irish soil would the Republic of Ireland consent to negotiate its constitution; only after the constitutional claim had been changed would Unionists consent to Strand 2 talks on Irish soil. Furthermore, the Unionists refused to accept Collins as Brooke's co-chair for Strand 2.

The Strand 2 dispute rumbled on for weeks, effectively stalling any substantive Strand 1 dialogue. Fairly early in the process, all but the Unionists agreed to a venue formula which allowed Strand 2 to open in London, move to Belfast for the most part of the process, and end in Dublin.

At the start of the third week, Brooke met the Unionist leaders to present them with a 48-hour ultimatum, which he and Collins had drawn up. The terms comprised the three-venue arrange-ment agreed by everyone else, and the idea of an independent Strand 2 chair. They rejected the ultimatum, but effectively outflanked the whole process by suddenly appealing to the Prime Minister, John Major, for a meeting at Downing Street to clarify the issues, while the SDLP and Alliance waited with increasing frustration. Afterwards, Major and Brooke on the one hand, and Molyneaux and Paisley on the other, were deeply at odds about what had been agreed. The week ended in a flurry of angry accusations thrown in all directions. With no resolution of the confusion at the start of the fourth week, the SDLP informed Brooke that as far as they could see, the venue problem was between Brooke and the Unionists, and that they would absent themselves from Strand 1 until he had sorted it out. By this stage, a large degree of cynicism had pervaded the talks, where dele-gates spent hours on end in their rooms, waiting to hear what the next argument would be about and wondering if the real talks would ever start.

By the end of the fourth week, the Unionists had accepted the venue proposals, and by week 5 the bilateral arguments had moved on to the question of the identity of the independent Strand 2 chair. The first proposed name from the two govern-ments, former British Foreign Secretary Peter Carrington, was angrily rejected by the Unionists. While the days passed into the sixth week with some bilateral progress on the smaller issues of standing orders for the Strand 2 meetings, the SDLP were still staying away from Stormont, insisting that the Unionists were the stumbling-block. Intense efforts by Brooke produced a com-promise: a starting date for Strand 1 plenaries could be set, pending agreement on the nomination of the Strand 2 chair before then. Without naming the favoured candidate, Brooke had clearly indicated that he was hopeful of reaching agreement on the chair quite soon. The SDLP returned to Stormont.

To the shock of all the world's press milling around outside, the party leaders suddenly appeared on the steps of Stormont to read a terse statement announcing their decision that plenary Strand 1 talks would begin in 11 days' time, in the confident assumption that a Strand 2 chair would be agreed by then. A week later, the two governments offered the parties their nomi-nation for the chair: former Australian Governor-General Ninian Stephen. By the end of the day, all but the DUP had agreed.

Paisley in fact waited until the first plenary was due to begin the following week before leaving for two hours to do some last-minute checking on Stephen and finally acceding to the nomination.

The Strand 1 plenaries finally opened, six weeks late, with a maximum of five weeks' negotiating time left, and with cynicism, ill-will and despair already rife among delegates. All three negotiating days of the first week, and one more the following week, were taken up with the leaders presenting their opening statements and answering cross-questioning on them. On the fifth day, Brooke moved them on to the previously agreed agenda. But already huge rows had broken out about the impending deadline: the Conference meeting was less than three weeks away, and almost everyone doubted their ability to make much progress by then. Many of the Unionists continued to argue for both an intensification of the negotiating schedule and a postponement of the Conference. Brooke was adamant on the Conference date. Some extension to the working hours was agreed, and the next two days of plenaries, as delegates discussed a comprehensive agenda covering almost every possible aspect of the Northern Irish conflict, consisted primarily of rambling, if occasionally interesting, discussions of well-rehearsed positions on the Irish constitutional claim to the North, the legal status of Northern Ireland as part of the UK, or the pros and cons of the Anglo-Irish Agreement. Outside this formal agenda, however, the arguments about the amount of time left continued to smoulder.

At the end of the seventh day, Brooke requested that the parties each prepare a position paper on Areas of Common Agreement, for discussion on the resumption of talks the following week. With any conclusion impossible before the deadline, his aim was to bring the talks to an end on as positive a note as possible, so to make a future resumption easier. The parties broke up for the weekend to work on the papers.

The eighth negotiating day rapidly degenerated into argument. The four papers had been circulated over the weekend, but there was very little in them about common ground, and indeed some of them completely ignored the brief to try to identify areas of agreement. In particular, the SDLP paper laid out a set of principles which should be agreed before any discussion of specific devolution structures could be initiated. By this stage, the Unionist parties were enthusiastically pursuing discussion of specific, detailed plans for devolved administration. Consequently, the two sides were talking from different approaches and on different levels. Brooke was absent from the talks all day, on government business, and it fell to Mawhinney to chair the day's rather bad-tempered and fruitless arguments. Outside the formal sessions, some of the Ulster Unionists were, unofficially, dropping hints that they would consider agreeing to an opening meeting of Strand 2 (and thus bringing in the Dublin government) in return for the two governments' postponement of the 16 July Conference meeting. That evening, however, Paisley left the talks session to announce to the press outside that he had no intention of having any such meeting with Haughey, and that he and his party would stand by their promise to withdraw from the talks as soon as the Secretariat returned to work (which was expected in less than a week).

On his return the following day, Brooke listened to Mawhinney's report and watched more of the acrimonious proceedings, and decided that there was very little point in continuing. By this stage, the Unionists were complaining that the SDLP were refusing to table their proposals for devolution and get into substantive Strand 1 discussion, while the SDLP were complaining that the high level of document leaking was making it impossible to risk airing any specific negotiating position, and insisting that they discuss general principles before getting down to such specifics.

Effectively, the talks were over. Brooke called the four leaders to a meeting and voiced his opinion that they should call a halt. There may have been some disappointment and surprise on the Unionist side, if indeed they had believed that a postponement of the Conference meeting was a possibility, but there was little dissension. The next morning, he convened a final plenary and formally closed the talks.

Blame for the end of the talks popularly fell on the Unionist parties in general and on their leaders in particular. But the politicians themselves mostly avoided acrimony, and indeed several spoke of the glimpses of insight gained during the final few days. Brooke himself insisted that he would try to restart talks in the autumn.

But by the autumn, the shadow of the British general election was looming large. The election was due by May 1992, but at this point was generally expected before the end of the year.

While Brooke embarked doggedly on another round of talks with the party leaders about a resumption of negotiations, election fever was having two major effects on his efforts. First, there was the very real possibility of a change of government in Westminster. Would deals and formulas negotiated with a Conservative government still hold under a Labour administration? In particular, would Unionists agree to work with a Labour Secretary of State, given Labour's stated commitment to Irish unity by consent? Secondly, amidst speculation of a hung parliament, the position of the nine Ulster Unionist MPs suddenly became very significant. If a re-elected minority Conservative government needed their support to stay in power, what leverage did that give the UUP to renegotiate their relationship with the government? In particular, would that increase Conservative support for Molyneaux's integrationist programme and thus devalue government commitment to devolution?

While in public both Brooke and Collins continued to speak confidently of a resumption of talks, in fact there was little chance of any such activity. As it became clear that the election would not happen before the Spring of 1992, the chances of resumption slipped even further away. The Unionists refused to make any commitment to negotiate beyond the election unless the Conservatives remained in power. The SDLP and Dublin refused to countenance such a precondition. The argument ran on for some time without any resolution in sight, and there was a widespread feeling that everyone was going through the motions merely for fear of being seen to be intransigent.

In mid-January 1992, Brooke was in Dublin for a weekend of official engagements when an IRA bomb killed eight Protestant workers at Teebane Cross, Co. Tyrone. Outrage was considerable among the Protestant community in the North, along with an expectation that the Secretary of State might travel back north to demonstrate solidarity and sympathy. Instead, Brooke continued with his engagements in Dublin, including an appearance on a television chat-show. During the interview he expressed deep and eloquent sympathy for the bereaved of Teebane, and then, apparently very unwillingly but under great pressure from his host, he assented to sing (rather poorly) two verses of 'Oh My Darling Clementine'.

Unionist anger was unrestrained the next day, as they contrasted the image of weeping families bereaved by Republican violence with that of the Secretary responsible for their security singing merrily on television in the Republic's capital.

It was an immense *faux pas*. Brooke offered his resignation to the Prime Minister, who considered it for a day before rejecting it. In the weeks that followed, Brooke continued to try to wind down the process. Rumours of Tory–Unionist deals were rife. Protestant paramilitaries took revenge for Teebane by killing five Catholics in a Belfast bookmaker's shop. In the aftermath, Major announced a 'security summit' with the party leaders, at which he overruled Brooke and demanded that the four party leaders meet to get talks restarted. They bowed to the pressure, and a symbolic four-hour meeting was held on 9 March, in which discussion centred mainly on the Irish constitution. Two days later, Major called the election for 9 April. Despite the speculation, the Conservatives were returned with a clear though reduced majority. In the ensuing cabinet reshuffle, Brooke was replaced by Patrick Mayhew.

2. BROOKE AS INTERVENOR

The picture of Brooke as one particular kind of intervenor – playing one discrete role in the talks process – has already become problematic because of the complex relationships and roles which bound him to the participants. He was simultaneously attempting both to be the neutral referee and to hold office as the most powerful player in the game. In his relations with Dublin, and in the context of the Anglo-Irish Agreement, he was an active partner in a relationship between two of the players in the game: he represented the deeply involved interests of Britain in that international context. In contrast, in the local Northern Ireland party-political context, he tried to play the role of impartial facilitator or honest broker, a third party role to which the British government, as a deeply committed player, was ill-suited.

In one sense, the two opposing camps in the conflict consisted of the SDLP and the Irish government versus the Unionists and the British government (as represented by Brooke): as the two governments acted in partnership to reach agreement, they took responsibility for pressuring their respective Northern Ireland clients to act according to their wishes. While this was a straightforward and relatively trouble-free role for Dublin, Brooke confused his side of the balance – perhaps unavoidably, it can be argued – by trying to appear simultaneously evenhanded and impartial. Consequently the Unionists, who might have looked for a partnership or protective role from him, saw his attempts at fairness as betrayal and were further encouraged in the deep distrust of British policy that had flourished since the Agreement.

The nature of his intervention may become clearer if we turn to the intervention typology provided by Fisher and Keashly (1991, pp. 33–4), and analyse how his technique maps onto their categories. As already noted, the typology identifies six styles of intervention. These can be grouped into two clusters around the resolution/settlement axis. Resolution strategies comprise pure mediation, conciliation and consultation, while settlement strategies comprise arbitration, power mediation and peace-keeping. If the Brooke Initiative was indeed a structural initiative, acting out the tenets of settlement theory, we should reasonably expect to find his efforts grouped mainly within arbitration, power mediation and peacekeeping, rather than within the resolution-based strategies.

Pure Mediation

Pure mediation involves 'the intervention of a skilled and experienced intermediary who attempts to facilitate a negotiated settlement to the dispute on a set of specific substantive issues . . . [using] reasoning, persuasion, the control of information and the suggestion of alternatives' (Fisher and Keashly 1991, p. 33).

As a pure mediator, Brooke tried to fill the role of impartial facilitator, or honest broker. He claimed that personally he had no 'blueprint or hidden agenda', but was rather a 'facilitator' (*Irish Times*, 25 June 1991). In his government role, too, he outlined British policy in similar terms:

> The British government has no selfish or strategic interest in Northern Ireland: our role is to help, enable and encourage. Britain's purpose . . . is not to occupy, oppress or exploit, but to ensure democratic debate and free democratic choice. (NIO Press Release, 7 November 1990)

Primarily, he tried to broker deals between Dublin and the

Unionists. This pattern recurred frequently in the initial stages of dealing with the Unionist preconditions, where he shuttled between Collins on the one hand, and Molyneaux and Paisley on the other. For example, during the negotiations over the suspension of the Maryfield Secretariat, Brooke 'adjourned' a meeting with the Unionists in order to consult with Dublin, and reconvened it a fortnight later to offer them a straight deal: Dublin would concede the suspension if the Unionists agreed to direct negotiations with Dublin later in the process.

Brooke's prolonged attempts to broker a formula of words to define the point at which Dublin would enter the talks process (June 1990–March 1991) addressed a more thorny problem because of the way in which both sides saw the issue as one of principle. The Unionists insisted that they needed to be involved in the decision to let Dublin in, to emphasise the point that the Irish government was a foreign one, while Dublin insisted on underlining their non-negotiable right to a say in the future of the North as enshrined in the Agreement. His Dublin–Unionist brokerage continued throughout the Initiative, from preconditions, through Dublin's entry, to the venue and chair for Strand 2.

But there were limits to how much Brooke could achieve with the tools of pure mediation. Particularly as time passed, and the complexity of the Initiative grew and the possibility of negotiation neared, the neutral facilitative role looked increasingly threadbare. Brooke admits:

> I think we got to the stage towards the end of the process . . . that the phrase 'facilitator' began to be disliked by people. But certainly . . . in the earlier stages, I think it was a good phrase, and it actually was an accurate description of what we were about.

So increasingly he resorted to the tactics of power mediation. Even while in his 'broker' role, he was stepping outside the bounds of pure mediation by employing pressure to achieve agreement. (For example, he faced both Dublin and the Unionists, at different junctures, with the pressure of taking the public blame for the Initiative's breakdown if they failed to accept his brokered deals.) By and large, pure mediation (in his terminology, facilitation) was too weak a tool, given the task he faced and the gulf between the two sides. Not only did he have to face the ever-present suspicion that Molyneaux in particular, and others at various points, were operating a wrecking strategy, but as Frank Millar of the *Irish Times* commented in late 1990:

> There are very few senior politicians, on either side, prepared privately to voice the belief that this is going anywhere. And this is not because they aren't anxious to move. Rather it derives from a reluctant acknowledgement that they operate on parallel tracks, and that their respective agendas are almost certainly mutually exclusive. (*Irish Times*, 18 December 1990)

Brooke had the power of his office at his disposal and for all that he described his (and Britain's) role as merely 'to enable and encourage', he needed a more muscular approach in order to keep the Initiative on track.

Conciliation

Conciliation involves 'providing an informal communication link between antagonists for the purposes of identifying the major issues, lowering tension and encouraging them to move towards direct interaction such as negotiation' (Fisher and Keashly 1991, p. 33). This description could apply to much of Brooke's preliminary bilateral 'talks about talks', as to King's before him, when he spent the time identifying issues and encouraging a move towards negotiation. Such talks, however, were almost all of a formal nature. Further, Brooke refrained from proposing solutions at this stage, but concentrated on defining positions and outlining agendas: these talks were aimed not at solutions but at building frameworks to facilitate solutions. It was a classic example of 'pre-negotiation' (Blair 1991; Rothman 1989, 1990; Stephens 1988). Brooke himself does profess an awareness during the plenary stage of the need to design the proceedings in such a way that they could be subsequently built on:

> We were seeking to do two things. In an ideal world we were seeking to secure the objective of a conclusion within the various Strands. And our second objective was so to conduct ourselves that were we to fail to do so, everyone would be prepared to return to do it again.

Implicit in such a long-view outlook is an appreciation of the Initiative as a preparatory stage in the process. However, his concurrent use of power mediation tactics constrains the degree to which he can be described as a conciliator only.

Consultation

Consultation involves a third party 'who attempts to facilitate creative problem-solving through communication and [joint] analysis . . . and to reveal the underlying emotional and relationship issues. It is assumed that an increase in understanding and trust will enable the parties to settle their differences' (Fisher and Keashly 1991, p. 33). There seems little evidence that Brooke utilised such procedures, and indeed the requirement that a consultant is from outside the conflict makes it unlikely he could have chosen so to do. In any case, neither Brooke nor many others involved in the Initiative are likely to have subscribed to the idea that any of the core issues under discussion were going to be resolved merely through an 'increase in understanding and trust' alone.

However, a broad-view argument can be made that his accomplishment in actually bringing the local disputants into talks for the first time in almost 20 years served as a relationship-building exercise for the subsequent post-Brooke negotiations and later events in 1994 and beyond. Such an accomplishment is of no little value, and the argument is reinforced by the comments made by participants after the breakdown of plenaries concerning the discovery of previously absent commitment, the genuine listening to each other, and the realisation that some positions were not, as expected, mutually exclusive (*Belfast Telegraph*, 4 July 1991). Such comments are resonant of the attitudes prevalent in the very early stages of relationship-building (or rebuilding) between alienated parties. Brooke acknowledges that the role was needed: 'There was this fundamental distrust in both directions, and you just had to work patiently to seek to break that down, so that actions in fact contradicted and disproved what the misgivings were.'

The greatest significance of the Brooke Initiative, of course, was that it happened at all. Not since Sunningdale in 1973 had anyone managed to bring Unionist and nationalist political leaders around a formal negotiating table to address the constitutional question. As Brooke describes it:

If you remain permanently immune from conversation with each other, then there is the danger that you just forget how to negotiate. And it's also true that, unless everybody actually sets out what their positions are, you can't discover whether there is . . . greater mutual ground than you think.

That the Initiative failed to reach a conclusion in a mere ten weeks surprised few people in Northern Ireland. Almost 20 years of violence, polarisation and protectionism had passed since their political representatives had been called upon to exercise negotiating skills: it was not to be expected that they would find it an easy task. This is particularly true for the Unionist politicians, of whom Brooke comments:

> One of the problems was that the Unionists had very little negotiating experience, because of the role that Unionism had played in Northern Ireland prior to the abrogation [sic] of Stormont, and the idea of negotiating was not one that was familiar to them. Curiously, they negotiated much better during the whole process which had been going on for more than a year in setting up the talks, than the SDLP did. And then when we actually got around the table, the SDLP were perhaps more skilful than they were.

But at least people now had proof that negotiations could happen (70 per cent of the Northern Ireland population wanted more talks; the figures were 80 per cent in Britain and 90 per cent in the Republic; Gallup/IMS: *Irish Times*, 6 July 1991). Undoubtedly in facilitating the dialogue, Brooke did help build familiarity into the Unionist-nationalist relationship, thus directly laying the foundation for further talks – and further progress – in late 1992 which, without the Brooke Initiative, might have been unthinkable. 'I think we did change the playing field,' Brooke asserts. 'We actually enabled a game to take place.' In that light only, Brooke could be said to have played a useful and successful consultant's role.

Arbitration

Arbitration is defined by Fisher and Keashly as 'a legitimate and authoritative third party providing a binding judgement to the parties arrived at by considering the merits of the opposing positions and imposing a settlement deemed to be fair and just' (1991, p. 33). O'Leary and McGarry (1993) argue convincingly

that, throughout the period of direct rule, arbitration has been
the self-declared policy of the British government towards Northern Ireland, and that in fact direct rule is, to government
thinking, arbitration in action. While they assert that it has been
a policy failure, none the less it is an accurate description of
British policy since 1972. In this sense, Brooke was the direct
inheritor of an arbitration policy: in his role of, as Prior described
it, 'Governor-General', he was both the power-wielder in Northern Ireland and the source of authority. So Brooke's Initiative can
be seen as a coherent continuation of the policy process.

However, as O'Leary and McGarry also point out, the Agreement had, in enshrining the Irish dimension, turned part of the
role over to Dublin; the Brooke Initiative was the clearest
illustration of post-Agreement 'joint arbitration' by London in
consultation with Dublin. As Brooke pointed out early in the
Initiative, he depended 'throughout the process . . . [on] a basis of
mutual understanding with the Irish government' (*Irish Times*, 30
May 1990). He can be seen continually gathering proposals,
formulas and conditions from the Unionists and then taking them
to Collins in order to work out a joint response.

This joint approach made problematic his effectiveness in
retaining the distance and independence necessary to maintain
the status of 'a legitimate and authoritative third party' (Fisher
and Keashly 1991, p. 33). The price he paid for this shared
responsibility was that he had to be party to a harder anti-
unionist line than he might have chosen himself. For example, as
a first move in wooing the Unionists in August 1989, on his own
initiative he carefully fabricated an 'alternative' wording of the
Agreement's Paragraph 29 (by which he implied that the Agreement was less resistant to replacement than the paragraph
actually suggests), incurring the wrath of Dublin, who saw it as 'a
blunder' (*Irish Times*, 17 August 1989). This is in striking contrast
to the joint Collins–Brooke decision, three months later, to
announce in advance the schedule for future Conference meetings, which was a starkly negative response to Unionist demands
for a suspension of meetings (to which Dublin was strongly
opposed). The strain which this shared role exerted on Brooke's
naturally conservative–unionist sympathies was especially evident
in the events of June–July 1990. As he strove to finalise a talks
formula by early July, he failed to move far enough towards
Dublin to accommodate their insistence on early involvement,

and arguably set the process back several months by taking a position very close to that of the Unionists, which he seemed extremely reluctant to relinquish. The role of joint arbiters was not one that could always come easily or naturally to representatives of two countries with such a long and acrimonious history of opposition. For Brooke particularly, the joint role was a source of tension, as he tried to act in the role of broker between the Unionists, for whose position he had a considerable British (and Conservative) predisposition, and the Dublin government, with whom he was an arbitrating partner.

The other implication of the shift to a shared role with Dublin was that Brooke would refrain from attempts to impose an arbitrated structure of devolution: rather he would try to facilitate the participants' agreeing their own devolution formula. Thus, in one sense the customary British arbitration framework continued as usual during the talks in the form of direct rule; in another sense, arbitration (that is, the imposition of a solution) was suspended for as long as the parties made progress towards their own solution. Brooke would occasionally remind the parties that if they failed, he might be forced to impose his own structure. But compared to previous Secretaries who had made the same threat, Brooke's capacity to threaten an imposed settlement was mitigated to the degree that he could no longer impose it on Dublin. Further, an arbitrated settlement had always contained the problem that at least one of the arbitrated parties (by which I mean the Northern Ireland communities) considered Britain insufficiently legitimate as an arbiter; the involvement of Dublin simply added to the number of arbiters whose legitimacy could be questioned. Arbitration, in short, in the sense of imposing solutions, had not worked effectively for Britain in the past, and post-Agreement relationships with Dublin further curtailed Brooke's capacity for arbitration.

Power Mediation

Power mediation is a development of the functions of pure mediation, but with the significant difference that the mediator's power resources are used to the full, so that the role 'includes the use of leverage or coercion by the third party in the form of promised rewards or threatened punishments. In a very real sense, the third party becomes a member of a negotiating triad and bargains with each party, using carrots and sticks.' The intervenor may also give commitments regarding continuing benefits and/or acting as 'guarantor of the agreement' (Fisher and Keashly 1991, p. 33).

Undoubtedly Brooke functioned as a power mediator. He used the resources of his position as Secretary to employ leverage and coercion, he attempted manipulation of the parties, he was a fully involved member of the negotiating triad, and the Agreement enforced his role as guarantor of any settlement.

Despite his claims for a British policy of neutrality, he was not slow to make use of the leverage his power and position gave him. In particular, this was his tactic towards the Unionists, regarding whom he could use his power of office to positive effect: his approach to them ranged from cajoling to ultimata and threats to impose his own solution. In his Bangor speech of January 1990, attempting to encourage them into negotiations over devolution, he offered the incentive that 'matters transferred to a new devolved administration would of course be outside the purview of the Conference' (*Irish Times*, 10 January 1990), suggesting that within a devolution framework they could themselves soak off the power of the Agreement and lessen the Irish dimension. In contrast, speaking in Ballymena in the following September, he warned that if progress was not forthcoming soon, he might need to 'set the pace and show the way' (*Irish Times*, 8 September 1990) by imposing his own devolved structures (with the implication that such a system would be built on the Agreement framework in a realisation of the Unionists' fears).

Again, as the Strand 1 bilaterals got bogged down and side-tracked in Unionist objections over the Strand 2 venue, he presented the Unionists with a 24-hour ultimatum. (The tactic was not effective, however, given that Molyneaux and Paisley responded by going over Brooke's head to appeal to the Prime Minister and managed to bury the ultimatum in a week of confusion.) In the aftermath of the Initiative, he returned to the threat of an imposed solution, should no agreement be forthcoming during the lifetime of the next Parliament.

His most successful use of leverage, however, was not directed at the Unionists, but at Dublin. After seven months of stagnation over the sticking-point of the timing of Dublin's entry to the talks process, during February and March 1991 he issued a series of dark warnings about 'putting up the shutters' (*Irish Times*, 6

February 1991), and forced Dublin's hand strongly by instigating a series of winding-down meetings with the political parties, knowing that the public blame for ending the process at that stage would fall on the Irish government. The strategy produced a major concession from Haughey (that the timing of Dublin's entry would be at Brooke's discretion) which saved the Initiative.

A less overtly coercive tactic was his role as agenda-setter, indirectly dictating in advance the substantive issues which negotiations would address. Early on, he forced all the parties into a commitment to devolution with which some felt uncomfortable, but with which they – notably Molyneaux and the SDLP – could not subsequently argue. Later, he was adamant that Strand 2 housekeeping details be agreed before permitting Strand 1 plenaries to begin. (Arguably, though, this was a distinctly unsuccessful tactic, and reflected his underestimation of the symbolic importance of such details, since it effectively delayed Strand 1 for seven weeks.)[11]

Such instances represent the explicit employment of the tactics of leverage from the power mediator's tool-kit. For Brooke, of course, the tool-kit came with the post of Secretary.

A somewhat subtler version of a similar kind of coercion is manipulation. While this is more difficult both to define and to recognise, there are grounds to argue that one ingredient in Brooke's approach to the Strand 1 talks was a manipulative strategy aimed at the Unionists. Implicit in the design of the talks, not least the large size of the delegations (10 per party; and thus 20 Unionists), was the expectation that there would be an empowering of the moderating influence of the Unionist second-tiers over their party leaders. Brooke rejects responsibility for this, attributing the large delegate numbers to Hume's insistence on having all strands of opinion within the SDLP represented in the delegation. Indeed, other party leaders may also have seen the sense in bringing in a broad spectrum of their membership, the better to sell any agreement or to share blame for any failure. Whatever the origins of the oversized delegations, Brooke accepts that it was a situation to be exploited: 'For the purposes of negotiation it was much more difficult if you had that number of people present. On the other hand, we went along with it. It did actually provide an opportunity for the Unionist delegations . . . to be a mix of opinions.' Right from the beginning, in his January 1990 Bangor speech, Brooke was publicly targeting the Unionist second-tiers, as distinct from the two leaders, with encouragement 'to develop their thinking . . . and to find ways to enable talks between the parties' (*Irish Times*, 10 January 1990). Similarly, the inclusion of the Alliance Party in negotiations introduced the voice of a moderate and basically pro-Union element with a strong commitment to successful negotiation and to devolution. Much depended on the greater flexibility and commitment to realistic dealing of the second-tier leaders of the three main parties (especially the Unionists) and their capacities to influence their leaders. For Brooke, a strategy of attempting to empower Unionist moderates and second-tiers 'was permanently the case'. But by and large, the Initiative failed utterly to facilitate any moderation on the hardline stances of Molyneaux and Paisley. As the talks broke down, significant numbers within both Unionist parties blamed the intransigence of their two leaders. Millar commented:

> The two men who have for so long dominated unionism remained firmly in control. Those of their colleagues most eager to get into substantive negotiations found themselves reduced often to the role of bystanders – frustrated by the rows which, from day one, soured the atmosphere and sowed the seeds of breakdown. (*Irish Times*, 4 July 1991)

Indeed, there is a degree to which Brooke could be said to have been manipulated in turn by the Unionists. In employing the tactics of power mediation and signalling that tools such as manipulation were acceptable within the Initiative, Brooke opened the door for Unionists to use these 'acceptable' tools to their own ends. Unlike them, he had too much at stake with the whole Initiative to risk having participants finding in his objectionable tactics an excuse to disengage from the process. But in this sense power mediation backfired on him. For example, in the midst of brokering a deal between Dublin and the Unionists on Irish involvement in the talks, he appeared to let his unionist sympathies outweigh his neutrality with a statement on the question which would have sounded quite appropriate had it come from Paisley:

> Clearly any talks relating to internal arrangements in Northern Ireland are matters for the British government and for the parties of Northern Ireland . . . . They are not talks which

involve the government of the Republic because they are internal to Northern Ireland itself. (*Irish Times*, 6 June 1990)

The statement angered Dublin deeply, and led directly to eight months of stagnation and delay which significantly increased Unionist distrust of both Dublin and Westminster, while serving Unionist delaying tactics well.

Again, Brooke can be seen as being outwitted by the Unionists over one small but significant matter during the final stages of reaching agreement to talk (April 1991), when by concentrating on his own tactic of putting pressure on them, he seemed to miss the Unionist tactics. When he warned that he would not enter into further 'textual barter' (*Irish Times*, 15 March 1991), except to give clarifications on the final document containing the formula for talks, the Unionists leaders took him at his word and received from him a letter containing twelve separate clarifications which, at later stages, they used as a written 'record of understanding' and as an extra bargaining tool, something he had not intended to provide and which no other parties received.

Finally, the meeting with Major was possibly the clearest example of Unionist strategy working to outmanoeuvre Brooke. While the Prime Minister's involvement made no positive contribution to the process, it permitted Unionists to claim they had overruled Brooke by going above his head, and led to dissatisfaction within the SDLP and Alliance, who complained that he had lost credibility by the meeting and that the talks were 'an unholy, confused mess' (*Belfast Telegraph*, 17 May 1991). The incident weakened his authority among all the participants.

Peacekeeping

Finally, there is peacekeeping, 'the provision of military personnel by an outside party to supervise and monitor a ceasefire between antagonists' (Fisher and Keashly 1991, p. 34). In the authors' sense, this has little pertinence to the Northern Ireland context. Peacekeeping could be said to be part of Brooke's role only in so far as Britain makes claims that its military presence in Northern Ireland is designed to keep the peace between the two communities. While this might have described the situation when the British army first arrived in 1969, tasked to intervene either between opposing rioting communities or between the Catholic

community and the Protestant constabularies, it is a long out-
dated view, as the military has for many years expended its main
effort on waging war against a Republican paramilitary force.[12]
Such a role is clearly partisan, and it is arguable that the war is
waged against the British army precisely because they are the
British army. By the time of Brooke's period in office, the
peacekeeping role applied only in the most general understanding
that he was the major initiator of security policy in Northern
Ireland. In the particular context of the Initiative, Brooke did not
employ the strategies of a peacekeeper.

CONCLUSION AND SUMMARY

The analysis offered above leads to a view of Brooke as incoming
Secretary capitalising on the opportunities provided by the post-
Agreement context which coincided with his arrival, simulta-
neously empowered and constrained by his office.

On the personal side, he came to the post aided by his image
as a genial, uncontroversial, low-profile Conservative, with some
distant family connections to Brookeborough, the former Northern Ireland Prime Minister, some prior understanding and em-
pathy for the province, a rapidly demonstrated capacity for fast
learning and universally low expectations that he would initiate
any significant changes. In all of these qualities, he was a distinct
change from his predecessor Tom King. It was an image he easily
encouraged, with his affable air and his sporting metaphors, and
the one which he promoted when he made overt his hope of
facilitating inter-party dialogue. He tried to present himself on
this level as a referee between the local political players.

But such an ingenuous image was problematic for Northern
Ireland politicians in so far as they could not for a moment forget
Brooke's office. He could not be simply a referee, however
personable he might be as an individual, because he was also the
most powerful player on the field. Moreover, this official role,
coupled with the post-Agreement context, meant that he had
contradictory relations with the protagonists. That is to say, not
only did he have an actively political relationship with each –
which alone would immediately complicate his position as a
facilitator – but in each relationship there were conflicting
elements of alliance and opposition. Indeed, his own comments

suggest that he was aware of the problematic of this contradiction between his stated neutrality and his duty as British minister. The example of his position on the Irish Constitution's territorial claim to Northern Ireland illustrates the difficulties he faced:

> There is no question that the Unionists did believe that [I] should not be wholly neutral on the matter, that the Republic's constitutional claim was an offence against the United Kingdom, and that therefore as a member of the UK government I should be resisting it. I understand the view they took, but it would have been very difficult to have played that role and still have been able to advance matters .... What they were wanting me to do was to define precisely – in private conversation – what my position was going to be in Strand 2 on the Irish constitutional claim. I said I was perfectly happy to play a role in seeking to get a solution, but I was not going to define how I would play it in advance. And had we got to that stage, I would have made it perfectly clear to the Irish government the difficulty I thought that the claim constituted. But ... in other words you had to retain an independence of hand, because otherwise then alternatively the Irish would have said we were taking sides.

His office, therefore, constrained his capacity to facilitate talks in the impartial terms of which he frequently spoke, simply because he was too deeply involved with the British agenda to be in any sense impartial at any level. At the same time, however, it was precisely the gravitas of his office as British Secretary which empowered him to exercise influence over the parties to bring them to talks. Thus, exactly that which disqualified him as a pure mediator was that which equipped him as a power mediator. His position was what James Smith describes as the mediator's 'two-hat' dilemma (1995): true impartiality might make him more welcome to the disputants, but only the power of his office, which rendered him partial, would enable him to have any positive effect on the situation.

But it is entirely arguable that no amount of impartial facilitation would have produced any results in the context of Northern Ireland politics at the time, no matter what the status of anyone who tried. Better then, it could be said, to have the power of the office exerted by an individual with a degree of comparative sensitivity to the situation, as Brooke undoubtedly did. Britain could not possibly just 'enable and encourage', given the significance of its political, diplomatic, financial and military investment in Northern Ireland, any more than Brooke himself could simply just 'facilitate', given his supreme position of influence and status in the arena. As *The* [London] *Times* commented, his own and his official agendas conspired against the neutrality to which he aspired, to consistently 'undermine the sense of him acting as an "honest broker" or an impartial facilitator in the process' (quoted in *Irish Times*, 5 November 1990).

But unempowered reasoning and suggestion were never going to bring the Unionists to the table willingly, or win the concessions from Dublin to bring them unwillingly. As the non-local facilitator of inter-party dialogue in Northern Ireland, Brooke can make some claim, as he did, to the strategy of pure mediation. But even in that Strand 1 context, and certainly in the wider context, he was much more frequently an employer of power mediation, in particular towards the Unionists and, when absolutely necessary, towards Dublin.

The main conclusion about Brooke's role as intervenor, then, must be that he operated as a power mediator, with constituent elements of an arbiter. The shadow of a British-imposed solution functioned, especially towards the Unionists, as the largely unspoken threat that first brought them into the process: if they refused to participate in the design of a voluntary structural solution, the arbitrated settlement they could expect would be worse than ever since it would be imposed, without their input, under the Agreement's continued auspices and with the involvement of Dublin. It was a powerful and effective threat, all the more so in the aftermath of the Agreement, which had proved that Britain could and would impose structures without Unionist input or consent; it was a threat that the representative of a neutral power acting as a facilitator could not have made.

Indeed, it is hard to see how any Secretary of State could have avoided the role of power mediator. And it is equally difficult to see, within the hard-nosed and unsubtle parameters of Irish politics in general and Unionist politics in particular, how Unionists would have expected – or respected – any other kind of intervention. From his first overtures to them onwards, he used a repertoire of threats, incentives, manipulation, pressure and ultimata. Furthermore, he was prepared to use similar tactics on the other parties when necessary.

There were, however, limits to the effectiveness of this strategy. While frequently his use of threat and pressure paid off, mainly as regards the Unionists, his tactic of manipulation failed on two counts. Not only was his goal of empowering the moderate Unionists at the expense of the party leaders not achieved in any significant way; he was also the victim of the tactic turned back on him by the two leaders, suffering a significant loss of credibility as he looked on occasion outmanoeuvred.

Additionally, there were instances of misjudgement on his part which weakened his mediating effectiveness. These included his miscalculation of the Dublin–Unionist gulf over Irish involvement in Strand 1 (or else his misunderstanding of the terms of his agreement with Collins on the subject), which led to months of delay; his underestimation of the symbolic significance of the issues of chair and venue for the Strand 2 talks, and his dogged insistence that they should be resolved despite the heavy cost in delay on Strand 1 (but see note 11); and, most dramatically, his peculiar appearance on Irish television singing 'Oh My Darling Clementine', while the unionist community mourned eight deaths at the hands of the IRA, an embarrassing incident which both alienated hard-line Unionists from him and his Initiative, and undermined his own estimation of his credibility in the subsequent talks process and opened the way for Major to overrule and further undermine him. (Political consensus in Britain and Northern Ireland has it that the gaffe was the prime factor in his removal from office in the post-election cabinet reshuffle three months later.)

Interestingly, however, his power mediation was made more subtle and more effective by encompassing some elements of conciliation and consultation. He fulfilled the communication channel role of the conciliator to some degree in the early 'pre-negotiation' stages. Any assessment of the effects of the Initiative must include the positive effects on the relationships between the participants from the simple novelty of engaging directly in dialogue: if such facilitation can be characterised as relationship-building and communication development, then Brooke played some element of the consultant. Both consultancy and conciliation, however, are by definition largely incompatible with power mediation, and thus Brooke's capacities for these roles were greatly constrained by his power-related strategies. The fact of their existence within his intervention strategy, however, does suggest some implications for cross-fertilisation between resolution and settlement styles of conflict management.

In his opening address to the first Strand 1 plenary session, he remarked that he had 'been variously described as a facilitator or sheepdog' (*Irish Times*, 25 June 1991). The phrase neatly (and perhaps unconsciously at the time) encapsulates this dual role: while Peter Brooke the affable facilitator tried earnestly to facilitate voluntary entry into talks among the local parties, the official sheepdog – the British Secretary of State for Northern Ireland – was snapping at the delegates' heels to force them towards the table.

Brooke's intervention strategy thus sits naturally within the characterisation of the Initiative as an implementation of the structural approach. Furthermore, utilising the power resources of the intervenor, accepting the impact of the intervenor's own agenda and resources on the process and the disputants, and aiming towards a negotiated settlement over the objective political issues, the Initiative is clearly also an example of settlement theory in action.

Was the Initiative a success or a failure? No agreement was reached in any strand of the talks, and indeed no strand even approached completion. Thus, there were no structural results which could be claimed as successes. Progress was made, however: the mere fact of bringing the parties into dialogue, and specifically of bringing the local political parties into direct negotiation, was a positive development. Subsequent talks under Mayhew in late 1992 when, however inconclusively, both Strands 2 and 3 were broached, undoubtedly benefited from the groundwork and familiarisation process completed by Brooke. Further, Brooke's initial three-stranded formula for talks, arrived at through 16 months of painful bargaining, has remained the accepted orthodox framework for potential negotiations over the ensuing years. The argument can be made strongly that Brooke's efforts forced a rethinking among all the parties that paved the way for the changes wrought in the later 1990s. In this sense, he successfully completed the pre-negotiation process which facilitated future talks and events. In February 1993, commenting on talks under both Brooke and Mayhew and the prospects for political cooperation in Northern Ireland, Molyneaux said simply, 'What we've done before, we can do again' (BBC Radio Ulster interview, 17 February 1993). What Brooke accomplished – and it was a considerable feat – was to prove to politicians, communities and observers alike, first, that the process could happen (by no means an obvious assumption after 18 years of stalemate); and secondly, that negotiation could be both possible and fruitful without implying weakness (an attitude previously prevalent, especially among Unionist politicians).

In the same interview, Molyneaux went on to criticise the structure of the talks as 'fifty-two people around a table, starting by answering the question "what nation do you want to belong to?" and having that set in concrete before continuing' (ibid.). Given his cynical view of the whole process, it is perhaps an understandably negative characterisation. But given that the whole Initiative was formulated within the parameters of a structural policy, and that the question he paraphrases concerns the essence of the structural approach – achieving a settlement-style solution to the constitutional question – he may be making a salient comment on the inherent limits of that approach. The central question over which Northern Irish politicians must engage in a structural process is indeed the constitutional question (see Chapter 1). However, the nature of that engagement may well benefit both from a cross-fertilisation from resolution-based approaches, and from a consciousness of the ability of resolution to address, in a complementary manner, elements of the conflict outside the capacities of settlement. These developments would suggest, first, a more comprehensive form of dialogue which includes elements of consultancy-style relationship-building; and secondly, the complement of another approach – a cultural approach – which asks the supplementary question concerning how relationships can be built to encompass the opposing answers to the constitutional question.

6 The Community Relations Council: An Examination of the Cultural Approach to Conflict Management

1. BACKGROUND

In Chapter 3, I traced the development of cultural initiatives from the late 1960s to the late 1980s, noting the gradual development of a coherent approach and a constituency of practitioners. After the failure of the flawed structural attempt to address intercommunal relationships in the Community Relations Commission (1969–74), the approach grew out of the strength of informal initiatives at community level, moving from simple contact work in the 1970s to focused community relations work in the 1980s. As Chapter 3 noted, by 1986 the realisation was growing that the approach could benefit from a more strategic and higher profile format.

In 1985, a report was commissioned by the Standing Advisory Commission on Human Rights (SACHR), a government-appointed body whose brief is to comment autonomously on any aspects of British government policy implementation in Northern Ireland. Recognising that the time might be right for a reassessment of community relations work in the late 1980s, SACHR was concerned to gain an understanding both of the current position and of possible ways to increase its effectiveness.

The report, 'Improving Community Relations', was presented to SACHR in 1986 by its authors, Hugh Frazer, then the director of the Northern Ireland Voluntary Trust (NIVT), a government-linked funding body for voluntary agencies, and Mari Fitzduff, then a researcher and trainer in conflict resolution in Northern Ireland, and a trustee of the same Trust. Their brief was to investigate, through consultation with a wide range of agencies in Northern Ireland and elsewhere,

(a) the adequacy and effectiveness of present structures for promoting improvement in community relations in Northern Ireland;

(b) whether a central body should be created to co-ordinate and fund community relations in the province. (Frazer and Fitzduff 1986, p. 6)

They offered a definition of what community relations work might mean in reality, conceptualising a continuum of what is desirable or possible, ranging from total 'reconciliation' to political accommodation. This was an importantly realistic note to bring to the debate, since it immediately differentiated between those groups who, for religious or idealistic reasons, aimed at some sort of ultimate 'peace and reconciliation', and those self-characterised pragmatics who aimed at an achievable and specific improvement in relationships. The lack of such a differentiation had previously only increased the problems for groups, like the NIPF, who in the past had attempted to spread an umbrella over all 'peace work' (see Chapter 3). But further, the inherent broadening of the definition of community relations work was an early portent of the breadth of approach the Community Relations Council (CRC) would subsequently apply to its operation. The ramifications of this for the cultural approach, as defined and operated during the 1970s and 1980s, will be addressed later.

The report also addressed the contact hypothesis (see Hewstone and Browne 1986), conceding that 'contact schemes are clearly an important first step in the process' (Frazer and Fitzduff 1986, p. 30). But it insisted that contact work was unlikely to bring breakthroughs 'unless accompanied by both active discussion programmes ["focused" work] and possibilities for long term involvement and contact' (ibid., p. 30). Furthermore, it argued that raising the profile of community relations work was a precondition for any successful overall settlement of the Northern Ireland problem:

A satisfactory constitutional settlement is dependent upon group relationships within the community. . . . To leave the problem of improving community relations until one has finally solved the constitutional issue may merely exacerbate not only the problem of relationships between the communities but also the task of finding an acceptable constitutional settlement. (ibid., p. 19)

Implicit in this statement was a clear elevation of the importance of community relations work, an attempt to rescue it from the periphery and make it an integral part of the search for a solution.

The report made two main practical recommendations. A new community relations agency should be publicly established to provide support, encouragement and direction to agencies working in the field; and this should be supported by an internal government policy unit which, apart from raising government's own consciousness on the issue, would also serve as an official endorsement of and public commitment to community relations work.

In 1986, quite independent of the SACHR initiative, the Department of Education in Northern Ireland (DENI, the government department charged since 1974 with responsibility for community relations) carried out its own internal review of the field. While it did not make concrete recommendations like the SACHR report, nevertheless it did provide impetus from within government itself for the development of a community relations initiative.

Around the same time, an informal group of interested individuals from academia, the media, education and the arts were coalescing into the Cultural Traditions Group. Their aim was to encourage the acceptance of cultural diversity in Northern Irish society, by promoting non-exclusive cultural pride within the two communities, and cultural tolerance and respect between them:

> Community relations and cultural diversity cannot be separated. While the first is a problem, the second is surely an asset, provided its richness can be celebrated in non-threatening ways. . . . There are many colours in our cultural spectrum, not just two. (Crozier 1989, p. vii)

In the aftermath of the two reports, Frazer, Fitzduff and a growing number of influential individuals, especially from the Cultural Traditions Group, entered into dialogue with government representatives concerning the way forward for community relations work. The discussions focused on the possibilities of new structures: a public agency and a government unit.

The first fruit of such discussions was the establishment in September 1987 of the Central Community Relations Unit (CCRU) within the Northern Ireland Office. Its brief was

to advise the Secretary of State on all aspects of the relationship between the different parts of the NI community. The
Unit, which reports to the Head of the Northern Ireland Civil
Service, is charged with formulating, reviewing and challenging policy throughout the Government system with the aim of
improving community relations. (CCRU 1993, p. 2)

Community relations had not been well served by the previous
government department established to deal with it, the Ministry
of Community Relations, 1969–74, which had in effect been
rendered peripheral to mainstream government. This time
around, there was a realisation of the need for a more committed
expression of government support for community relations.

The CCRU was to be a central unit, rather than a discrete
department, so that it would report directly to the Secretary of
State, and would have access to all government departments
rather than be sidelined into any one. 'The intention was to
ensure that at the centre of the decision making process in
Northern Ireland, the crucial community relations issues, in their
very widest sense, were given the fullest possible considerations'
(CCRU 1991, p. 1). The definition here of community relations
in the 'very widest sense' was a highly significant, if subtle,
development in the field, the effects of which would be increasingly evident once the CRC was in operation. The CCRU was
charged with primary responsibility for policy formation and for
funding.

Within the terms of my overall argument, such a Unit is clearly
a construction of the structural, rather than the cultural, approach. As an instrument of government, it was by definition a
structural agency, yet geared to address issues from the agenda of
the cultural approach. However, the NIO clearly recognised the
inability of its structural operation to provide a complete solution
to Northern Ireland's problems:

Progress in overcoming terrorism and in creating political
structures which command support across the community
would help to improve community relations. However, even if
such progress can be made, the underlying community divisions will still have to be addressed. If they are not, they will
continue to threaten and undermine any political and security
progress. (CCRU 1993, p. 1)

Consequently, the CCRU outlined the initiatives which government, through it and DENI, felt were important to support and develop. These comprised education reform, instituting statutory cross-curricular themes in all schools of Education for Mutual Understanding and of Cultural Heritage; the Cross-Community Contact Scheme, which grant-aided joint activity programmes by schools and youth groups; a District Council programme, which would provide funding for each of the 26 elected Local District Councils to cooperate on a programme of cross- community activities under the supervision of council-appointed Community Relations Officers; core funding for established reconciliation groups; administration of a funding programme to support regeneration of the physical and social environment; and the establishment of the CRC (CCRU 1993).

Once set up, the CCRU continued its consultations with informal and formal groups from the statutory and voluntary sectors, to explore the possibilities for a new public agency for community relations. The embryo Cultural Traditions Group was influential in these consultations, and when the design of the new agency, the CRC, was complete, it included both themes of community relations and of cultural traditions work.[13] Indeed, the CRC's first chair was James Hawthorne, who had previously chaired the Cultural Traditions Group. (He was replaced in the latter post by Maurice Hayes, first chair of the NICRC in 1969.)

In 1989, Fitzduff published another paper which greatly influenced the debate. Developing some of the earlier report's themes concerning both the philosophy and the practical implementation of community relations work, this paper provided a comprehensive typology of community relations work which for the first time effectively bridged the gap between the erstwhile amorphous concept of community relations and the forms in which it could be implemented on the ground (Fitzduff 1989). While the descriptive content of the paper was not particularly original (she based the variety of types of work on existing examples of community relations organisations), the act of describing, analysing and categorising the practical projects involved in terms of their goals, their practices and their origins provided the first solid basis on which a future strategy for community relations might be based. When the Community

Relations Council, with Fitzduff as its director, was established in 1990, it set about its task very much on the basis of this typology.

What follows in this chapter focuses almost exclusively on the work of the CRC. But this does not imply any lack of awareness of the significance of the CCRU, on the structural side, and its overseeing and support for the CRC's operations. Likewise, the CRC was chosen as the focus of this case-study primarily because of my desire to explore the potential of complementarity, as I hope will become clear through the rest of this and the next chapter; but such a focus in no way diminishes the real significance of the many agencies and individuals in Northern Ireland who carry out the actual work of community relations, and for whom my great respect is, I hope, made very clear in Chapter 3.

2. ESTABLISHMENT

The CRC was initially fully funded through the CCRU, with a third of its 21 Council members appointed by the Secretary of State from the voluntary and statutory sectors.

'The ultimate aim', its strategic plan asserted, 'must be to assist in the creation of just and sustainable solutions to the many issues that divide the communities in Northern Ireland' (CRC 1991, p. 4). Within this goal, 'the main strategic aim of the Council is "to increase understanding and co-operation between the political, cultural and religious communities in Northern Ireland" ' (ibid., p. 6).

This assistance role was envisaged in two ways. Community relations work was seen to be both 'pre-political, i.e. work that is necessary for political solutions to be achieved, and sub-political in that it will continue to be necessary for the foreseeable future in order for any solutions to be sustained' (ibid., p. 5).

The CRC, further, was designed to support community relations initiatives, rather than to carry them out itself. 'On the contrary . . . the Council will seek to multiply the effective development of community relations through co-operation with *all other agencies who have the capacity to contribute to the work.* The Council itself should thus aim to remain a small organisation, while helping community relations work to proliferate throughout society' (ibid., p. 8; emphasis added).

This represents a change of attitude from the NICRC, whose

aim was to implement a major programme of community development under its own auspices and through a policy of expansion. However, a more important aspect of this design lies behind the phrase 'all other agencies who have the capacity to contribute to the work'. This is a key point, and will be developed at length later, but some remarks must be made here concerning the CRC's envisaged clientele. It was noted that the NICRC decided at the outset that its role towards reconciliation groups would be secondary (see Chapter 3). The few such groups that were in existence were considered rather too middle-class and thus too removed from the geographical areas of conflict to be charged with carrying the community relations torch. The NICRC put its faith more in the vision of a network of confident and cooperative community groups which would grow inexorably out of the community development programme. Chapter 3 argued that the inherent limits of such a structural approach to a cultural agenda, at least as constrained by a partisan and cynical government structure, left a major flaw in the logic.

But the CRC made the same decision. Despite 20 years of development and expansion within the cultural approach, the CRC, like its predecessor, wanted to cast its remit wider:

> One of our first decisions was not to concentrate on reconciliation groups. To a certain extent, they needed to be worked with, to be supported, to garner from them what was best in practice, but certainly not to depend upon them. And I think that's actually been the right decision, because it is much more often the wider groups that can actually help move. (Fitzduff)

However, the CRC was not aiming to take over the work of community relations, as the NICRC largely had. Nor was the criticism of reconciliation groups so closely focused on their possible middle-class bias. (Not only is the criticism less justified in the 1990s, but it is also more widely accepted that sectarianism is not the prerogative of any particular class.) The aim from the first was clearly to develop community relations *beyond* the existing audiences or constituencies of the cultural approach. Such a change was an inevitable consequence of the broadened definition of community relations work in the 'very widest sense', upon which the CRC was based. So the CRC targeted not only those groups that had an overt desire to address community relations, but also the many other social agencies that, while having other primary aims, also had 'the capacity to contribute to the work'. In other words, the CRC set out with the task of convincing these non-cultural approach agencies of the need for their involvement. Fitzduff asserts:

> There's hardly anything that we can't undertake, if the Council agrees to it. . . . In a sense there is nothing now left that is not a community relations issue. . . . We really feel it is up to us to engage as many as possible. Our task is to make sure that all of them – in the same way that one would become aware of gender or race – would actually become aware of sectarianism and community relations.

This expansion of the arena of community relations – viewing it as the business of every social grouping or agency – involves an incremental development of cooperative processes, according to Fitzduff:

> Cooperation is the key, going from the easier levels to the harder levels, by cooperating on the social issues, by cooperating on the environmental issues, etc., moving then to what we call long-term quality contact, and then moving on up to the more difficult issues of security, constitutional issues. And in the end we are moving towards a just and sustainable constitutional solution.

In this significant sense, then, the CRC is not an embodiment of the cultural approach, or one part among many within it. The CRC is attempting to take the tools and procedures of the cultural approach, and expand it and them beyond one sector of society until it infuses every sector. Reconciliation, indeed, is only one among five interest areas defined by the CRC (see below). At the same time, however, its tools and methodology are drawn almost exclusively from that approach; it concentrates on relationship-based tactics; the practitioners it supports and utilises come from within that approach; and part of the basis on which it was established was broad consultation with those practitioners. Thus locating the CRC at any one point within the cultural/structural framework becomes problematic. It has developed out of the cultural approach, and its *modus operandi* is based on that approach. And yet it has links, through its government-sponsored foundation and through the CCRU, with the structural approach, it targets elements within the statutory sector, and states as its primary aim a contribution towards the achievement of a structural settlement in the form of 'a just and sustainable constitutional solution'. This mirrors to a large degree the CCRU's own conscious policy of reaching out beyond its own structural approach to interact with the cultural agenda. The implications of this entanglement of both approaches will be examined in Chapter 7.

Operationally, the CRC translated its aims and goals into a clearly delineated practical framework from the start. Three sub-committees were formed (including co-opted non-Council members) for each of three core areas of interest: cultural traditions, peace and reconciliation groups, and work and community groups. (This last area – work and community groups – constitutes the significant expansion beyond the reconciliation sector.) Additionally, two important support functions were identified: skills training and information dissemination. Under the director, a development officer was appointed for each of these five headings. They were supported by an administrative staff of six. In its first Annual Report, the Council outlined the substance of the five areas of operational interest. First, skills training recognised the

> substantial volume of knowledge and skills . . . accumulated by a variety of individuals located throughout the peace and reconciliation organisations, within youth work and holiday organisations in particular, and throughout the voluntary sector. . . . The immediate role and purpose of the Community Relations Council in its training function has been to provide access for as many individuals and organisations as possible to that accumulated skill and knowledge. . . . The Council's first task was to establish a trainer network to allow the development and sharing of community relations skills. (CRC 1991a, p. 42)

The offer of training was positively received by community relations activists, and the first CRC training schedule included workshops on prejudice reduction, non-violent action, human rights education, facilitating political discussion, socio-psycho-drama skills, publication skills, mediation skills, anti-sectarian work, cultural traditions work and church-based community relations work. The networking implicit in the provision of this training service developed rapidly and significantly into a means of drawing practitioners closer together in a forum for contact and discussion.

Secondly, information dissemination took three forms: CRC publications, which ranged from relevant pamphlets (for example, reprints of Frazer and Fitzduff's SACHR report and Fitzduff's community relations typology) to a news magazine which served the purposes of publicising the Council and its work and of discussing publicly the development of community relations work; a reference library on community relations issues for public consultation (later, a community relations 'shop' was opened in central Belfast's commercial district); and a series of information days in conjunction with Local District Councils aimed at raising public consciousness of the CRC's programmes.

Thirdly, the cultural traditions programme

> involved supporting local groups, educators, arts groups, publishers, broadcasters and film makers among others, in promoting a more general public awareness of, and sensitivity to, local cultural diversity. This has been done by means of three CRC grant schemes, cultural traditions awards, fellowship schemes and conferences. The aim has been to develop a greater cultural confidence in the community and a respect for difference. (ibid., p. 14)

The work involved liaison with public arts bodies, museums, galleries, universities, broadcasting bodies, etc., and with localised groups pursuing an interest in aspects of local cultural heritage.

Fourthly, the peace and reconciliation group program was aimed at those groups who hold reconciliation as a primary focus of their *raison d'être*. It involved:

> supporting the many peace, reconciliation and church groups in Northern Ireland in their efforts to promote greater cross-community contact and understanding. The Council aims to assist them in their development and to encourage the emergence of new groups. (ibid., p. 35)

This support took varying forms, including skills training for practitioners, facilitating conferences and seminars on issues of common concern, producing a directory of the many groups involved, administering both the Intercommunity Grant Scheme for mixed-group activity programmes (previously administered by NIVT), and the Organisational Development Scheme, which provided resources to those groups wishing to 'take some time out to reflect upon their organisation e.g., its aims, membership, and the work it was doing, and to use such reflection to make their programmes more effective' (ibid., p. 37). Thus the Council interpreted its role towards the main constituents of the cultural approach as involving moral and financial support, facilitation, direction, provision of fora. By carrying out such functions, it also served as a focal point for such groups and such work, and thus concentrated the approach into a recognisable public form.

Fifthly and finally, the work and community group programme was aimed at developing the concepts of community relations approaches in groups who, in distinction from reconciliation bodies, had not overtly embraced reconciliation within their remit, but for whom some element of such work could be introduced. These included:

> the wide range of groups and organisations which have a capacity to add a community relations dimension to their existing work. The aim of the Council is to help integrate community relations into every aspect of the life of the community, whether at the level of the workplace, the housing estate or the community association. (ibid., p. 23)

Consequently, the Council entered consultation 'to encourage groups in the voluntary, community, statutory and business sectors to add community relations work to their existing work agendas' (CRC 1991, p. 16).

These five interest areas formed the basis of the CRC's operational approach in its first three-year strategic plan. Within each area, a set of objectives was defined under five headings: to provide a forum for pertinent issues and thereby stimulate debate within the interest area; development work, to assist individuals, agencies and groups in the interest area to further their work in terms of focus, effectiveness, strategy, efficiency, etc.; grant aid, through the re-channelling of funds previously distributed by government (for example, by DENI) or by other bodies (such as NIVT); training, both in skills specific to the programme of any particular organisation or individual, and in organisational development; and research and evaluation, of the CRC's operation, of that of the agencies it engaged, and of public attitudes to community relations work.

3. IN OPERATION, 1990–3

The CRC itself struggles with the problem of evaluation of its work. Levels of activity can be monitored and quantified, but relationships and attitudes are impossible to measure accurately. Thus a simple question like 'Have community relations improved?' does not afford a simple answer. None the less, a set of 'very minimal indices' is in use by the CRC in order to gain some generalised measure of effectiveness. Fitzduff offers the following synopsis from January 1993 in response to the question of evaluation:

> The following have all shown [a numerical] increase over the past three years:
> a) Cross community interactions . . .
> b) Adoption of anti-sectarian policies/programmes [by] Trade Unions, Sporting Bodies, Probation Board, major voluntary and statutory bodies, and community groups . . .
> c) Integrated schools . . .
> d) Post-crisis work. . . . Now communities often cross territorial lines to mourn with one another, and display a desire for an end to such tactics . . .
> e) Local Councils. . . . Over half now exercise voluntary power-sharing and approximately 94 per cent of Nationalist and 68 per cent of Unionist local councillors now say they are in favour of it . . .
> f) Acceptance of cultural differences . . .
> g) Church co-operation. Some churches traditionally hostile to community relations work are now actually employing people to develop it. . . . Clergy in Belfast have, since [1993], put out joint statements vis-à-vis murders.
> h) Workplaces less divided and safer. Workplaces are increasingly becoming integrated places, as our legislation on monitoring/discrimination becomes effective . . .
> i) Attitudes. The British Social Attitude Survey in 1992 showed that three times as many people now, as opposed to five years ago, believe that community relations in Northern Ireland have improved . . .[14]

Most of these comments indicate trends rather than irrevocable shifts. Consequently, of course, they are difficult to prove or disprove. Certainly, as the Social Attitudes Survey suggests, most people in Northern Ireland would probably endorse the general trend of Fitzduff's comments. More difficult to assess is the question of any causal link between the CRC's establishment and the noted improvements. It is quite possible to argue that these phenomena and the existence of the CRC are both the results of a deeper attitude shift in the Northern Irish community, and certainly the CRC is not claiming exclusive responsibility for these improvements. But it is fair to say simply that such observable phenomena as there are indicate a trend towards a more positive view of the importance of community relations work, and that there is no reason to exclude the argument that the CRC is contributing to such change.

However, what is more relevant for this study is the qualitative nature of the work undertaken during the CRC's first three years. Without accurate measurement of results, the questions can still be usefully asked, and usefully answered, concerning the nature of the CRC's development over this period: What work has it taken on or supported? What directions have been taken? How has it fulfilled its own five-category objectives (see above) for evaluation? Further, these questions are particularly useful if addressed in the context of the cultural approach during the same period.

As I noted above in section 2, the CRC's strategic plan defined its objectives in terms of providing a forum, assisting development of individuals and agencies in the field, administering grant aid, providing relevant skills-based and organisational training, and enabling research and evaluation. As regards practitioners within the cultural approach, the argument can be confidently made that the CRC has enhanced their practice with regard both to providing a forum and to providing training. Much of the increased networking which characterises current practice has centred on skills training – an obvious focal point of interest to practitioners – and has also served to reinforce the consolidation of practitioners into a self- conscious community. Fitzduff points out that there are over 100 groups in the 'reconciliation' sector, and that the CRC has worked with a total of 800 groups in three years:

> We provide fora rather than a forum, and there are often loads and loads of interlocking networks within that. . . . So we're talking about a variety [of events] within which people will meet, but they may not *all* meet together.

Joe Hinds is the CRC's Development Officer for Reconciliation and Church Groups (and thus his caseload largely encompasses the groups that comprise the cultural approach as described in Chapter 3). His view concurs:

> This year [1993] instead of getting a conference which is trying to address a theme of importance to all peace and reconciliation groups, I found that large-scale umbrella type of scenario not to be relevant to a great deal [of groups]. Because of that natural diversity in so many of the groups, it's hard to find too many common denominators. . . . This year . . . there are going to be more local-based, thematic seminars and fora.

Practitioners themselves support these claims and see direct benefits to them from the CRC in terms particularly of opportunities for cooperation in training, networking and debate, and in general terms of raising the profile of both the work and the practitioners as a group. For instance, Martin O'Brien, Director of the Committee on the Administration of Justice (CAJ) as well as a long-standing office-bearer in the Peace People, comments that the CRC

> has probably brought just a lot more energy into the arena, and there are a lot more resources around. There's a lot of activity and a lot of training, and the concepts and the thinking are being passed on to more and more people. . . . They do provide opportunities for people to come together. There is certainly a sense now that there is a [body] of people who are doing this work, and I think the CRC have developed that idea to a degree.

David McKittrick, Field Officer of PACE (Protestant And Catholic Encounter), one of the longest established groups in the field, explains the process:

> My experience brings me into touch with other community relations workers, because of the way that the CRC has been organising and networking. Therefore I begin to know what is going on elsewhere, and I get influenced by that and in turn I hope to influence. . . . So there has been a networking of the best practice, a proliferation in terms of agreement about what the practice should be. That's a change in the last couple of years. . . . There also has been money to run innovative pro-

jects and to try out ideas. . . . [CRC] have produced a leaders' manual: name, address, organisation, what you offer, who to contact. So it's not only that we know each other, but it's organised. We put our wares out in public, and people can buy them in.

Joan Broder, Chair of the Conflict Mediation Network, endorses the benefits of the higher public profile that CRC has brought to the work: 'people feel more validated in their work now, because they are recognised as trainers; there is a better sense of that'.

Jerry Tyrrell is the Director of the Quaker Peace Education Project in Derry[15] and a consultant trainer in prejudice reduction; he spent over 15 years as director of a reconciliation holiday organisation, and is the Northern Ireland affiliate of the National Coalition Building Institute of Washington, DC. He believes that the CRC has had a validating role for many practitioners:

A lot of the approaches and philosophies and outlooks and methodologies which were on the periphery . . . have now been put central stage. So it's a recognition of experimental stuff. . . . It's a forum, yes. My main interest in the CRC is around training, and I think they do an excellent job of making it accessible, of encouraging people, and also of encouraging people to be critical, and of ensuring there's dialogue. . . I do see it as an agency which creates opportunities and encourages good practice . . . it breaks through the isolation and competition that is often inherent in this kind of work. . . . There's a body of people who see themselves as delivering [community relations work], and [CRC] is making it more the norm, rather than something left to a minority of people to do. . . . Something the CRC does which is useful, is that it insists on people getting together.

Such comments suggest that the CRC has been successful in its aims of providing a higher public profile for community relations work and its practitioners, of providing them with a forum for debate on good practice, and of providing them with practical skills-based training. On the provision of relevant research, a service which entails a degree of time-lag, the results of studies commissioned by the CRC will be slower to arrive, and evaluation will have to wait for more of the studies to reach the publication stage.

However, the CRC's two other areas of provision for cultural-approach practitioners require examination in some depth because, for the purposes of this study, the direction of that progress raises pertinent issues concerning the development and future of the cultural approach, of the CRC itself, and indeed of the entire community relations project in Northern Ireland. These two areas of provision are development work – assisting groups and individuals to further their work and their effectiveness – and grant-aid – a role that CRC has embraced at a speed foreseen by few. The ramifications of activities in these two areas, and of the underlying policy of widening the arena of community relations, comprise the subject matter of the rest of this chapter.

Development Work

As the CRC's Development Officer for Reconciliation and Church Groups, Hinds defines his client groups thus:

> a group or an organisation or a collection of individuals who want to singularly address an issue arising out of the conflict. . . . I work with a constituency whose sole focus and sole reason for being is that they are addressing the conflict in some way.

Hinds sees his role as, initially, one of support, 'to validate and affirm whatever brings people into the work'. But this is preparatory to the development element of his work:

> It would be my job to try and support, to bring a bit more networking, to give a bit more insight and knowledge, and to develop the project and the group so they become more effective in their practice and their application, and become as healthy and as strong and as self-sufficient as possible. . . . So it's not just support and affirmation, but there's a degree of challenge, saying [for example] 'Yes, that was your mission in 1973 . . . but this is 1993. Circumstances have changed, therefore your programmes and practical activities must be changed and adapted to new environments.'

Frazer and Fitzduff's (1986) report noted that 'a major and perennial difficulty for many groups working in the area of community relations has been their difficulty in adequately defining what they see as the objectives of community relations work in Northern Ireland. This confusion has frequently been reflected in their difficulty in formulating strategies' (1986, p. 15).

Fitzduff expands on this lack of strategy which they discovered as they prepared their report, and on the Council's approach for dealing with it:

> The sense was a lot of good will, a lot of hopes, but absolutely nothing in terms of planning, absolutely nothing in terms of objective-setting, no looking at quality beyond contact. And certainly I was quite shocked that this important work was very much going by default. . . . It has been problematic, the idea of evaluating what you're doing, the idea of us saying 'it's not enough that you've got good will, it's not enough that you've the best intentions, you've actually got to look at who you're trying to change, what you're trying to change, and how you will know when you've got there.'

Development work has two intertwined aspects, related to both the process and the content of the groups' work. Hinds has clear ambitions in both respects. Developing better process for groups is concerned with improving their organisational structure, their effectiveness, and their strategic planning. Developing better content comprises helping groups to question and evaluate fundamental aspects of their policy and their activities to ensure they remain relevant to changing contexts.

Developing better *process* involves Hinds in a management consultant role, where he can provide 'an outside perspective into the workings of their organisation, into their practice to see if it's still relevant. . . . It's practical, it's strategic, it's about organisational development and maturity.' Most practitioners in the field would accept the necessity of such assistance. Because the work tends to be activity-centred, labour-intensive and under-resourced, especially as regards personnel, time out for strategic planning or long-term reflection is considered a luxury which few can afford. Additionally, practitioners may often be so closely involved with the work – so close to the ground, so to speak – that they have difficulty finding the appropriately broad perspective from which to indulge in such evaluation or planning. It is exactly this need which Hinds aims to satisfy, although he accepts that this kind of intervention on the part of the CRC requires a degree of sensitivity:

My main thrust is critical, but I and the Council would like to
see as strong and as vibrant a reconciliation sector as possible.
And that's the way I sell it: we're not coming in to threaten,
we're coming in to try to improve or give them the opportunity
to improve. . . . To some extent you must respect the individual
integrity of the groups. So I can only give so much leadership.
Or – I wouldn't call it leadership – I can provide clues, I can
provide openings. . . . I have to be very careful about making
suggestions about change. . . . I can't dictate.

Hinds cites the example of Corrymeela, a Christian-oriented
residential centre for the facilitation of dialogue and contact
between the communities, and also the reconciliation group of
longest standing and highest international profile. At first Corrymeela greeted the new Council with a degree of 'natural suspicion' but three years later,

it's got to the stage now where we do have a very strong and
vibrant relationship, where we can talk about the most contentious and difficult issues, whether it be staff induction and
recruitment, staff training, follow-up provision, proper review
or evaluative structures, information management systems. . . .
So we've identified, through a mutually agreed process, about
12 or 13 large-scale issues which have to be addressed.

In sum, Hinds' aim for organisational development is that 'the
more strategic thinking is happening at the senior level in
organisations along these lines, the better. . . . There are very few
examples of that happening yet, where reconciliation organisations have such a sophisticated strategic approach.'

The CRC's thrust to develop the *content* of such groups' work
runs in parallel to efforts to improve their strategic capacity and
their efficiency levels. Again, Hinds is engaged in a process of

talking to individual organisations in confidence, with their
executive, with their professional employed people, with their
volunteers, taking them through steadily, over a period of time,
a process where they can talk to me about issues of concern.

The end-result of such a process is to ensure that the members
of the agency in question 'are now assured that what they are
doing is relevant and is focused and is actually answering a
demand, providing a service which is beneficial' (Hinds). But

rather than simply facilitate or encourage the organisations in their own policy development, the CRC has its own opinions about the direction in which their work should go. Hinds accepts readily the analysis of reconciliation work as developing from the contact activities of the 1970s through to focused community relations work in the 1980s, but he is certain that the 1990s should see a new stage, one of what he terms *empowerment*. Too many reconciliation groups, he argues, still see themselves as intervenors in a problem of which they themselves are not part, saying 'it's someone else's problem; let's work with the disadvantaged and deprived . . . let's go into deprived areas and let's educate people.' The ramifications of such an attitude are important, he continues, in that they limit the effectiveness of the work:

> Very often if you talk to community groups in interface areas about peace and reconciliation groups, they spit at you. They say, 'We don't want those eejits in here. They don't live here, they don't understand our problems, they don't understand the context in which we have to live. They come from outside, and they're preaching. They preach some sort of message to us which is of no practical significance whatsoever.'

Many reconciliation agencies continue to work with the same community groups for many successive years. 'By that stage', argues Hinds, 'the institutions that you should be targeting or focusing your efforts on should be capable of doing their own community relations work.' The new phase of the work should involve:

> empowering communities to realise their own potential, to realise what they should or could be doing in their own local context. Acting as a catalyst, a facilitator, an empowerer of skills, of methodologies, of strategies. Acting as a resource, but then stepping back.

The CRC has an important role to play in this process, not only in advocating this policy of empowerment, but in assisting groups to achieve it, and indeed in leading groups towards it:

> There's a Community Relations Council out there now, who will dictate the pace or will to some extent say what is good practice and what isn't, or who will say to groups, 'Would it not be better for you to do something like this now?' Or 'Working in that way is not enough, you've got to find – and

we will help you find – a way to get out of [for example] Ballymurphy, a way to educate and empower Ballymurphy so that they can do their own community relations work and build up local capacity and support'. (Hinds)

The drive towards this new policy of empowerment, demanding as it does a reorientation by reconciliation groups, will inevitably cause some painful self-examination by practitioners. 'They're still, I think, doing things to communities, rather than enabling communities to do things for themselves' (Hinds). But Hinds argues strongly that it is a necessary expansion of community relations work, and one that will challenge practitioners to open out the whole arena of community relations work beyond the confines of the cultural approach as traditionally defined by those working within it:

> The difficulty with reconciliation groups is that very often they're preaching to a converted and self-selecting audience. It would be more useful if a lot of their energies were placed into developing and targeting new constituencies, which would be the difficult end of the work.

In sum, then, the CRC is hoping to offer a challenge to the established order of the cultural approach. In the first place, it demands greater organisational effectiveness and clearer strategic planning. In the second place, it is also demanding a shift of emphasis in operation which will fundamentally broaden the target audience for community relations well beyond merely those who choose voluntarily to become involved with a reconciliation group. This latter widening process into 'the difficult end of the work', however, is of greater significance than merely demanding that reconciliation groups broaden their constituency. I shall return to this point below.

Funding

In the process of developing community relations work towards the aims outlined above, the CRC's role as funder becomes an important means by which to encourage the adoption of community relations programmes. 'We get half our money from Europe, but most of our money would come *through* government' (Fitzduff). Over 90 per cent of the CRC's income is therefore effectively British government money: in 1992–3, this comprised £840 378 from the CCRU of the NIO, and £729 372 from the European Regional Development Fund (CRC 1993, p. 46). From its inception, the Council administered several funding schemes. These comprised the Intercommunity Contact Scheme, previously administered on behalf of DENI by the NIVT; grants for publications and media work on cultural traditions themes, previously administered by CCRU; and two new schemes, for local cultural traditions projects and for organisational development. Most significant for the purposes of this study was CRC's takeover of the Intercommunity Contact Scheme, which provides government money to cross-community projects and which had been a major source of funding for the activities of reconciliation groups. In 1992–3, the CRC disbursed a total of £198 766 under the scheme (ibid.). Meanwhile, from its own inception in 1987, the CCRU took over from DENI the so-called 'core-funding' programme. Core-funding is government money given annually to a number of the major established reconciliation groups (currently 23) to meet ongoing and recurring administrative costs (salaries, rent, etc.). Core-funding money goes to organisations for recurring expense, while Intercommunity Contact money goes on a one-off basis to specific activity programmes (including, of course, those operated by core-funded organisations).

Thus, from the first, the CRC and CCRU together comprised the dispensers of government money to the cultural approach. (The rest of the CRC's grant schemes are focused more on intra-community cultural traditions projects, and less on direct inter-community contact.) With the announcement in late 1993 that, from the following year, the CRC would also take over administration of the CCRU's core-funding scheme, the Council was effectively becoming virtually the sole source of government funding for community relations work. The absolute significance of this becomes clear in the light of O'Brien's comment: 'There are now, I suspect, very, very few groups in the mainstream peace movement who don't rely on government funding for their existence.' Although there are other government departments which are tapped for funding by various reconciliation groups – for example, DENI's Youth Service Department by groups who work with young people, or the Department of Agriculture by groups who include an element of rural development – in effect funding is now controlled by – and therefore groups depend crucially upon – one source, the CRC. Small wonder that Hinds admits that this may significantly shape practitioners' perceptions of the CRC: 'To some people I'm probably just a bureaucrat: I sit on a grant-scheme.'

Whether the practitioners of community relations work like it or not, financial control gives the CRC the ability to improve their client groups' lack of self-examination, by the simple expedient of tying funding provision to accountability and monitoring of funded activities according to a set of criteria overseen by the CCRU and the CRC itself. Fitzduff notes about the mid-1980s situation:

> There were very few resources going in, so groups didn't actually have to be too accountable, it was just £5000 here and £5000 there. But as the decision was taken to put more resources into them, along with that went the requirement to actually look more closely at what they were doing. . . . To a certain extent it went along with the extra cash.

Thus, as Hinds speculates on the CRC's imminent acquisition of the core-funding program, he notes that:

> Each core-funded organisation, for instance, from next year will be giving monitoring returns on assessments of political affiliation of participants in the particular programmes they run in terms of their activity base. . . . And that will be a monitoring point, which will be supervised in one sense or another.

In this way, the sanction of continued funding becomes dependent upon performance. Whether wholly intentional or not, the CRC's control of funding gives it the muscle to encourage its client groups to follow the direction and the policy it wants them to. The core of CRC development policy is (1) to make cultural approach groups more effective and more strategic in their policy and their implementation, specifically in the direction of empowering their clients, and (2) to make other social groupings adopt an element of community relations into their practice. Given that the conceptual foundation of the CRC, as encapsulated in the 1986 SACHR report and in Fitzduff's typology (1989), was based on the experience and perceptions of practitioners in the field, there should be little necessary friction between the CRC and its cultural approach clients in terms of

seeing eye to eye on policy matters. (Certainly, for example, holiday organisations were expressing commitment, at least in
principle, to a policy of empowerment several years before
the arrival of the CRC.) However, control of the purse-
strings risks a change in that relationship. Hinds himself
notes that where previously practitioners have seen the Council
'as an ally, as a lobbyist and as a supporter, that distinction may
be blurred slightly because now it's a big funder'. Further, he
accepts that the significance of the CRC in the role of core-
funder may have unwelcome implications for some previous
recipients:

> We were able to inherit a core-funding picture in which certain
> groups have [continued] in existence because they've been
> heavily subsidised for a long number of years. I suspect that
> when we [take over], over a period of time we'll be starting to
> ask more radical questions about the validity of the work, the
> quality, whether it is relevant, what successes can be attributed
> to it. That may act so that if funding is gradually withdrawn
> over a period of time from a particular group, they may say
> 'Well, we can't survive . . .' So the natural wastage may get
> some assistance, but that's part of the process, where resources
> are put where resources are most needed and you have to
> respond to shifting priorities.

Given that there are, according to Hinds, a number of groups
who have been newly approved for core-funding subject to the
funds becoming available, it is logical to foresee a heightened
sense of competition between core-funded groups. But of greater
significance is the implication that groups' perceptions of, and
relationships with, the CRC will change significantly. In
O'Brien's words, the core-funding role will

> fundamentally alter the relationship which CRC has had up
> until this point with the [reconciliation] sector. Everybody
> knew that [CRC] had an influence over whether grants were
> awarded. But now they are the people making the decisions.
> And so if people have a problem with something, are they
> actually going to tell the CRC about it? Are they going to ask
> for help? When CCRU were [administering the core-funding]
> people could think 'Well, we can talk to the CRC about this,
> they'll help us to overcome this, they're our advocates, they're

our allies'. . . . The nature of the relationship will change
entirely.

McKittrick concurs:

Unfortunately the CCRU has now handed over funding and
policy to the CRC. So they now have to be the police as well.
Now they have to police the field, as well as inspire the field
to engage in 'best practice'. . . . Because they're now having to
decide who gets bits of the cake and how much they get, then
it's becoming more difficult for them to work in the way they
did before. Their hands are tied to satisfying criteria that to
some extent are laid down. They're not as exploratory and as
free as they were initially, not as independent. . . . I don't know
to what extent they'll find their hands tied by some of the
functions that government has landed them with.

McKittrick's observation is a sharp one. Behind this modification of the CRC's role, manifest in its growing financial control,
lies a more fundamental issue: the relationship of the Council to
government. This brings us back to an issue considered earlier in
relation to the old Community Relations Commission (NICRC)
of 1969–74 (see Chapter 3): when does the relationship between
the structural agency of government and the Council begin to
constrain operational effectiveness in the cultural approach? How
can the CRC walk the line between the financial and political
support it needs from government for its continued existence on
the one hand, and the independence from government and from
structural agencies which it needs in order to carry out the work
of the cultural approach on the other? How can it remain both
advocate, on behalf of community relations practitioners whom it
exists to support and develop, and judge, in the sense of assessing
the work of those very practitioners to decide whether they
receive the funding that enables their continued existence?

Fitzduff has clearly learnt lessons from the saga of the Commission–Ministry relationship: 'Looking back, [the NICRC] were
tremendously confused, they confused the Ministry enormously.
They were caught up in their own enthusiasm . . . they never
brought their parent Department along with them.'

She accepts there is a constant dilemma created by the
relationship, not only because of the potential for suspicion of the
CRC by the government, but also due to the potential for

suspicion of the government's motives by practitioners: 'It's a very interesting game to play, because you're dealing with funders who might be either suspicious or nervous or hostile, and yet, no, you can't do without them. And at another level you're dealing with a field who may see them as actually [suspect].' The lesson for her in the history of the NICRC was that 'politicians' needs are not always the same as our needs, and engaging the politicians' support is really quite important if only for survival's sake'. Consequently, the CRC has seen the necessity, from the earliest stages, of both engaging government in its process and of delineating its area of operation clearly to government: 'Really, we have staked our boundaries fairly clearly in the first year . . . stated clearly what we are about, and retained a kind of status [in government eyes].'

Much of this dilemma can be reduced to the question of independence. For the incipient CRC, this meant making clear, early decisions with the government's CCRU about the degree of independence needed in terms of both policy-setting and funding. As early as 1986, Fraser and Fitzduff were considering the merits of independent funding for any projected new community relations agency. They agreed that it would have been possible to find such funding outside government, but that not only was government funding possible without the accompanying restrictions that so hamstrung the Commission, there was a positive benefit in bringing a committed government along with them: 'Government can influence you, but what's actually much more important is that you can influence government,' Fitzduff argues. She believes that the CRC has successfuly worked out the relationship, complaining of nothing more than 'the odd bit of bureaucratic pressure' and even querying the degree to which the CRC, rather than the CCRU, has in practice taken on more than its share of the CCRU's brief for policy development.

The CRC's sense of security over its position and its relationship with government is evident in its preference for its current legal status as an independent voluntary agency, although that status is less secure than some of the alternatives which have been considered. This attitude reflects a degree of self-confidence on the Council's part, and a belief that, unlike the former Commission, it has no need to fight for its continuing existence. It has the confidence that it can justify its existence by convincing the politicians of its worth, rather than needing to protect itself against their opposition:

> It's an interesting balance for us. There has been a suggestion that we should become an official public body, which is one set up by parliament, on the basis that it's less easy for us to be got rid of. [The government] found it quite hard to understand why we didn't want to go for that. . . . But I do think that if the politicians do not come to see us as worthwhile, then in fact we have failed and deserve to go. . . . You cannot set up a dichotomy between yourself and the politicians which is just not useful in the circumstances. (Fitzduff)

In the CRC's own eyes, then, the question of independence of operation has been successfully resolved by developing a pragmatic relationship with the government that acknowledges the unavoidable link that exists with the state structure, rather than trying to fight free of it. Fitzduff's attitude is that community relations work applies to politicians too, and that it can only be made to do so by working with, rather than despite, them:

> We will go out of business in our own time, I would hope. If we cannot persuade our politicians and our funders then we're not worth being here. Because our job is about persuading as many as possible, particularly those who have power, that there's merit in doing things a certain way or seeing things a certain way.

Widening the Arena

I have been considering the CRC's roles of development and funding in terms of how they impinge upon practitioners operating within, by my definition, the cultural approach. But, as has been a constant thread throughout this chapter, one of the CRC's fundamental strategic decisions was to go outside that approach, and to apply its techniques and principles to a broader constituency than merely the 'reconciliation sector'. Perhaps above all, this principle has the most important consequences for the future of the cultural approach.

The effect of this basic principle is that the CRC wants to see the entire arena of community relations widened far beyond mere expansion of the role of reconciliation groups. In essence, it wants to make community relations the task of all social groupings in the community:

> There are reconciliation groups. . . . But then you have the churches, trade unions, you have the workplaces, you have businesses, you have politicians, you have security forces . . . rural networks, district councils. (Fitzduff)

The starkness of this fundamental change is embodied by the fact that Hinds himself, with his responsibility for heretofore cultural approach groups, represents only one of the five operational areas of CRC staff. In contrast to his own work with groups whose existence is based on direct addressing of some aspect of the Northern Ireland conflict, he is quick to point out that another Development Officer takes responsibility for groups who have no overt remit for community relations work:

> So he's trying to get community relations onto their agenda in the voluntary sector, in the community sector, in business, in trade unions and so on, so that they can realise that they have a contribution to make addressing sectarianism in the workplace, within their community, within their association, within their tenants' group.

Community relations work, argues Fitzduff, will only finally succeed when it is absorbed into every aspect of social interaction. And that demands a simple but fundamental shift in placing the work within society: it must no longer be the preserve of specialists — as it has been as long as it was contained within the cultural approach — but it must become a component part of all social relationships. In the process, it may become less of a distinct area of work — as, again, it has been, with its body of practitioners and professionals — and more of a constituent part of many other kinds of work:

> [Community relations work] should happen not even using the term 'community relations'. It should happen as an inclusiveness that becomes part of our systems much, much more. . . . The term has now become respectable. It was not half as respectable four or five years ago; it was seen as soft. But when you see the number of people who now feel able to put it down on their agenda because it's not a soft issue, and similarly the number of people who also feel able to come in [to address

community relations issues] at their own level, it is very, very heartening. . . . There is certainly a movement towards the hard, hard edges of issues, and I think to a certain extent we [the CRC] have actually pushed a lot of those boundaries. (Fitzduff)

The logical conclusion of movement in such a direction, then, would be this novelty: rather than a person needing to make a conscious decision to seek out and get involved in a specific community relations project, the person would be examining various aspects of her or his own social interactions for a community relations element, or for a gap requiring such an element. Should this shift happen in Northern Ireland, the consequences for the cultural approach, as for the society at large, would be hugely significant.

This widening process involves three strands: first, an expanded definition of what community relations work is and who carries it out; secondly, a packaging of the work involved – its processes and its techniques – so that it can be transported across contexts and implemented with some degree of standardisation; and thirdly, a formalisation or accreditation of the status of the practitioner-trainers who do it, so that they can move among the various contexts with acceptance and recognition of the status both of themselves and of their work.

In terms of expanding the definition of who is a community relations group, the CRC's position has been noted earlier, that 'there is nothing now left that is not a community relations issue' (Fitzduff). Hinds sees this expansion process as one of benefit to a previously introverted practitioner group:

I think the peace and reconciliation sector has seen itself as a sector, in isolation. They talk to each other but very rarely to anyone else. And I think that's a bad thing, if we're always going to be insular in our perspectives. If we talk to [other sectors] we get an attitude that, yes, community relations or reconciliation has still got to happen in our little focused network, but that it's going to be a success if we can draw in the community sector, the adult education agencies, peace studies, the churches, youth service training, vocational training for teachers, etc. It's going to broaden the base.

Consequently, he uses the example of the CRC's *Guide To Peace and Reconciliation Groups*, first published in 1990 (CRC 1990). In that edition, 77 reconciliation-related organisations were listed, almost all of them very recognisably located within the cultural approach. But in preparing an updated version, the 1993 *Index of Peace Groups*, he has expanded the inclusion criteria so that there are now over 100 entries:

> The new Index will have groups like the Northern Ireland Council for Voluntary Action (NICVA), the Workers' Education Association (WEA), the Forum for Community Work Education (FCWE), East Belfast Community Development Centre, and other bodies whose main thrust is not to develop a community relations strategy or to improve mutual understanding or to reduce prejudice ... but because they have a community relations Training Officer or a mutual understanding Training Officer. They have developed a dimension which is significant.

Building community relations programmes into the work of these non-community relations organisations is a process of expanding on the work of the original practitioners, exporting their expertise:

> There's going to be a greater recognition of the role of peace and reconciliation groups, that they can provide the skills and the insights and assist people to achieve the different perspectives needed to develop and widen the work and the networks. Initially, they're also going to be used to provide the basic induction skills and advice. (Hinds)

This is the process by which the cultural approach practitioners gain some level of formal status as recognised trainers, and by which their practice becomes a set of skills and techniques which can be packaged for teaching. But not all the practitioners themselves are completely happy at the price that may be required in this modification of both themselves and their work. And once again, their fears are heightened by the influence of the CRC's funding role. There are suspicions that a wide variety of voluntary or statutory groups with little effective interest in practicing community relations will develop minimal programmes of questionable content merely because, in an increasingly competitive funding race, the CRC is a comparatively approachable source of government money. The resultant tension with such groups is acknowledged by the CRC and encapsulated in Hinds' characterisation:

> The tension is always: 'They're trying to get money out of me, and it may not be for community relations purposes. I'm trying to get community relations on their agenda, and they're trying to get hold of the money.'

Of course, the argument can legitimately be made that whether or not the agency in question is committed to the CCRU and CRC's goals is less important than whether or not, willingly or otherwise, it actually engages in community relations activities; and, further, that getting such activities onto its agenda will lead to a genuine commitment to community relations faster than waiting for the commitment to come first before the engagement. In other words, perhaps doing the right thing for the wrong reasons is preferable to not doing it at all. Jerry Tyrrell – himself a cultural approach practitioner of some standing – argues, in the case of the voluntary sector at large, that there must be considerable value simply in terms of the widespread acceptance and validation of the concepts of community relations work:

> Whereas ten years ago you'd have reconciliation agencies, community relations bodies, whose sole function was community relations, now everybody, every single agency has had to have built in some sort of community relations or fair employment or equal opportunities policy. So . . . it's making it more the norm, rather than something which is left to a minority of people to do.

Tyrrell's point of view as a practitioner is valid: community relations, as a general concept, has gained a new respectability in the eyes of the Northern Irish public, and has developed for the first time a public profile in the form of the CRC. O'Brien is happy to confirm this opinion, but he is aware that the price of this progress is a steep rise in the centralisation of the work into the CRC, and he worries about the effects of this on practitioners' autonomy:

> [Although] I don't think anybody could say that they are behaving in an autocratic way. . . . I think people would worry perhaps if [CRC] were seen as the voice of community relations in Northern Ireland, and that if for example all your

contact with government was mediated in some way through them I think that would be a disaster.

It is not my aim here to do more than point out the potential tension involved in this transitional widening process. However, it is worth noting that even someone as supportive as Tyrrell can also recognise the potential for community relations issues to be abused in the cynical race for funds:

> I have been aware of being asked to lead a prejudice reduction workshop on a [government Youth Service] outdoor pursuits weekend. And it's obvious from the fact that the children fall asleep exhausted during the process that it has been tacked on to the program in order to get the grant.

The defence against such situations, he argues, is that the CRC and the CCRU must be consistently challenging and monitoring good practice. O'Brien, however, sees dangers in that process, too:

> All of this may lead to a kind of professionalisation: the disabling professionals who resolve your conflicts for you, these professional peacemakers. I have some concern about accreditation . . . the idea that you can go off on a course and in some way be accredited to do the work. . . . And there's a jargon, and this is linked into 'evaluations' and 'outputs' and 'monitoring' and all those kinds of things.

Broder goes further:

> I do think that with community relations, a lot of people now think 'CRC' and think 'money'. . . . Money is drying up in the voluntary sector, and CR work is the only expanding area for funding. I'm not saying it's the total reason, but I know it's a major part of the reason for an organisation that wants to survive. . . . I do think it's good that it has been integrated into organisations. But I think it needs to be carefully monitored as to what they're doing and the quality of what they're doing.

One of the major achievements of the CCRU and, in a supporting role, the CRC, in their programme of expanding the community relations agenda has been to persuade all 26 Local District Councils in Northern Ireland to employ a Community Relations Officer (CRO). The significance of this is heightened given that, for the duration of the Troubles, these councils have often appeared as focal points of sectarian tension and community conflict. Frazer and Fitzduff noted in their report to SACHR that 'the sensitive nature of community relations work makes support for it unacceptable to most local [council] politicians' (1986, p. 11). Involving Local District Councils in community relations work was therefore both a priority and a challenge, and the CCRU are understandably proud of this achievement. However, while the placement of CROs has been generally welcomed, there are also widespread reservations which again concern the quality of the work. Broder sounds a note of caution:

> It's common knowledge that a lot of the councils took on community relations to look good. If you talk to [the CRC Training Officer] who was involved in training and supporting some of [the CROs], he will tell you that some of them had great scope in their job, while others had no scope.

McKittrick also detects a cynical motivation, but one related to money rather than public relations:

> The CCRU has managed very successfully to create that local council involvement in that they have a community relations role now. . . . They all call it the same thing; but they don't *do* the same thing. What each CRO is doing is very much circumscribed by the kinds of tensions within the local council. . . . [Money] is what some local councils largely came on board for, you know: 'Let's get this extra £10 000 (I think it was) into our budget and have a CRO,' and they don't really have to do anything too radical in order to be seen to be fulfilling the [funding] criteria: 'We can have a few mixed choirs, and so on, and that'll be all right.'

Indeed, McKittrick, although he might be regarded among his colleagues as perhaps more of a 'purist' than others in terms of protecting the integrity of the cultural approach as essentially interpersonally based, has reservations about the viability of the whole process of 'packaging' the work so that it can be added to pre-existing and different agendas:

> It's kind of a distorted way of going about it. . . . There are some negative things about the way in which groups are being

asked to take on board community relations, as if it's another 'thing', instead of something that's been there all the time. . . . When an organisation starts to have a community relations element as a kind of extension of their programme, I think it's sometimes difficult for them to do that successfully. . . . Having to take it on as a 'thing' is very dodgy and distorts the practice. . . . I think it [should be] much more all-embracing, it permeates into everything we're doing.

It is clear that practice within the cultural approach is changing, and will change further, under the influence of the CCRU and CRC. The days of the specialist, single-purpose reconciliation agency are numbered if, in Fitzduff's confident assertion, 'reconciliation has now become the additional work of so many others'. Hinds is similarly confident in predicting a future where this shift of community relations away from the specialisation of reconciliation groups into an all-pervasive element of social interaction will continue, and he accepts that to some degree the logical conclusion of such a shift may well spell the end for those organisations who choose not to adapt accordingly:

If the record in, say, 20 years' time is a further large shift in the acceptance of community relations as being a positive thing, and that starts to have significant political ranifications – voting patterns start to shift, there's a degree of local devolved government, there's responsibility-sharing in more Local Councils – that will be evidence that the policies and the efforts of voluntary agencies have shifted. That's not to say that they all have got to go out of existence, but they've got to take stock of those developments and then make . . . their programmes relevant to the needs of the day. . . . Some groups are purely contact, and that's it. If there's no need for that, if that's happening in all sectors, then there will be no reason for those groups to survive. They're going to have to say, 'Listen, circumstances change, we've got to be more focused or targeted, we've got to complement particular policy initiatives.'

CONCLUSION AND SUMMARY

The establishment of the CCRU and the CRC was a major development of community relations in Northern Ireland in

166   *Peacemaking Strategies in N. Ireland*

recent times. It is clear that the CRC will continue to be a main agent of influence and change within the field for some time to come, and that it will set the tone for the nature of the work throughout the 1990s.

The basis on which the CRC was designed and constructed was one of widespread consultation with practitioners during the late 1980s. As such, it ought to reflect accurately the needs and aspirations of those practitioners. But it is equally clear that it has produced effects which they might not have foreseen and with which they have reservations, and some of its founding principles are causing inevitable change and challenge to that very approach. Supporters will argue that this is a positive effect, and that the cultural approach has developed to the point where it can now break out of its self-defined confines and contribute to the question of Northern Irish communal relationships in a more widespread and fundamental way. Most practitioners will accede to this view, while also expressing important reservations which have to do with what happens to the nature of the work during the process of widening. There may be a trade-off between, on the one hand, the quality and content of the work and, on the other, the breadth of application of the work: will quality be reduced as quantity increases?

A key element in that debate is the CRC's relationship to government. Unlike the earlier NICRC, the CRC is clearly more at ease with a view of government as partners rather than opponents. As a government-sponsored agency, the CRC has a foot in the structural camp. Furthermore, it brings to a cultural context a degree of organisational formality (monitoring, assessment, effectiveness criteria, funding control) which sits more familiarly in a structural setting. Thus, in at least one fundamentally significant sense, the CRC is straddling both the structural and cultural camps. So while it has grown out of, and would not exist without a pre-history of, the cultural approach, it represents the development of something that no longer sits completely comfortably within the two-approach picture.

The effects of this shift of relationship with government structures can be seen on the ground. Previously, cultural practitioners retained complete autonomy over their work as they approached government for funding. Now, however, their funding source (which is still ultimately government) is mediated by an agency which is much more actively – and proactively – monitoring the qualitative nature of their work. One positive result of this is that they are forced to be more organised, strategic and accountable in their formation and execution of policy. But it is at least arguable by some, at this early stage, that such formal accountability may constrain the originality and individuality of so much of the work to date. Hinds, for example, argues that he would not dare to dictate to groups in his care the degree of organisation they must have or the policy they must follow, since they are autonomous and free to decide their own policies in this regard. But, on the other hand, he does have strong opinions on the optimum structure and policy for such groups, and as the conduit for the money which provides their main lifeline, the criteria he operates for such funding must perforce dictate their activities to some degree.

The single most important effect of the CRC on the cultural approach stems from the policy of widening the arena of community relations, of 'helping community relations work to proliferate throughout society' (CRC 1991, p. 8). Community relations therefore is no longer the preserve of the reconciliation sector, but must expand out into the whole voluntary sector, the statutory sector, the business sector, politics and all aspects of society. Looking far ahead, and taken to its logical conclusion, this would spell the ultimate demise of the specialist agency and the rise of community relations on the agenda of every organisation and grouping, or at least all those which are susceptible to control via government funding. (In Northern Ireland, that in effect means most social activities groups in existence.) It would be pure speculation to try to guess the nature of the structural influence that this might bring to bear on the relationship-oriented methodology of the cultural approach, but the influence will be there and it will be significant.

Finally, in the overall context of this book, clearly the cultural approach corresponds closely to the ideas of resolution theory. The methodology of the cultural approach is primarily concerned with relationship issues. Facilitating contact through focused dialogue, and developing relationships of trust, respect and understanding: these constitute the main tenets of community relations work in Northern Ireland. They represent the working out, in the specific Northern Ireland context, of the tools of resolution. This process of translating the general resolution tool-kit into specifically relevant methods is more the detailed subject matter of Chapter 8, but it will suffice to say here that this study of the CRC bears out the earlier proposal that the cultural approach is the practical, and therefore observable, functioning of the theoretical approach of resolution, to the same degree that Chapter 5's examination of the Brooke Initiative illustrates and elucidates the theory of settlement in the practice of the structural approach.

7 Complementarity in Practice: Northern Ireland

Complementarity between the two practical approaches in Northern Ireland is more than merely a hypothesis advanced in an academic study. Practitioners from within the approaches themselves make implicit or explicit acknowledgement of an underlying complementarity. The review in Chapters 2 and 3 of the history of these approaches may give the impression of two largely discrete processes in independent operation, which Chapter 5's analysis of the Brooke Initiative in the main does little to contradict. Chapter 6's examination of recent development trends in community relations, however, contains a significant thread of argument which challenges that view. The consequent argument to be proposed here is that such a view is – and will be increasingly – challenged by the movement from within the cultural approach to address constituencies and/or issues which were formerly the preserve of the structural approach. It should be pointed out that this challenge is to the structural *approach*, rather than to the structures themselves; that is, it is directed towards the policy areas in which the structural approach operates. Indeed, by means of acknowledging complementarity, the cultural approach is also acknowledging the importance of the structural approach, rather than challenging its efficacy or its ability to secure solutions. The cultural approach's challenge thus does not aim to take over from the structural approach, or indeed to tackle structural issues solely by cultural means. It simply suggests that, given the complexity of the interconnection between issue-based and relationship-based elements in the Northern Ireland conflict, most structural problems will have a cultural element (and vice versa) and so structural solution-seeking must be complemented by its cultural counterpart. Thus, the impetus for the development of complementarity in Northern Ireland has grown initially and primarily from within one (cultural) side of the equation. The response from the structural side has been largely reactive but none the less positive: the CCRU's and the government's implementation of a new policy and their decision to establish the CRC is a very significant endorsement of the importance of a dual approach. The aim of this chapter is to examine the interrelationship between the practice of the two approaches for evidence of potential or actual cross-fertilisation and interdependence.

1. THE POTENTIAL FOR COMPLEMENTARITY

Even at the earlier stages of the period under consideration here, a significant undercurrent in the thinking of both approaches has been that practitioners retained some sense, however vague, of the limits of their approach. From the earliest days of direct rule, British policy included expressions of the limitations of a structural initiative. Such expressions can, of course, also be read as the British government's careful strategy of distancing itself from responsibility for the problem and for its solution, and passing that responsibility back to the people and politicians of Northern Ireland. None the less, the terminology of these statements is enlightening. Whitelaw's 1972 discussion paper declared that

> Both political theory and practical experience show that no scheme of government, however carefully drawn, can do more than present an opportunity for progress. It is in the hearts and minds of the people of Northern Ireland, and not just in the aims of Government or the words of Acts of Parliament, that the capacity for working and living together must flourish. (HMSO 1972, p. 37)

Whitelaw expanded the theme in the subsequent and seminal 1973 policy-setting White Paper, describing the need for a 'community settlement' of the conflict, for which any 'governmental settlement' could only be a starting point:

> Constitutional proposals clearly have a significant part to play in the restoration of stability, because the institutions of government touch at one point or another the lives of all the people . . . . Yet the problems extend in one way or another into countless aspects of the life of the community – into patterns of education, housing and employment; into general social attitudes and responses; *into history and culture and tradition.* Thus the solution to 'the Northern Ireland problem' is not to be found in any set of political proposals or institutions alone.

However skilfully and fairly framed, these can do no more than provide opportunities which the people of Northern Ireland themselves may take or fail to take. . . . Many of the steps which remain to be taken will be for new Northern Ireland institutions, and *many more will be outside the field of government altogether*. . . . Unless, in the future, a greater sense of community can be fostered amongst the young people of Northern Ireland, it is difficult to see how this *mutual distrust* can be broken down. (Cmnd. 5259, pp. 6–7; emphases added)

The resonance of such comments grows with the hindsight of two decades. As Whitelaw struggled to manoeuvre the politicians into rebuilding a new and cooperative structure of government at Stormont, he was nevertheless aware that matters of 'culture and tradition', and problems of 'mutual distrust' – key definitional terms for the CRC 17 years later – needed to be addressed if such a structure was to succeed. But while the White Paper acknowledges the problem of community relations, it gives nothing in the way of positive suggestions for means of addressing the problem 'outside the field of government'. For his day, Whitelaw deserves credit for at least this acknowledgement. At that time, the sum total of the government's attempts to address community relations had been encapsulated in the NICRC, which Britain, having foisted upon the Stormont government in 1969, let slide into rapid decline after assuming direct rule (see Chapter 3). Indeed, the failure of the NICRC provided an early and clear instance of the limitations on the structural approach. (Hayes' comments in his resignation letter indicate his frustration that the Commission was never freed from the constraints of the structural/governmental approach (NICRC 1972, p. 20). See Chapter 3.)

Following the collapse of Whitelaw's hard-won power-sharing Executive in 1974, Rees tried to recover momentum with a Constitutional Convention, but in laying out his plans for this he too acknowledged briefly that

No political system will survive, or be supported, unless there is widespread acceptance of it within the community. There must be participation by the whole community. (Cmnd 5675, p. 16)

For Rees, as for Whitelaw, Northern Ireland was primarily a

political problem. His comment touched on the core difficulty for British politicians then and subsequently: avoiding the double veto implicit in the criterion of 'widespread acceptance'. How could a political structure be devised that would encourage not just the politicians but the people in two divided communities to cooperate? In today's Northern Ireland, many would reply that the relationship-building process of community relations work is precisely the path to such cooperation; in other words, the answer does indeed lie in some supplementary process outside the political arena, and that process is what has developed into community relations work. Indeed, that argument goes to the heart of what justifies the existence of community relations work. For Rees in 1974, however, and for everyone in Northern Ireland who had watched the sad demise of the ineffectual NICRC, such a response would have been far from obvious. Nor was it particularly obvious to Atkins in 1980, who commented in similar terms in his second White Paper:

> The key to stability in Northern Ireland is the healing of the divisions between the two communities. . . . What Her Majesty's Government can do in this is limited. It can create. . . . fair and workable institutions. But governments cannot create the will to make the institutions work: *that will to work together must come from the people of Northern Ireland themselves.* (Cmnd. 7950, p. 4; original emphasis)

More recently, in July 1989, the outgoing British Secretary of State for Northern Ireland, Tom King, told the press:

> You can have all the written constitutions or the new political plans that you like, but if there is basic distrust between the two communities, if there is this defensive attitude . . . that is not the sort of climate in which you get any generosity or outgoing approach. (*Irish Times*, 10 July 1989)

Peter Brooke himself believed firmly that some of the progress in his Initiative was made possible by improved underlying communal relationships.

It is noticeable, then, that expressions of the need for some kind of supplementary process outside a political settlement have appeared frequently, and from an early stage, in official government pronouncements concerning possible solutions. The need is expressed, but what is much less noticeable is any positive proposal for satisfying that need. This implies no great criticism of the British politicians involved, who were, after all, professional politicians trying to practice politics. To criticise them for being too political in their outlook would be pointlessly unfair. But what it does suggest is that if there were to be any real complementing of the structural approach (as practised by the politicians) by the cultural approach (aiming at the mutual understanding and cultural tolerance and generosity that they deemed vital), the impetus was unlikely to come from the structural side. Rather, while the structural approach allowed for the possibility of complementarity, and even permitted the space for a non-structural complement, suggestions as to the shape and substance of that complement would have to come from outside its approach.

A similar awareness of the need for other, external, elements to contribute towards a solution can be discerned at various points in the development of the cultural approach too. For example, the central problem which fractured the Peace People in the mid- to late 1970s was the irreconcilable tension between those who wanted merely to heal relationships and reconcile the two communities without recourse to the political arena, which they saw as beyond their remit, and those who saw the need to embrace the political (structural) reform agenda within their approach. Martin O'Brien has commented:

> In the early days of the Peace People I remember that opponents used to angrily chant 'Peace with Justice' in an effort to explain their opposition. We were seen by many as the 'peace at any price brigade'. Later, attending meetings of the Northern Ireland Peace Forum . . . I recall how any mention by the Peace People of justice issues could frequently provoke a raging controversy: 'Let's keep out of politics'; 'What's that got to do with peace?' (O'Brien 1993, p. 3)

By the mid-1980s, Frazer and Fitzduff were arguing that the primary task of community relations, the healing of communal relationships, was distinct from the structural goal of a 'constitutional settlement' (1986, p. 19), a goal which they implicitly designated as outside the confines of the community relations work of the cultural approach.

However, and much more significantly, Fitzduff's typology of community relations work does not stop at categorising the cultural range of tasks and of organisations. It concludes with a discussion of 'contextual necessities' in which she identifies the 'vital parallel work' that lies

> beyond the capacity of voluntary agencies. . . . Such work can be undertaken by the Government directly, by various statutory and semi-statutory bodies, and by other institutions. (Fitzduff 1989)

This work is essentially structural, both in its nature and in the agencies involved; it includes community development, economic development, political agendas, security policy, etc. This differentiation is a very clear statement, however implicit, of the interdependence of the two approaches.

So the impetus for complementarity comes indeed from the cultural side of the debate. Fitzduff's differentiation between cultural 'community relations work' and structural 'contextual necessities' forms the first positive offering of a mode of operation based on complementarity. Thus, as the structural approach reached a clearer understanding of the need for something extra outside its remit, the cultural approach, began – even if only by implication – to define not only what that something extra might be, but also how the interrelationship might be framed.

Over a considerable period of time, therefore, we can discern in each approach some strand of understanding of the need for supplementary work. The CRC itself is a product of the tentative and initial convergence of both strands. Its formation grew from, and required, some mutual understanding from within both approaches that the aims of each would both be assisted by the cooperative effort of establishing the CCRU and the CRC. On the cultural side, the Council drew much of its form and its *modus operandi* from being based on wide consultation with practitioners from that approach. On the structural side, however, government was sufficiently exercised on the problem of supplementing its own approach to both direct the initial question of potential development to cultural practitioners and to carry out its own internal review of the situation of community relations work. Such cooperation between the approaches itself further underlines the acknowledgement from both sides of the need for complementarity. Recognition, therefore, must go to those within government who identified the need for such a cultural development, as it must go to cultural practitioners for identifying the need for a partnership approach with government through the CRC.

The Community Relations Council initially defined its area of interest in terms of relationship-building, supporting the structural level by 'developing an infrastructure of understanding and tolerance' (Fitzduff 1991, p. 9). Thus,

> the CRC sees its work as pre-political, i.e., work that can enable the development of a solution to the Northern Ireland problem that is just and sustainable. It recognises that it is, eventually, on the wisdom and capacity of our [political] spokespersons that our success in resolving conflicts will depend. (ibid., p. 4)

None the less, Fitzduff's differentiation of 'contextual necessities' demonstrated that she had a more concrete idea of what contribution the structural approach, in its turn, could offer to the cultural approach. If this can be accurately characterised as the impetus for complementarity arising from within the cultural approach, it will be useful to examine to what degree this understanding is shared by the practitioners of the cultural approach, and in what manner it is being shaped and developed from within the CRC.

Martin O'Brien's comments go straight to the heart of the matter. Writing in *Peace by Peace*, the magazine of the Peace People, he reflects:

> There is undoubtedly still some tension around between those who see peacemaking as principally about building relationships, and those who have an interest in addressing structures. In many ways this is a very false division. Good relationships are essential, but very often structures inhibit the relationships from becoming good. Clearly what is needed is an approach which addresses both of these concerns. (O'Brien 1993, p. 3)

As he expands on these ideas, his remarks reinforce the idea that the movement for a drawing together of the two approaches is indeed coming from within the cultural approach. He reflects that in the early years of the reconciliation groups, there was a conscious avoidance of structural or political issues. This stemmed from the purported desire to be 'impartial' because of a perceived danger of contamination:

There was one approach [within the peace movement], and
that approach has been challenged as being insufficient. . . .
Peace People certainly took the view that 'we aren't involved
in party politics, and we aren't involved in the constitutional
question; in a sense it's nationalism and unionism which are
the problem'. . . . There was this idea that peace groups should
not take sides, and that once you got involved in these
structural issues the whole parameters of the debate around
those issues placed people on sides . . . I think part of it has to
do with trying to keep your hands clean, trying not to be seen
to be taking a side.

So while an awareness of the existence of the structural arena
– the political issues – was there from the start, it was viewed as
something to be avoided, possibly even as the source or the
exacerbator of the cultural problem, rather than as something to
be complemented. Clearly, such a view was a long way from the
idea of government as the structural partner in a complementary
process. But this awareness has deepened in recent times, as
O'Brien illustrates:

You need to approach the problem from two ways; one of
those is the interpersonal and the other is the structural. And
there are structural things . . . which impede the forming of
good relations on the interpersonal level, and if you want to
address the conflict here you have to approach it from both
these perspectives. . . . Peace movements are not simply about
stopping the Provos or stopping the UDA or UVF. There's
undoubtedly still an element of that within the peace movement here . . . but there is also a growing debate and awareness
about tackling those more difficult issues. And I think certainly
more and more people in the peace movement are beginning
to look at the harder issues – and by that I mean policing,
prisons, emergency laws, justice and fairness – as opposed to
holding discussions on why our religions are different, or, not
even discussions, [just] sport or meeting for tea.

Fitzduff herself offers the example of PACE, a group singled
out by the NICRC in the early 1970s for criticism as a typically
middle-class reconciliation agency comfortably insulated from
direct involvement with the issues of conflict, but one which, she
insists, has changed dramatically:

Those who don't know what's been happening in PACE think, oh, Protestant and Catholic encounter, coffee-cup mornings, a middle-class coffee party. . . . [But] a lot of them are articulate, hard-hitting, thinking people, not afraid of some fascinating work. [Portadown PACE group] took out a full-page ad in the local paper when Portadown was bombed: 'To the IRA from the Catholic community in Portadown: why are you bombing our town in our name?' Very, very brave stuff. They had a meeting before the last political elections, and they brought together all the political parties and they asked them all sorts of questions about community relations and about other things.

The result is not merely a broadening of the scope of reconciliation work, but an understanding of the need for a diversity of approach. O'Brien attributes some of this reorientation directly to Fitzduff:

There is more acceptance now that we're all working on these issues, and we don't all do the same thing but we're all pushing in the same direction. Work by people like Mari Fitzduff has been quite significant on that, like her typology [Fitzduff 1989] which said, 'Look, here's the problem and there are all these ways you can address it, and it doesn't matter if you're doing this and someone else is doing that, because all of those are valid.' There's been a process of validation of different [methods] which has been very healthy.

Brendan McAllister, the Director of the Conflict Mediation Network (CMN), locates his organisation's work within the same framework:

The work of peace-making in Northern Ireland will go on at two levels. Firstly, the party political level wherein political leaders negotiate on the shape and detail of a political agreement. At another level, the two traditions in Northern Ireland, Catholic and Protestant, have become embittered . . . and estranged [to the extent that] in addition to a political agreement, there is a need for communal reconciliation. . . . Peace-makers and conflict resolvers can most usefully assist this process at the grass-roots community level . . . CMN's contribution in the future will be to facilitate creative dialogue among grass-roots people. This is not in itself an answer to all our problems. It is simply a component in the process. (McAllister 1993, p. 5)

Joan Broder, Chair of CMN, readily supports his analysis, concurring also with O'Brien's view that there has been a reluctance among reconciliation groups to address the 'hard' issues. But she has fears about the communication processes necessary to make a complementary strategy workable:

> You have to operate on different levels and in different areas. . . . In terms of a long-term strategy, you're going to have to look at how we are going to get these different [practitioners] to talk to each other in a meaningful way. While they 'hear' what other people are saying, they don't actually internalise it because it's a different language that's being used, it's not within their remit, if you like. . . . Yes, you need to be working on all aspects, but I don't think there's a linking between them; they talk on different tracks. . . . These people are ploughing their own furrows, and never really communicating . . . and we could end up with, say, ten parallel lines going for the one end, but never actually crossing over. A way needs to be found for people to appreciate what each is doing and see it in its overall context.

Her analysis implies a need for some mechanism to provide communication and coordination between approaches.

2. THE BRITISH GOVERNMENT AND COMPLEMENTARITY

In an important sense, community relations is the responsibility of government, even if it must delegate some of the actual work to other agencies. The British government defines its current community relations policy as aiming to achieve three 'fundamental objectives':

> – to ensure that everyone enjoys full equality of opportunity and equity of treatment;
> – to increase the level of cross-community contact; and
> – to encourage greater mutual understanding and respect of the different cultures and traditions. (CCRU 1993, p. 2)

But the main governmental tool, legislation, is a very blunt instrument for such goals. It is not possible to legislate for relationships. It is possible to legislate for the first of these aims, and the government has attempted to do so, with mixed results, through, for example, Fair Employment and Equal Opportunities legislation in the 1980s. Increasing contact and encouraging mutual understanding, however, are more difficult to achieve with structural tools, precisely because they involve straying into the cultural arena. The British government's achievements on these objectives are largely limited, first, to education reform in 1989 (most notably, the legal requirement that all schools now include curricular elements of Education for Mutual Understanding (EMU)[16] and of Cultural Heritage, and a funding scheme for inter-school projects); and secondly, to the establishment in 1987 of the CCRU with its responsibility for the CRC and for the District Council Community Relations Programme. Elements of economic development programmes (such as Targeting Social Need, Making Belfast Work, Londonderry Regeneration, and so on)[17] impinge on community relations in so far as they aim, among other things, to increase economic and social parity between the two communities and thus enable more equitable relationships. But these are, first and foremost, structural initiatives with structural (economic) goals. Community relations benefits are, at best, spin-off.

Whether the British government has learnt (for example, from its experience of the NICRC) its limits in affecting communal relationships through legislative channels is a moot point. But its policy of addressing its three objectives by such means as EMU and the CCRU/CRC, as supplements to legislation, is at least an implicit expression of its commitment to a complementary approach. Complementarity is not an overtly expressed policy of government, or of the structural approach at any level, but current structural policy and practice suggest that complementarity is passively and implicitly supported and welcomed.

This characterisation of government's involvement as passive should not, however, be read in critical comparison to the more active role of the cultural approach. There is a major constraint on a British government's public endorsement of any initiative: public reaction. The British government *per se* is highly suspect in the eyes of many in both communities. For example, should the government give a high-profile official endorsement to the

Community Relations Council, sections of the nationalist population would then dismiss the CRC as a British initiative and thus, by definition, something to be shunned. Indeed, at the CRC's launch in January 1990, one Sinn Féin councillor dismissed it as 'a cosmetic propaganda exercise by the government' (*Irish Times*, 5 January 1990). The same doubts are rife among unionist or loyalist opinion: in Fitzduff's words, 'There is suspicion in some quarters that we are just an alternative form of Anglo-Irish Agreement. But if you see everything as an Anglo-Irish plot, then we would so easily fit into that.' It is therefore imperative for the CRC's sustained and effective operation that its partnership with government does not delegitimise or taint its status, and that the relationship between the two does not become too close in public perception.

In short, however deeply committed a British government might be to a community relations programme within an approach of complementarity, to come out too strongly and say so in official terms would risk the destruction of the very program it wishes to support. This double-bind sets clear boundaries on its capacity to take a proactive role in developing community relations. The backstage work of the CCRU, and of the Northern Irish civil servants who have developed it and other initiatives as support/partnership structures to the CRC, is perhaps as much as can be reasonably expected of a beleaguered structural approach with a no-win public relations situation.

3. THE COMMUNITY RELATIONS COUNCIL AND COMPLEMENTARITY

The commitment to complementarity is more active, more overt in the cultural approach. Broder asks the key question:

> There are enough people out there taking on the political agenda, and enough people working on the reconciliation agenda, but how can you actually get them to work together?

In her own opinion, she suggests that the CRC might be the agency to fulfil such a coordinating role, ideally positioned because it interacts at both levels:

There needs to be a way, and it needs to be in the CRC's plan. I think the Council is well placed to do this, to be able to look from a distance at all that's going on, and to look at how you get people to appreciate the other's views and incorporate them. . . . I know [the CRC] are probably doing work with politicians, and they're doing work with church people. But in some way they're going to have to get people to really talk to each other, and to begin to value and hear each other. Because I think a lot of the 'peace' people see it that reconciliation is the only way, and that constitutional issues are neither here nor there. Whereas they are; that's reality – you have to have both.

O'Brien agrees with Broder's analysis that although awareness of complementarity has increased, so that it becomes a viable concept, it still has some distance to cover in order to be implemented to its full potential:

I would agree with [that image] that we're all in our little furrows. But better that than if we're messing up each other's furrows, which was what people were doing previously. . . . What is going on at the moment is that people are tolerating what other people do, and they are no longer prepared to dismiss entirely what other people do. And that is a welcome change. But we haven't got to the point where people fully understand. . . . In the past, work on structural issues (which is my term for it) would have been dismissed as politics and as not relevant to peacemaking. Now there aren't quite so many people who would say that. They [still] wouldn't want to get involved in it, they'd be quite frightened by it, they would be suspicious of it and wouldn't really understand it. But they'd be prepared to say, 'Well, they're doing that bit, and we're doing this bit, and all these bits have to be addressed.'

This development can be viewed as an object lesson in appreciating diversity, as cultural practitioners, themselves proponents of the need to embrace cultural and political diversity in more inclusive ways, apply the same principle of accepting diversity within their own practice. Once again, O'Brien attributes some of this development to the directional role of the CRC towards its client groups:

It's quite interesting how this idea can actually take on something of an orthodoxy, and I think Mari Fitzduff has been quite clever about that. But I'm not sure how deep it goes.

Indeed, while Broder is prepared to speculate that the CRC could act as the coordinator and so be instrumental in bridging the divide between the two approaches, O'Brien is more sure that the CRC is already privately active in both areas, but that the gap cannot be narrowed further (and, thus, complementarity increased) until such activity is made public:

> Visibly, the work which the public know the Community Relations Council is doing, and indeed the work that [practitioners] know they are doing, is in the relationship end, the interpersonal end. It's not in the structural end. I mean they *are* doing work in the structural end. But that's not public. . . . It is about time they started to be getting *publicly* involved in some of the structural aspects of the problem.

As with Broder, he accepts that, for a reconciliation group with a previous agenda centred on the interpersonal and on relationships and communication, addressing structural and/or political issues involves leaving behind the safe areas and entering the most difficult and controversial regions of Northern Irish discourse. None the less, he argues that the CRC's public profile and its leadership role within the cultural approach give it the opportunity – perhaps even the duty – to turn into the reality of practice what has so far remained a theoretical position:

> I'd like to see the Community Relations Council doing more public work on some of the more controversial issues. In particular, some public critique or comment on the impact of various government policies on community relations. If they took on that role, that would provide space for other people to do that in a more open and direct way. And it would firmly entrench the idea of these two models. But while the jargon and the legitimacy of them exists – and Fitzduff's typology is very good from that point of view – you don't see it being followed through by the Council, and I'd like to see that happening.

The concluding argument of Chapter 6 suggested that the most significant development of community relations work in the early 1990s was, via the CRC, the widening of the arena in which such work would be implemented. Where this impinges directly upon the cultural approach is both in broadening the agenda of community relations to include an increasing amount of the 'hard issues', and in broadening the target audience of community relations to include non-cultural elements and agencies. Comments from both Fitzduff and Hinds noted in Chapter 6 illustrate that this is a conscious, explicit process by the CRC. Both Broder and O'Brien explicitly identified the potential of the CRC to bridge the gap between approaches. Hinds also recognises this:

> We've access to funding, we can lobby government . . . we have operational plans which allow a multifaceted approach to the whole conflict. We challenge particular government departments on community relations issues. And we can make representations to the Orange Order [for example], to Northern Ireland security ministers, we can talk to the churches and to the police; we've even talked to the paramilitaries. . . . We have connections with every district council, we have a connection with every interchurch group, we've a connection with every peace and reconciliation group. . . . There isn't a corner of Northern Ireland where a [CRC] Development Officer hasn't been at one stage or another. We have a unique perspective on the totality of community relations work, at whatever level it happens.

Few, if any, agencies in Northern Ireland have anything approaching such a degree of access across the cultural/structural spectrum. Where the essential overlap lies, for Hinds, is in the fact that both approaches aim to affect the working of society at large. The aims of the cultural approach – to achieve a set of social relationships based on respect and trust – necessarily, he argues, call for structural efforts too:

> We're trying to create a much more pluralistic society which can respect diversity rather than suspect it, and in a sense there has got to be a great deal of structural and social engineering to create those 'normal' spaces. . . . What community relations means in practical terms [is] that there is some compromise and accommodation.

The overlap is dramatically illustrated by Hinds' own terminology: 'compromise and accommodation' are key terms – and usually exclusively so – in the structural/settlement vocabulary.

Yet they are clearly important and effective concepts to this cultural practitioner. Tyrrell describes the overlap in similar terms:

> I think you can only change structures by having or changing relationships with people – even if it's just withdrawing from that relationship. . . . [My work] is about relationships, but ultimately if it's about trying to make significant change, then it's actually about making relationships with people in power, too.

The way in which community relations work thus feeds in to this dual approach process is fairly clear to Hinds:

> A lot of community relations work is in a sense preparing ground, allowing constituencies which otherwise have been closed to engage in dialogue and discussion about, say, political developments or political options. By allowing the development of such work, it creates an atmosphere and a precedent: it makes people more comfortable with the idea of consensus, of having relations, of taking account of another perspective. That's got to be good in terms of building up more of a consensus base or a consensus style for democratic principles, rather than an us-and-them, majority–minority view. . . . Community relations work will have to be ongoing regardless of what happens in the political arena, *but you can't divorce the two.* . . . If [politicians] get more and more signals through the Social Attitudes Survey, or there are more and more politicians at local council level co-operating and sharing responsibility, if there's a greater profile of cross-cultural and multi-cultural events, then that's bound to create a changing environment and atmosphere. . . . There's a changing environment, and *there is a greater focus of attention placed on the issues*, and all of that should contribute to the macro-political process. (emphases added).

In Hinds' view, perhaps the greatest contribution of community relations would be to put people – politicians included – in a position to address the political issues in a more positive, inclusive light:

> A lot of the value of reconciliation groups is in their facilitation process, that they can allow different perspectives to be shaped and developed. They can produce a degree of enlightenment between otherwise intractable or mutually hostile communities

or visions. . . . But that will get people only so far. I'm not sure that it will in itself provide all the answers. It will generate an atmosphere, give people skills which they can bring to bear on difficult issues, create an environment where problems may be solved more in a politics of accommodation. . . . *There is great complementarity.* (emphasis added)

Community relations work, then, constitutes in some way an effort to produce the necessary relationships within which contentious politics can then be addressed differently and more positively:

[Community relations] groups shy away from producing a preferred option, either a political or a cultural one. Their work is process-oriented: they want people to get to the stage where they can. . . . have the ability to accept diversity and difference, which our society hasn't really provided us the skills to do. . . . Now, what that denotes in political terms – whether it's dual sovereignty, or a federal Ireland or a federal UK – is up to the individual. They're not going to provide a favoured outcome, they're process-orientated. (Hinds)

Fitzduff echoes his comments as she describes the 'pre-political' role of community relations work:

Unless there's enough community relations work done, in effect it's much more difficult to reach a solution. Inevitably, our solutions are going to be complex: if people have not at some level come into contact and understood that complexity, it will make the solution harder for their political leaders to sell.

The underlying hypothesis here, then, is that as community relations work operates to develop more inclusive communal relationships, that will facilitate politics in working out more inclusive political settlements. That is the heart of complementarity.

Such clear statements of community relations work's essential complementary role to the political arena, and particularly the implied clear understanding of the difficulties of operation in that arena, would suggest that the CRC has indeed, as O'Brien argued, entered the arena itself. Fitzduff confirms this, but accepts that there is a dilemma involved. She believes that, at a general level, 'We have been seen to fund and resource quite a lot of difficult stuff'. But in relation specifically to work with politicians, she accepts a behind-the-scenes role: 'We will have a hand in it, but much of the work will never come out under our name. Nor should it.' At least for the present, O'Brien's plea for greater publicity on the CRC's structural role cannot be satisfied given its currently tentative and delicate nature:

> There is that kind of engagement with, and sympathy to, the difficulties of the politicians; in so far as is possible, trying to work with them, challenging them and encouraging groups to challenge them. . . . *There's a lot more stuff going on quietly than is known about publicly.* . . . That kind of quiet facilitation is something we try to encourage . . . We have tended to either leave the politicians alone or work very quietly with various of them, simply because we are very conscious that at a private level there is a lot more complexity available on the part of politicians than there is at a public level. We would know enough to know that at many levels many of the things that seem problematic in public have already been talked about in private by the young politicians. But they find it hard to move on them. . . . So it's that bit of work around the private to the public, we're working very much around that at the moment. (Fitzduff; emphases added)

So as the development of community relations work is characterised as moving from the 'softer issues' of relationships to the 'difficult end' of political issues (see Chapter 6), the development of greater complementarity proceeds in tandem:

> Look at the way in which we have validated different approaches within CR. People were vying for attention. Justice and rights workers were saying, 'It's justice and rights, not community relations.' Somebody else was saying, 'It's political process.' [Another was saying,] 'No, it's equity.' What we are saying is, 'It isn't one or the other, it's a combination'. Within our own work we're saying that prejudice reduction, for example, is frankly not the answer. It is one part that is extremely useful in certain workshops. Because the reality is that if you read every book in George Mason [University] or the Harvard Program on Negotiation, you'll know that there is not, and never is, one answer. It always appears to be a

combination of. And therefore to do other than look at the combination that seems to be most pertinent is non-truthful in terms of the knowledge we actually have. It doesn't mean that one won't come to the fore at a certain time. For example, at the minute we are talking about [work with] politicians and paramilitaries; but we can talk about that because to a certain extent equity [for example] has 'been done'. (Fitzduff)

If, then, cultural practitioners are incorporating the 'hard, hard edges of stuff' (Fitzduff) as they broaden their agendas and arenas into the more contentious issues of politics and structural change, is there a reciprocal broadening of interest from the politicians towards community relations?

Some of the politicians still hold themselves quite aloof; although the local [council] politicians do not. . . . The number of local councils I've seen where they actually now boast of their community relations programme – and I know that two years ago they weren't boasting of it, they were fighting the bit out about it – means that to a certain extent a lot of our politicians have seen that perhaps CR is not as problematic as they had thought. So at the local level there is no longer a dilemma about it. But the dilemma is more at the [party] leaders' level, who are beginning to feel, I think, a bit uneasy about all the movement that is around. . . . We have the odd problem with them . . . partly because their defences are so great. But to a great extent we've managed not to alienate those and we've managed to bring on board most of the others. . . . I can't think they wouldn't cooperate with us. (Fitzduff)

For Fitzduff, the whole process of engaging politicians – at whatever level – is rewarding and productive, but as yet very delicate. At the general, public level, it can be done fairly simply: 'We went to Derry last year [1992] for our Annual Conference. And we invited everybody, including Sinn Féin, publicly all their councillors. So at that level we're validating that kind of inclusion.' And the CRC has a direct inroad to the politicians at Local District Council level via its supporting role to CCRU in establishing the Community Relations programme in all 26 District Councils: 'We will often provide for District Councils to come together, not just the workers but the councillors and the CROs and their line-managers.' But for the higher level politicians, a clearly strategic approach is in use, as the CRC initially targets the younger, more moderate and less rhetorically bound party members:

> For instance, we have a seminar coming up which we have helped to facilitate with young Ian Paisley [son of the DUP leader] and Alex Atwood who is one of the bright young sparks of the SDLP. They're co-sponsoring a conference on identity. So that kind of quiet facilitation is something we try to encourage, as well as which we've been trying to encourage the younger politicians to provide forums among themselves. That can be problematic in terms of the fathers, but we manage to maintain relatively good relationships with the fathers. (No mothers as yet!)

But, tellingly, she explains the necessity for the CRC to be involved in the political arena in clear terms of complementarity, of progress in each approach acting in a mutually supportive manner:

> In a sense, it's a chicken and egg situation. It's harder for the politicians to get there if we haven't done enough qualitative work. But [community relations] work is also limited because people actually can get quite dispirited if there's not some sense of politicians holding on.

Further, the CRC takes advantage of its uniquely central perspective in the conflict, its 'overview in a variety of settings' (Hinds; and see above). With this perspective, the CRC can look at both arenas and, if it can identify an element in either one which might significantly help or hinder progress in the other, then it has access to address such elements. In terms of structural elements which affect the cultural arena,

> If the Council sees something is not happening that it believes is significantly affecting community relations, it has the capacity to address it. For instance, the whole question of housing planning is something that we're hoping to present a report on to government, [or] for instance industrial development and economic development . . . the interface with the security forces . . . agricultural development, the positioning of schools . . . (Fitzduff)

Transfer can operate in the other direction too. First, Fitzduff sees that the methodology of community relations work can be fruitful in the structural arena:

> We can offer some things to the politicians. We've had a lot of the Local [District] Councils along to a lot of our venues, our seminars. We're developing local conflict resolution/community relations training for councillors. . . . I'm also working on a feasibility study to set up a political development trust . . . that looks at the whole political process. That will involve all the political parties looking to what they need in terms of developing themselves. (Fitzduff)

This tallies with Chapter 5's concluding suggestion that some of the relationship- and trust-building skills developed in the cultural approach could have a very positive contribution to make in the facilitation of better political dialogue processes. Hinds supports the view, arguing specifically that the reconciliation sector may possess exactly the skills and methodology necessary for this development:

> For the peace groups, because they have access to a process of facilitation . . . there might be a significant role for them to play in bringing people into a much more constitutional-type political process, or bringing them in from the cold, or instituting dialogue, or widening the debate. (Hinds)

Secondly, not only methodology can be transferred, but substantive work too. Certainly, the CCRU – the CRC's structural partner – has adopted initiatives which try to offer at least legislative backup and at most structural forms for addressing the cultural questions of relationship-building, mutual understanding, and so on. The CCRU's initiatives include the Local District Council community relations programmes, the detailed contents and form of which the CRC has done much to develop, and, in particular, education reform including a new common curriculum for both Protestant and Catholic schools:

> Unique to the NI curriculum are statutory cross-curricular themes covering Education for Mutual Understanding (EMU) and cultural heritage, and their objectives must be promoted through the curriculum for all pupils. . . . Other initiatives include the development of a core syllabus for religious education. This was prepared with the co-operation of the four main

churches and will be taught in all grant-aided schools. (CCRU 1993, p. 3)

For Hinds, the approaching challenge for community relations groups and workers is to adapt to this interdependence of approaches, to recognise that 'circumstances change, you've got to be more focused or better targeted, you've got to *complement* particular policy initiatives, like Education for Mutual Understanding, for example' (original emphasis). This increasingly combined approach to both politics and community relations is, according to Fitzduff, still at an early stage. But it is the way to future progress in both approaches:

> There are certainly some areas, particularly middle-class power, both Catholic and Protestant, that we really do need to engage a lot more in the participative process and that includes both politics and community relations. . . . [But] it has begun, it's beginning, and that work won't stop when we get our political solution. It has to go on, that kind of networking and interlocking, for quite some time.

CONCLUSION AND SUMMARY

It is appropriate at this juncture to attempt to sketch a picture of the state of play of complementarity as it currently exists in the practice of conflict management in Northern Ireland. From the foregoing comments and analysis, several points can be drawn out for consideration. First, the degree of *awareness* of the need for complementarity can be considered, as distinct from, secondly, the *implementation* of complementarity in practice. The nature of the interrelationship of approaches within complementarity can be considered in terms of, thirdly, *encroachment*, as distinct from, fourthly, *cross-pollination*.

Awareness of the need for complementarity has undoubtedly increased significantly, especially in recent years. The first stage of this can be discerned in the ways in which various practitioners since 1968 indicated an appreciation that their own approach would not suffice to solve the conflict. This was more evident on the structural side, in various British government statements from 1972 onwards throughout the 1980s, about the limits of a 'political' versus a 'community' settlement. But while such statements implied the need for some kind of complement to the political process, they included little suggestion of the form it might take. In short, the structural approach at this earlier stage permitted the space for a complement, but saw no shape to it. On the cultural side, there were few, if any, corresponding statements on the need for other approaches. Partly this is because formal statements on any policy-related subject were not in the nature of these informal cultural projects, partly because there was no central organising focus among the disparate cultural agencies which could take on a representative role, and also partly because cultural practitioners spent the 1970s looking inward to develop primarily their own practice and, within resource constraints, some modicum of strategy for their own approach. Indeed, it must be recognised that some cultural initiatives were started specifically out of frustration or despair at the perceived failure of political/structural efforts in the 1970s. It was really only in the mid-1980s that, on both sides, heads were raised to look outwards. The British government began to reconsider the question of what might fill the complementary space. And at the same time, the community relations sector was flagging the distinction of approaches in an initial terminology of 'community relations' and 'contextual necessities'.

Thereafter, the two sides began to draw closer, as government considered concrete suggestions as to how to fill the space, and as cultural practitioners considered how the governmental/structural system might best assist their efforts. The resulting CCRU and CRC represented, in their establishment, some new degree of mutual respect between approaches. Clearly, by this stage awareness of complementarity was well developed in a general sense of accepting the need for a diversity of approaches. Comments noted earlier in this chapter suggest that this awareness has accelerated since the establishment of the CRC in 1990, and that it has become more specifically and clearly defined.

However, awareness is not the same as *implementation*, and this chapter suggests that implementation is in an initial or transitional stage. The way in which each approach defines its goals is instructive. On the one hand, the structural approach's view of its goals is well expressed in the words of the CCRU, where the emphasis on the interdependence of approaches is explicit:

Community relations programmes are designed to bring the two sides of Northern Ireland's community towards greater understanding and respect. Progress in overcoming terrorism and creating political structures which command support across the community would help to improve community relations. However, even if such progress can be made, the underlying community divisions will still have to be addressed. If they are not, they will continue to threaten and undermine any political and security progress. (CCRU 1993, p. 1)

On the other hand, Fitzduff's own definition of the CRC's ultimate goal has similarly evolved into something far beyond the bounds of simply improved community relations: 'A just and sustainable constitutional solution is our goal.'[18]

These are clearly 1990s definitions, and what is most interesting in both cases is that they are obviously not limited to the areas of operation of the relevant agency making the statement. Thus, both approaches have demonstrated, from their increased awareness of complementarity in principle, some convergence in their definitions of ends. As regards their definitions of means to achieve these ends, some degree of integration can also be seen. The inter-reliance of approaches is clearly stated in the CCRU's statement above; the same understanding is demonstrated in Fitzduff's remarks, quoted earlier, about the 'chicken and egg' relationship between politics and community relations.

This interrelationship has two facets. First, there is some evidence of *encroachment*, that is, of each approach broadening its interests into the other's arena. Chapter 6 documented the cultural approach's efforts to widen its arena beyond the voluntary sector by making community relations the business of all social groupings in all sectors. In this way, we can see community relations encroaching on what has previously been the territory of the structural approach – community relations programmes for District Councils, community relations aspects to school curricula, community relations elements for all aspects of social activity – and putting cultural subject matter on the structural agenda. Similarly, as community relations workers have begun to address the 'harder' issues of Northern Irish discourse within their own arena, they have begun to accept structural subject matter on their cultural agendas. Justice and rights work, equity work, security interface work, dialogue with paramilitaries, and so on (see Fitzduff 1989), were absolutely excluded from previous definitions of community relations work. Now they are increasingly central items on the agendas of many cultural practitioners: thus, structural items have also encroached on the cultural agenda, and the boundaries of both arenas are blurring.

Distinct from such encroachment is another way in which the approaches have developed a mutual support mechanism: a *cross-pollination* of methodologies. On the one hand, the concepts of inclusiveness and relationship-building are creeping in to the political process. Comments at the end of Chapter 5 suggested that the Brooke Initiative might have benefited from a greater element of relationship-building in its process of dialogue; and elsewhere in that chapter I argued that Brooke's efforts played some significant role of relationship-building among the party representatives which facilitated subsequent progress under Mayhew. And the argument can certainly be made that the concept of inclusiveness has since become significant to the British government as regards the role of Sinn Féin in the political process. Brooke made overtures to Sinn Féin during his period in office, but the overtures were outside the context of political dialogue. (Indeed, that rare thing – an easy point of unanimity – was achieved over the need to exclude Sinn Féin from the dialogue.) Subsequently, and especially since early 1993, a main thrust of British policy has clearly been aimed at identifying the terms on which Sinn Féin can be included in dialogue. The basic requirement of this – that they renounce support for political violence – has been upgraded to the central aim of virtually every effort Britain has made (including direct and secret communication with Sinn Féin) since the end of the Mayhew talks in late 1992. It cannot, of course, be proved that this is due to any influence from the cultural approach; but the case can reasonably be made that inclusiveness and appreciation of diversity are two important threads in the cultural approach that have gained significant salience and currency among all sectors of Northern Irish society in the late 1980s and early 1990s. But more directly attributable to a cultural influence is the development at the Local District Council level of an acceptance – grudging or positive – of the viability of community relations programmes. These aim both to improve a Council's internal relationships[19] and to draw Councillors and staff into action and responsibility for relationship-building work in their community.

In the other direction, the cultural approach has also adopted or co-opted some of the strategies of the structural approach. The CRC has encouraged – perhaps even forced, to some degree – community relations agencies to develop accountability, strategic planning and management skills which have traditionally been the preserve of the public and private sectors. It has further developed a directional role, guiding them towards a widening of the arena of their work by controlling access to the structural sources of money. And it has, finally, encouraged such groups and agencies to address the 'hard edges' of their work: the aspects of Northern Irish society which have traditionally been left to the politicians, security forces and paramilitaries to handle. The future logical conclusion of this last development can be glimpsed by recalling Hinds' adoption of the settlement vocabulary (quoted above) as he speculated on the future convergence of complementary approaches into a fully integrated process, one where 'compromise and accommodation' meet 'process-oriented facilitation'.

There is, then, a degree of convergence between the two approaches. Such convergence of views does not, of course, necessitate ultimately identical ends and means. Indeed, complementarity would become meaningless if both approaches simply duplicated each other's work or merged totally into one. However, it suggests that both approaches are well into the process of seeing each other in the light of partnership, sharing similar ends and apportioning the means to those ends between them.

But what it further suggests is a degree of confusion for the two-approach model. Where the approaches begin to truly complement each other in their methodologies and their means, is at the point where their boundaries become indistinct. This can be simply illustrated if one takes a moment to ponder for example on the people – the individuals – whom I have generalised into a category of 'cultural practitioners' for the purposes of my argument. While that is what they are, and they carry out that work on the basis of a belief in the relationship-building orientation of tha: approach, it would be a gross error to believe that that is all they are. In so far as each of these individuals has a political viewpoint on the conflict, has an opinion of the shape a 'constitutional settlement' should take, and on the way negotiation and bargaining should be used to achieve that, then each is clearly an interface between the two approaches. Proponents of the cultural approach do not exist in a political vacuum where the only salient goals are relationship-building and mutual understanding. They too interact in the structural realm as citizens, as political beings, as members of society and components of those structures. As such, they made no decision to 'drop politics' in order to become community relations workers: they, like everyone in Northern Ireland, exist simultaneously in both spheres and in many other spheres too. The same argument, in reverse, can be made against viewing 'politicians' as creatures of only a structural dimension; on the contrary, they too invest significance in their communities, their communal identities, and necessarily in inter-communal relations. It must not be forgotten for a moment that the artificiality of dividing conflict-solving efforts into structural and cultural approaches stems from the process of analysis, rather than from what or who is being analysed. It is the neatness of the division that is artificial; it is the confusion and complexity of social life that is real. This train of thought will be explored further where it most appropriately belongs, in Chapter 8.

8 A Model of Complementarity in Conflict Management

This chapter aims to relate the information gathered from the foregoing discussion of Northern Ireland practice (Chapters 5–7) to the theoretical debate from Chapter 4 on a model of complementarity in conflict management.

In Chapter 4, I suggested that there is a direct practice–theory relationship between, respectively, the cultural and structural approaches to practical conflict management in Northern Ireland and the prescriptive approaches of resolution and settlement theories. I therefore argued that analysis of the practical approaches and their interrelationship could enlighten the debate about complementarity at the theoretical level. Chapters 5 and 6 offered a degree of analysis of the dynamics of each practical approach *per se*, and Chapter 7 subsequently addressed the interrelationship. From the picture which develops of the current interdependence of cultural and structural approaches, significant validation can be gleaned for the concept of complementarity: practice backs up the theoretical concept; more pertinently, the practice *grounds* the theory.

Directly relating to the hypotheses of Chapter 4, four observations can be made:

- There are indeed two corresponding practical approaches in operation.
- These approaches operate concurrently and most often in different arenas.
- The practitioners of each approach have always had some awareness of their own limits and of the others' existence. Until recently, however, they have tended to operate independently.
- Finally, their relationship has more recently developed from exclusivity to inclusivity, from the initial coolness of mutual disparagement (somewhat like the theoretical positions until Fisher and Keashly entered the fray) to a warmer

proto-partnership with an increasing degree of mutual respect and a growing awareness of inter-reliance and complementarity.

Specifically relating to the practice of Northern Ireland, three further observations can be made. First, the mutual respect between the two approaches has become more explicit, and its public expression has become an important source of validation for each approach. But the question arises as to how far the explicit expression of this respect can go. For example, while government support and cooperation is necessary if the CRC wants to develop its interpositional role between both structural and cultural approaches, too much overt expression of such support could either undermine the CRC's confidential work with politicians, or alienate it from sections of society antipathetic to the British government. In the current atmosphere of dynamic transition, this problematic of explicit expression of this respect – and its significance as a factor in both approaches' progress and efficacy – is being more seriously, if as yet inconclusively, addressed.

Secondly, in the process of this transition, the boundaries between the approaches in Northern Ireland are beginning to blur. As regards these two context-specific observations, it may merely be noted at this point that there is a resultant tension. On the one hand, the blurring of boundaries may operate as a force for greater integration of approaches. On the other, whatever limit there may come to be on explicitness of support could well operate as a brake on that same force, a factor resistant to closer integration. This may have something to tell us about the limits of complementarity.

Thirdly, we can observe that the practical question of coordination is becoming increasingly pertinent. Coordination, however, seems to have more base in, and relevance to, the specific context of Northern Ireland practice, although it seems reasonable to assume that it would inevitably arise as a problem to be addressed in any practical context where complementarity is in operation.

So far, then, the case studies offer a reasonable validation of the earlier speculations about the nature of complementarity: resolution and settlement approaches do seem to be complementary, do appear to operate simultaneously, and do increasingly validate each other in active complementarity. On the basis of these findings, it is now possible to speculate on the shape of a model of conflict management which more effectively enables a complementary approach. This is the main task of this chapter, reviewing and developing the earlier arguments from Chapter 4 in the light of the subsequent empirical evidence. First, though, section 1 examines the core concept of complexity in model-building, and relates it to the ideas of generalised and embedded criteria as proposed for the model. Section 2 then lays out the shape of the complementarity model.

1. COMPLEXITY IN CONFLICT: IMPLICATIONS FOR MODEL-BUILDING

The notion of complexity was introduced in Chapter 4 in relation to the tension in model-building between off-the-peg generalisation and bespoke specificity. Social conflict, especially the protracted variety, is a highly complex phenomenon. Certainly in Northern Ireland, there are 1.5 million potential disputants who comprise between them an entire society, with all the dynamism and fluidity, all the complexity and contradiction which that entails. But the more widely applicable we want our models to be, the less we can afford to build into them the degree of complexity which would represent the reality of any context to which the models may be usefully applied. Consequently, generalised theories – like Fisher and Keashly's contingency model – become too simplified: mapping the descriptive elements of their model on to Northern Ireland shows the weakness of (1) squeezing the conflict into the constraints of a unitary one-stage-at-a-time diagnosis and a consequent one-approach-at-a-time prescription, and (2) assuming degrees of consensus and homogeneity within heterogeneous and dynamic constituencies.

Johan Galtung likens the process of conflict modelling to steering a course between Scylla and Charybdis:

> Real life conflicts are usually very complex; elementary conflicts are for textbooks. . . . The problem, the Scylla, is that the complexity may become too high for the human mind to handle. . . . In other words, simplification may also be called for, with the danger, the Charybdis, that simplification

becomes polarisation, down to elementary conflicts. The crucial problem is how to steer a course between Scylla and Charybdis. (1993, p. 18)

Polarisation is a popular term in conflict analysis, and carries with it a pejorative or problematic connotation (indeed, it is one of Fisher and Keashly's escalatory stages). As conflict intensifies, we speak of the parties becoming polarised: as they move further apart they shed their links and communication channels, with a concomitant reduction of sophistication in their perceptions of themselves, their opponents and their conflict. Generally, the process of polarisation is seen as a negative one in which accuracy of perception is sacrificed to simplicity in an us-or-them view. Galtung is suggesting that the same danger that lies for disputants in the process of polarisation – a problematic process in the view of analysts – also lurks for conflict analysts in the process of simplification.

Galtung's theoretical Scylla and Charybdis, the poles of complexity and simplicity, also relate to inductive specificity and deductive generalisation. Deduction – moving from the starting point of general principle to deduce consequences for the specific – privileges generalisation, the process at the heart of most model-building. It carries with it the temptation to universalise: to encapsulate an explanation of all instances of a phenomenon in an overarching theory or model. This search for theoretical universality in turn encourages such dangerous generalisation, because it brings with it a process of simplification that flies in the face of the complex realities it tries to explain, as Sandra Harding points out: 'consistent and coherent theories in an unstable and incoherent world are obstacles to both our understanding and our social practices' (1986, p. 649).

Johan Jorgen Holst recognises the same pitfalls:

I am not arguing against intellectual order, of course. Nor am I arguing against attempts to build theory, to develop generalisations from which may be derived normative prescriptions and operational principles. I want, however, to sound a note of caution about a propensity to derive those prescriptions and principles from abstract models by the deductive route. . . . I favour the inductive route to generalisation, and I favour humility and caution about the scope for generalisation. (1990, p. 19)

This study takes to heart his plea for caution. Northern Ireland again provides the illustration. As Whyte has remarked,

> [Academic] researchers appear to have reached unanimity only on the barest matters of fact. . . . Thus, after twenty years of study by hundreds of researchers, there is still only partial agreement on the nature of the problem, and none at all on the nature of the solution. (1990, pp. 244–6)

In the face of such diversity and confusion among the experts, it behoves the conflict analyst to embrace humility in trying to describe even that conflict in itself, let alone attempts to outline general similarities or principles about that and other conflicts. This is certainly not an argument for rejecting generalisation wholesale, but rather for accepting that there are grave constraints on the process.

Can some balance, then, be reached between induction and deduction, between generalisation and specificity, between complexity and simplification? In particular, is there a way to resolve this trade-off in the complementarity model? Some progress can be made in this direction by means of attention to the criteria for prescribing specific tools within the model. The way to do this is to open up a channel from the specific conflict under consideration, so that it has some access to shaping the theoretical model in such a way that, without sacrificing the benefits of some generalisation, it becomes more accurately representative of the specific conflict. In other words, we want to keep the general aspects of the model so that it is applicable to a variety of social conflict situations, but we also want to ensure that, each time it is applied, the model is tempered by a degree of sensitivity to the particular situation. If that were possible, then the context would actively influence the shape of – rather than being passively incorporated into – the model. How can such a channel be opened up from context to model? John Paul Lederach's work has something to offer in this respect.

Lederach is a practitioner and trainer of conflict management and of intervention (in the terminology of this argument, he is from the resolution approach, from a tradition associated primarily with pure mediation, unofficial intervention, community-level facilitation and empowerment, and so on). While he is particularly concerned with practical methods of training conflict managers, the principles behind his approach can be harmonised with the argument under discussion here. Lederach (1995) addresses the problem of culture in conflict management training. He presents two Weberian 'ideal types' of training, locating them at either end of a spectrum. These are the *prescriptive* and the *elicitive* models. First, he identifies the prescriptive approach to training as one which grows out of his own Western, North American tradition. The prescriptive approach is based on a trainer–trainee hierarchy, where the trainer relies on her or his own expertise:

> First, the prescriptive approach ... assumes that the expert knows what the participants need. ... Second, throughout the [training] event the explicit and expert knowledge of the trainer is assumed to be and is valued as more trustworthy and relevant. ... Third, the primary goal of the training is to learn the model. (1995, pp. 48–50)

In contrast, Lederach offers the elicitive model as one which begins from the vantage point that

> training is an opportunity aimed primarily at discovery, creation and solidification of models that emerge from the resources present in a particular setting. ... The starting point of elicitive training involves a reconceptualisation of roles. ... [T]he trainer sees himself or herself primarily as a catalyst and facilitator rather than as an expert in a particular model of conflict resolution. ... Simply put, the foundation of the elicitive model is that implicit indigenous knowledge about ways of being and doing is a valued resource for creating and sustaining appropriate models of conflict resolution in a specific setting. (ibid., pp. 55–6)

He further distinguishes the prescriptive approach as content-oriented, and the elicitive as process-oriented. Most critical for the argument presented here, he comments that

> prescription assumes a certain amount of universality. The model is transfer-based: knowledge and experience that has emerged from and has been applied in a particular cultural context is now moving to another. The premise of universality suggests ... that such a transfer can successfully take place across lines of culture, class and context. (ibid., pp. 65–6)

For the elicitive model, however,

Cultural context and knowledge about conflict-in-setting make up the foundation through which model development happens. Participants' natural knowledge, their way of being and doing, their immediate situation, their past heritage, and their language are seen as the seedbed in which the training and model building will be rooted. (ibid., p. 67)

In sum, a prescriptive trainer brings a pre-packaged, generalised, universal model and transfers it wholesale and largely intact *to the specific situation*; whereas an elicitive trainer comes as a catalyst to the specific situation with the intention of eliciting *from that situation* the most appropriate model. The prescriptive approach employs a top-down process, where the flow of information travels almost exclusively from the outside 'expert' to the trainees within the context; the emphasis of the elicitive approach is on a bottom-up process, where the 'experts' are those involved in the context, and their 'expertise' arises from, and is validated by, the very fact that they are from within the context. Lederach accepts that these models are archetypes, and that most conflict management training lies along the spectrum between the two extremes. None the less, he argues convincingly that the dangers of the prescriptive approach lead to the sacrifice of the real complexity of the situation for the sake of the model:

The assumptions of cultural universality that underlie the prescriptive approach do not always hold. In fact what becomes universal may be the homogenisation of people to fit into the approach. (ibid., p. 68)

He advocates the elicitive approach because it

suggests that we consider what is present in a cultural setting as the basis for identifying key categories and concepts as foundational building blocks for a conflict resolution model. . . . Practically, this means that [participants] dig into the mines of their own knowledge and setting. Rather than learning the language of a new model . . . and then needing to ferret out the implicit assumptions from that model for a particular cultural context, the elicitive approach initiates learning with the implicit but constructive images and assumptions present in the culture and builds toward an explicit model. (ibid., p. 100)

Lederach's prescriptive/elicitive tension between universality and 'conflict-in-setting' mirrors the simplified/complex tension between generalised models and context-specificity. There are two important differences, however, between Lederach's argument and that presented here. First, while he argues within the debate on intercultural transfer, I make a broader statement about contextual influence: in modelling conflict, *all* relevant factors of the specific context – subjective and objective, and not only the cultural – must be included. Secondly, Lederach refers specifically to the building of conflict management training models; I again range more widely, arguing that the same principle of contextual input must apply to model building across the whole approach of conflict management usage, methodology and practice, including its training practice. By re-utilising the term 'cultural' in its broader, and broadest, sense, to refer to every contextual aspect that makes a particular society what it is, then the core of the inductive approach is laid out in Lederach's sentence: 'cultural context and knowledge about conflict-in-setting are the foundation through which model development happens' (ibid., p. 67).

And the route by which 'conflict-in-setting' gains access to, and influence within, the model of complementarity is by means of *embedded* criteria at the prescriptive decision-making stage. The use of these embedded criteria ensures that model development begins from, in Lederach's terms, what is present in the setting, in order to identify the building blocks for the model. The provision of these criteria will ensure that a comprehensive range of strategies for managing the conflict are *elicited* from, and translated to, the setting, within a flexible model where they will complement the more generalised information or data built up from the identification of tentative patterns, types, and correspondences from many diverse conflict formations.

2. A MODEL OF COMPLEMENTARITY IN CONFLICT MANAGEMENT

In order to elaborate the model at greater length, it may be simplest to take as a starting-point Fisher and Keashly's contingency model of intervention, and outline its short-comings before presenting an alternative model in some detailed form. To assist the discussion, the reader is referred once again to Table 4.1 in Chapter 4 (p. 82).

The contingency model aims to diagnose the developmental stage of a conflict by means of assessing the elements of the conflict along six different axes. These axes are: communication and interaction modes, perceptions and images of self and other, the state of the interparty relationship, emphasised issues, perceived possible outcomes, and preferred methods of conflict management. There are four points on each axis, each point corresponding to one of the four developmental stages: discussion, polarisation, segregation, or destruction. Thus, having examined the conflict in terms of the six axes, it is then consigned to one stage. A different type of intervention, based largely on the difference between resolution and settlement approaches, it is argued, is appropriate for each different stage. Thus the criterion for assigning an approach to a conflict is the diagnosed escalatory stage: lower escalation stages require a more resolution-oriented approach; higher stages a more settlement-based approach. Because the conflict is seen as being in only one stage at a time, only one approach is prescribed.

In Chapter 4, I critiqued the contingency model on two specific points of over-simplicity. First, I argued that complex social conflict tends to exhibit a range of characteristics (axis-points) from more than one stage at the same time. Secondly, I also argued that groupings in complex social conflict are too unstable, dynamic and heterogeneous to be characterised as speaking with a homogeneous or coherent voice, or from one unified viewpoint. The result for the contingency model is that analysis of a complex conflict will produce an inconsistent range of axis-points which together indicate no clear, single escalatory stage.

The conclusion was that, given these weaknesses in the descriptive base, the subsequent employment of sequential stages as the criteria for developing prescription was too simplistic. Instead, it was suggested that a more sophisticated model might more accurately reflect the complexity of social conflict by rejecting these sequential criteria in favour of a combination of (1) *generalised criteria* employed at the first, descriptive, stage to develop a suitably complex picture of the conflict under study, and (2) *embedded criteria* from within the specific context employed at the subsequent, prescriptive, stage, to develop a more comprehensive and properly complementary prescription consisting of a mix of resolution and settlement strategies. The ideas behind these categories of criteria will be fleshed out below.

The shape of the complementarity model, then, comprises two phases: description and prescription. In the first, a set of four open-ended, information-gathering questions based around what I term generalised criteria, are asked. These generalised criteria are based on an adaptation of Fisher and Keashly's six axes. The questions (whose provenance is detailed below) take the following form:

- Who is communicating over which element(s) of the conflict by what means?
- Who utilises which perceptions and images of themselves, the conflict and the other, in relation to which elements?
- Who envisages which possible outcomes over which elements?
- Who utilises which means of conflict management over which elements?[20]

Simple as these questions appear, the resulting answers provide a complex and detailed picture of the conflict, its elements, its actors, its themes and its modes; and once the elements are thus identified, they can be separated into subjective and objective elements. Following this descriptive process, the various elements of the conflict can be generally assigned, according to whether they are subjective or objective, for either resolution or settlement approaches. In the second phase, that of prescription, the generalities of resolution and settlement are translated into practical strategies specific to the context of the conflict in question, by means of filtering them through the embedded criteria elicited from the context. Thus, appropriate strategies are allotted to appropriate elements. In other words, the general ideas of resolution and settlement become, in this second stage, translated into a set of *context-specific methodologies for action* targeted at specific elements in a complementary and coordinated form.

The overall shape of the model, then, begins in the specific conflict context, moves to the theoretical level, where it intersects with the concepts of objective and subjective conflict, of resolution and settlement, and of complementarity, and then returns to the specific context in order to devise and prescribe the most appropriate methodologies for that particular context. First, information specific to the conflict (its issues, actors, etc.) is drawn out and collated. Then it is inserted into the generalised level so that we can draw general conclusions about which elements are subjective, which are objective, and which broad approach (resolution or settlement) applies to each. Thus we have, at the generalising or theoretical level, some sense of the complementarity of approaches and where the various elements fit in to that theoretical structure. But the model then turns towards the specific again, as the theoretical approaches of resolution and settlement become translated in specific, context-relative practical strategies most appropriate to each element.

The significance of this process of translation into context is vital. The point can be illustrated simply by drawing a comparison between two different conflicts. For example, both the Northern Ireland conflict and that in Israel/Palestine contain the same subjective element of negative mutual stereotypes arising from a lack of communication and understanding. The complementarity model would prescribe a resolution approach focused on consultation and facilitated dialogue in both cases, and yet the appropriate practical forms of consultation in each conflict could be very different. For example, one of the forms consultation takes in Northern Ireland is that of encouraging or facilitating focused dialogue on stereotyping and discrimination in work practices within workplace groups. This is effective because many such groups are religiously mixed and so the process involves interaction between the two communities. In Israel/Palestine, consultation would also be prescribed but, given the segregated nature of most workplaces there, there would be little point in developing such a specific practical strategy: consultation would have to be translated into some other context-relevant action. Likewise, it could be said that the conflicts in both Northern Ireland and Israel/Palestine involve the objective issue of resource competition between two communal-ethnic groups, and that negotiation or power mediation is the prescribed means to solve both problems. But while resource competition in Northern Ireland is mostly over government-sourced economic development schemes and public and private employment, in Israel/Palestine the competition is much more complex: for example, it includes the fight for access to water, and to water-bearing territory. It is unlikely that the same procedure for bringing together community leaders to negotiate with government over its economic policy in Northern Ireland will work to solve conflict over water in Israel/Palestine. For a start, the water debate cannot be addressed comprehensively without involving several external sovereign states. In each situation, the context-relevant translation of negotiation over scarce resources will follow a radically different form. This may become clearer in the detailed outline below.

A schematic representation of the model is given in Figure 8.1(overleaf). The sketch is unashamedly untidy and incomplete, precisely because, as I have argued, neat models arise from the tendency to over-universalise, while my whole aim is to restrain universalising in order to make the model more sensitive to the untidiness, the uniqueness, and the confusion of its subject matter: complex social conflict.

The Descriptive Phase: generalised criteria

The model's first aim is to build a complex description of the conflict. The degree of complexity is necessary to ensure that all relevant elements of the conflict are included. While by no means ignoring the conflict's history, the picture to be constructed is less concentrated on time and development and more interested in reflecting accurately the current state of the conflict and its dynamics. In this sense, the complementarity model emphasises (though not exclusively) a synchronic description which includes all current elements, in preference to the heavily diachronic emphasis of the contingency model. The implication of this, of course, is that in order to take into consideration both the temporal dynamic of the conflict and its history and develop-ment, this synchronic 'snapshot' needs to be taken and retaken regularly, as the pattern of elements changes with time. In other words, the model would need to be reapplied at intervals in order to remain flexible to the shifting dynamics of conflict.

The objectives of this descriptive phase are twofold: to achieve a complex view of the conflict, and to identify the main elements and the main actors or groupings involved with each. The means to these ends can be found in using the generalised criteria. This process involves asking a series of questions based on an adapted version of Fisher and Keashly's six factors or axes. The process of adaptation needs comment, and reference can again be made to Table 4.1 (p. 82).

As Chapter 4 argued, the contingency model's factors (or axes)

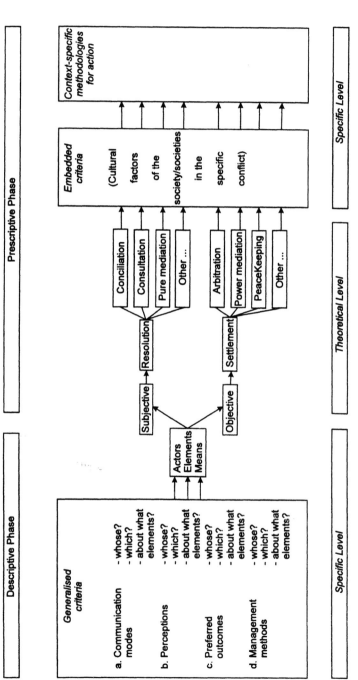

Figure 8.1 A Model of Complementarity in Conflict Management

for diagnosing the conflict stage can be transformed by detaching them from the framework of escalatory stages. They become instead a series of elicitive, open-ended (rather than either/or) questions through which will be achieved an initial view of the complexity of the conflict. As they stand in the contingency model, the factors are limiting since they lead to defining and categorising questions with a very limited range of only four possible answers. But detached from their prescriptive purpose, and from the idea that each axis-point indicates a temporal stage of the conflict, these then become the cues not for a prescriptive decision about 'the adoption of one strategy over another' (Fisher and Keashly 1991, p. 34), but for drawing a complex descriptive map of the conflict's elements.

For example, instead of asking which alone of four modes of communication is in operation at the moment (and using the answer to assign the conflict to a stage), a much more sophisticated descriptive answer can be drawn from asking the open-ended version of the question: which constituencies or groupings (or sub-groupings) are communicating over which elements of the conflict in which manner? Transferring the set of factors to the complementarity model in this way, they become the *generalised* criteria by which we gauge the nature of the conflict.

However, we can dispose of two of the six factors in the contingency model. These are the state of the relationship, and the emphasised issues. These become extraneous in the transition from factors to criteria, for the simple reason that they become not descriptive factors so much as the substance of the conflict, the categories (objective issue-based, and subjective relationship-based) into which we want later to put the elements identified through the other four criteria. Translated into criteria, these two factors ask the questions: what are the subjective (relationship-oriented) elements of this conflict? and what are the objective (issue-based) elements of this conflict? But the answers to these two questions are the end-result of the questions asked about the other four criteria, and so they are in this way already superfluous. If the four questions based on the generalised criteria are answered as comprehensively as possible, all the relevant elements of the conflict, subjective and objective, should already have been made apparent. If we did not expect to find problems relating to both the relationship and the issues – a subjective–objective mix – we would not be bothering with complementary approaches and would have no need for a model designed to energise them.

Consequently, if it is taken as read that the other four criteria – communication modes, perceptions, perceived outcomes and preferred strategies – exist largely to illustrate the balance of relationship elements and issue elements in the conflict, we can collapse the six factors into just four, and proceed by asking the open-ended questions surrounding the four remaining generalised criteria. Finally, with the original diagnostic factors now operating as purely descriptive criteria, there seems no good reason to retain the four-only pattern of possible answers to each question. While the possible answers identified by Fisher and Keashly are by and large valid and informative, we might allow for the possibilities of finding in use, for example, a means of communication or a preferred means of conflict management other than the four possibilities listed in the contingency model. This reflects the complementarity model's inductive approach of drawing out the information about the conflict under consideration from the specific context, without any pre-definition of what will be found, rather than turning to the context to look for pre-defined phenomena.

The difference between Fisher and Keashly's factors and the complementarity model's translation of them into generalised criteria is at its clearest when comparing the different questions each provokes. The questions asked by Fisher and Keashly are as follows:

- First, which single one of four communication modes is in operation in this conflict: discussion and debate, indirect (mis)interpretation, threats, or silence and violence? As a generalised criterion, this becomes: Who is communicating over which element(s) of the conflict by which means?
- Second, which single one of four modes of perceptions and images is in operation in this conflict: benign and accurate images, rigid and simplified negative stereotypes, a good v. evil dichotomy, or views of the other(s) as non-human? In the generalised criteria, this becomes: Who utilises which perceptions and images of themselves, the conflict and the other(s), in relation to which element?
- Third, which single one of four possible outcomes is preferred in this conflict: win–win, mutual compromise, win–lose,

or lose–lose? As a generalised criterion, this becomes: Who envisages which possible outcomes over which elements?

- Fourth, which single one of four methods of conflict management has preference in this conflict: joint decision-making, negotiation, defensive competition, or outright destruction? In the generalised criteria, this becomes: Who utilises which means of conflict management over which elements?

The descriptive phase therefore comprises looking for the answers to four open-ended questions. Such a re-use or re-interpretation of Fisher and Keashly's original factors as generalised criteria immediately provides a far richer and more sophisticated picture of the conflict under consideration, while at the same time dispelling any possibility of categorising this richness into one simplistic escalatory stage and applying either resolution or settlement. The descriptive phase of the complementarity model thus produces a far more intricate tapestry of material with which to work.

The Prescriptive Phase: embedded criteria

Once description has been worked through sufficiently, it identifies an array of elements which go to make up the conflict. A distinction can be made between those which are objective or substantive issues, and those which are subjective or relationship-oriented, and some very general prescription can be attained by initially assigning them, according to this subjective–objective mix, for a resolution or a settlement approach. Further, the description provides a picture of the actors most involved over each element, and also a view of the means each of them use to address that element and the goals they are working towards. Prescription now demands that practical strategies are outlined for addressing each element. The means by which these methodologies are identified, designed or modified is via the use of embedded criteria, for it is at this point that we look to the internal context to see what is needed, what is possible, what is relevant and what is appropriate.

The embedded criteria, however, are implicit in their context. They comprise all the cultural (in its widest, systemic, sense) factors – social, historical, political, economic, geographic, psychological, and so on – which make the society (or societies) involved in the conflict unique in its own right, and which then determine the most relevant translation of the generalised tools of settlement and resolution into specific methodologies of action. Even for those on the ground who act as the practitioners of particular approaches or strategies, it is difficult to express the criteria upon which they decide what strategy to develop or adopt. Indeed, in the course of the case studies for this book, asking why people chose one approach over another in interviews produced a mystified response in every case, which suggests not that the people involved simply did not know the answer but that the wrong question was being asked. No one was aware of having adopted one exclusive approach or strategy or arena of operations while rejecting another. Most people who become involved in reconciliation work in Northern Ireland, for example, did not make a conscious choice to adopt reconciliation and reject politics. The choice was largely unconscious, dictated by the situational factors surrounding any given individual. As I have remarked before, individuals in Northern Ireland do not cease to function as political citizens because they become community relations workers (and vice versa.) None the less, different people address the conflict in different ways: in Fitzduff's words, 'People start from where they are and with the resources they have.' In a real sense, then, the embedded criteria are by definition implicit in the context. They comprise all the specific aspects of the context from which can be elicited the resources for translating general approaches into specific action. They are, in Lederach's words, the 'implicit but constructive images and assumptions present . . . [which] build towards an explicit model' (1995, p. 100).

The initial descriptive phase provides a picture of what the elements of the conflict are, and which should be amenable to a resolution or a settlement approach. On the basis of that distinction, it would then be possible, in the manner of Fisher and Keashly, to make broad prescriptions for consultation, arbitration, pure mediation, and so on, as appropriate. But such general terms still require a translation into context before they can be implemented.

This is not usefully possible at the level of the generalised, universal model. It can only be done effectively from a starting point within the context. It is a dual process of elicitation from, and translation to, the context. Generalisation advances us to the point where the question can be asked: 'How then can the approaches of resolution and settlement – and their methods of power mediation, pure mediation, arbitration, conciliation, consultation, peacekeeping, and so on – be applied to this conflict?' The answer can be developed only from a starting point internal to the conflict. Thus, all a generalising, universally applicable, model can offer at this point is to provide a gap, an empty space in its workings where the theoretical strategy can be translated into relevant practical methodologies. For example, even if a variety of conflicts produce generalised prescriptions of resolution and settlement, and even if for all of them those translate into cultural and structural approaches, the practical forms of those approaches will likely still be unique in each case, because the context-specific questions still remain: what culture(s), and which structures? Use of the embedded criteria within the empty space of the generalised model ensures that such questions are asked and answered, and that the results draw on the context to prescribe strategies most suited to it.

At the initial specific level, in the descriptive phase, the generalised criteria are applied. This produces complex and information-rich answers concerning the actors, elements and means present within the conflict. When these are inserted into the prescriptive phase, where we rise briefly to the theoretical level, the elements in particular can be assessed as generally subjective or generally objective and assigned to resolution or settlement approaches. Then, returning again to the specific level, the tools of these approaches are filtered through the embedded criteria to produce the context-specific methodologies for action which best suit the conflict in question. Of course, the theoretical model at this point offers only a blank space where the methodologies fit, precisely so that the model can only be completed by means of input from the real circumstances of the conflict.

Imagine a complex social conflict, Conflict X, to which the complementarity model is applied: the application indicates that it has both subjective and objective elements, and so needs a complementary mix of resolution and settlement. Further, the translation of these approaches into the specific context of Conflict X produces both structural and cultural strategies for management of the conflict. Would these practical strategies then be identical to the cultural and structural strategies identified in Northern Ireland? No: because the embedded criteria – the unique social, cultural, political, economic, historical, etc., aspects of the conflict which provide its context – would be different in Conflict X.

The descriptive phase produces a complex description of the conflict: a sense of what the objective and subjective elements at stake are, who the involved groupings are in relation to each element, and what processes have been and are used by those groupings over those elements. The prescriptive phase then asks: what is to be done, and by whom? The implication of complementarity is that it should be possible to apply resolution techniques to the subjective elements and settlement techniques to the objective elements. But this goes no further than saying, for example as regards Northern Ireland, 'on the objective elements of territorial sovereignty, structures of governance, physical security, resource competition and so on, the range of settlement techniques including power mediation, arbitration and peace-keeping are prescribed'. While certainly putting us on the right track (for example, so that we do not prescribe power mediation for non-negotiable matters of cultural identity) this remains too general. The key question of the prescriptive stage is: who can address which element, and by which means? Thus, we now employ the embedded criteria to translate into a context-specific form the practical methodologies which these general approaches prescribe.

In the case of Northern Ireland, these context-specific methodologies for action are, in fact, what constituted the subject matter of earlier chapters: the structural and cultural practical approaches. It is important to note that I am not arguing that the structural and cultural approaches in Northern Ireland are the same as, or synonymous with, settlement and resolution. The whole point is rather that the structural and cultural approaches are settlement and resolution *translated into practical action in the context of Northern Ireland*. This translation is predicated on the basis of the embedded criteria, the various relevant context-specific aspects of Northern Ireland.

The resulting context-specific methodologies for action comprise a detailed set of prescriptions -- worked out in a complementary framework – targeted at specific elements of the conflict, involving specific groupings within the conflict. The aim of this complementary approach ultimately is not either resolution or settlement of the conflict: rather, both approaches combine through complementarity to produce in concert a stage where the conflict is transformed, gradually but comprehensively, into a more positive and healthy, less destructive and negative, formation.

CONCLUSION AND SUMMARY

The complementarity model includes three simple improvements over the contingency model. First, it greatly increases the degree of descriptive input into the model. A far more complex and realistic picture emerges of the conflict under examination, which provides a much richer information base from which to progress to prescription. Second, by leaving the space for embedded criteria, it significantly increases the amount of elicitive information in the model. The model becomes immediately more sensitive and responsive to the conflict in question, avoiding the degree of generalisation in the contingency model that results in blanket prescriptions across what may be widely diverse contexts. And third, in providing a means for complexity of description, it improves on the simplistic and mechanistic tenor of the sequential, stage-based view of conflict dynamics, and permits a far broader repertoire of simultaneous strategies for conflict-solving.

While these are significant improvements, together they comprise one very small contribution to understanding the dynamics of divided societies. The main thrust of this book has been to illuminate theory in the light of realities in the Northern Ireland conflict. In the process, however, I have, via the mechanism of the complementarity model, attempted to illustrate the particular nature of the divided society of Northern Ireland. At the heart of that argument has been an understanding of the importance of learning from real experience; of theory-building that begins inductively from the starting point of real life; of the need for humility in the academy when balancing the asymmetry of neat models and untidy realities; and finally of an inclusive prescriptive approach that retains the potential to range across all possible resources of help and, crucially, leaves room for the invention of specific strategies for change from within specific conflicts. Underpinning my entire argument is a belief that such principles can improve both our theory and our practice in conflict management in tangible ways, at the acceptable, even welcome, cost of a reduction in the overarching theoretical ambitions sometimes rampant in the field of conflict analysis.

It is to the shame of conflict management theorists that a scholar of the standing of John Whyte could express disappointment that his attempt to apply their literature to the Northern Ireland context was 'largely a waste of time' (see Introduction). It is my contention that such criticism arises in large part because too many theories and models of conflict lose much of their relevance to reality in the course of their search for overarching universalities, and that the remedy lies in redressing the balance through an increased emphasis on learning inductively from reality and in making such theories and models more sensitive to the contexts they aspire to explain.

9 Concluding Remarks

1. COMPLEMENTARITY

In the Introduction, I referred to the pressing need, in the post-Cold War context, to broaden the definitions and approaches of conflict management beyond the old power-based strategies of containment in order to take account of those more subjective, but no less potent, factors clustering around issues of identity and communal security. This study has in part tried to demonstrate that to ignore, or to under-represent, the perceptual layers which surround complex social conflict and to reduce the dispute to one of only objective issues, like territorial sovereignty, is to simplify matters in such a way as to curtail the possibilities of successful transformation. To do so would necessitate the dismissal of all the Northern Ireland evidence from Chapters 1, 3 and 6, which demonstrates both the importance of such issues in the minds of protagonists and the extensive attention being paid to addressing those issues.

Similarly, to concentrate a diagnosis of conflict on matters relating only to identity and perception, and to aim to heal relationships without addressing incompatible positions over political or resource issues, would produce an equally partial and incomplete picture and subsequent prescription. The popular short-hand description of the conflict(s) in former Yugoslavia as essentially 'ethnic' comes to mind. To dismiss what has been happening in Bosnia as simply a war between ethnic factions bent on destruction is at best unhelpful and at worst obstructive: while it makes the problem very simple to understand from outside, it completely elides the political elements of territory, power, resources and control which contribute forcefully to the conflict's dynamic. (It also, of course, implies the outsider's insult that 'they' are caught up in some sadly atavistic quarrel that 'we' are too civilised ever to fall into.) Likewise, to describe events in Rwanda and Burundi as simply a matter of ethnic hatred between Hutus and Tutsis is to concentrate on the tribal 'boundary factor' of that conflict, without an appreciation of the social and economic differences which parallel the 'ethnic' divide.

217

When the term 'ethnic conflict' is bandied about, there is always the danger of mistaking the wrapping for the contents: Northern Ireland's protagonists use religious labels as the badges by which they differentiate and identify themselves, but – as this study soundly demonstrates – the conflict is not waged over matters of religious observance. Ethnic difference often creates fault-lines in a society which mirror other non-ethnic cleavages; but, for example, to describe Northern Ireland's conflict as one merely over religious or ethnic issues completely devalues and dismisses the aims and intentions of the whole Civil Rights reform movement there in the 1960s. Those mostly Catholic protesters were identifying themselves as some sort of 'ethnic' group suffering discrimination; but their goals had little to do with religious freedom and everything to do with social and economic issues. Likewise, most of those Protestants who opposed the protesters cared very little about Catholic religion *per se*, but cared supremely about the political disloyalty and subversion of their unionist state which they perceived among the Catholic protesters. These Catholics were, first and foremost, a political threat rather than a religious one, despite their primary recognisability as Catholics.

I have attempted here in a small way to answer that call for broader strategies of conflict management by offering the concept of complementarity. I have argued that by using the complementarity model to analyse, diagnose and prescribe in relation to a complex conflict, the product is guaranteed to be broader in its understanding of the conflict's elements and in its prescription for the conflict's transformation. This is the result of two aspects of the model: first, the model's insistence on the inclusion of a much wider range of context-specific information at the descriptive phase; and secondly, the use of complementarity itself to energise a more comprehensive and coordinated range of prescriptive strategies which are aligned with the generalisations of conflict management theory but also attuned to the specific context under consideration.

The arguments offered in the development of the model concentrate both on deepening and enriching the understanding of conflict and on broadening the repertoire of responses, in such a way that neither subjective or objective issues, nor cultural or structural approaches, can be overlooked. This has implications not merely for conflict management theory. It also relates to practice. If more evidence were needed, the arguments for complementarity deny the possibility of addressing complex social conflict with the old tools of power-based containment or coercion alone.

This is to suggest that the ideas developed here have both an applicability and a validation in other contexts. In particular, the idea of complementarity has potential in situations of intervention in complex social conflict, specifically for third-party intervention such as that of the UN. Indeed, one can argue for a refinement of the concept of peace-building to include an understanding of the positive role to be played by parties internal to the conflict in addressing relationship issues at inter-communal level. That could then enable an argument for complementarity between peacekeeping and peace-building which might greatly increase the effectiveness and comprehensiveness of UN operations in such contexts. That is, however, a debate for another time.

The initial presentation of the complementarity model here also suggests themes for further research. Clearly, the detailed application of the model to another context would yield useful information. For example, my study identified the momentum for complementarity coming from within the cultural approach in Northern Ireland. In another context, could it come from the other side of the fence? Or is there something inherent in the components of the resolution approach which gives it a greater potential for instigating a drawing together of approaches? Seeking answers to such questions will help to broaden the information base about the functioning of complementarity in the real world, and will also feed back a clearer picture of where the model is helpful and where it fails. As long as any proprietary feelings towards the model are held in check, knowledge of its limits and failures can be the most informative means of progressing.

More study, especially on other conflict situations, would help to clarify several key questions. Does the inductive–deductive balance shift according to the situation, or is it a theoretical constant irrespective of the specific context? Northern Ireland has remained largely free of what can be unproblematically identified as third party intervenors: what dynamic would a significant third party bring to the model and to the resolution/settlement debate? Are the strategies of resolution and settlement best practised by separate agents, as they largely are in Northern Ireland, or are they as effective when encompassed by the same agent/s? In particular, how might complementarity best be structured in a situation of UN intervention? Would complementarity there refer to the relationship between different UN policies (say, between peacemaking, peacekeeping and peace-building) or between different UN agencies (between military and civilian operations)? Or would it refer to the relationship between the UN as a third party and 'peacemakers' on the ground from within the conflict? In a situation of international conflict, how about the potential for complementarity between the diplomatic and the unofficial spheres? How would the conscious development of a complementary strategy affect that situation? Would it go some way to address the major obstacles to inter-agency coordination which are so often encountered in international conflict situations? Could it help to underpin coordination between short-term UN peacekeeping initiatives and longer-term UN and NGO aid work? How exactly would the dynamic of complementarity operate in such situations, and how could that assist the refinement and improvement of the model? The distinction between generalised and embedded criteria proved useful, if somewhat inelegant, in the Northern Ireland application: would more theoretical development of the criteria produce a more elegant formation, or is inelegance a worthy price to pay for applicability? Northern Ireland fits the description of protracted social conflict. Application of the model to other protracted social conflicts would broaden the information base about the model's usefulness through a comparative approach. But what of applying it to other kinds of conflict – international, interpersonal, intergroup, and so on? Certainly, approaching the model from the widest possible variety of different angles will most quickly help to validate or falsify its components.

Throughout this book, one important theme has underpinned the argument for complementarity. That has been the recurring tension between generalisation and specificity, between simplification and complexity, between the universality of theoretical models and the uniqueness of the situations to which they are applied. This thread of argument has to do with fundamental issues in the methodology of conflict management research. In that context, then, I have argued for a methodological complementarity which more evenly permits the processes of both induction and deduction in the generation of theories and models. The main argument presented here for complementarity in conflict management models stands as an example of the issues involved around this tension between modes of theorising. Real social conflicts may well be confused, complex, contradictory and messy processes, but these problems will not serve as excuses which permit the scholar of integrity to take exclusive refuge in the cool, rational clarity of theory. Theory can indeed bring useful clarity to bear; but it should not do so in order to bring neatness at the expense of realism. Generalising theory can offer a degree of overview essential in achieving a more balanced framework for analysis; inductive ideas based on real examples, messy or otherwise, can assist in the construction of that same framework by keeping it relevant and, quite literally, grounded.

2. NORTHERN IRELAND

While Northern Ireland has to some degree served a secondary role in this study, acting as the real-world foil for a theoretical debate, none the less some interesting conclusions have emerged which have a salience specific to the conflict. The analysis of the conflict presented in the previous chapters has both clarified and validated the various ongoing efforts there at conflict transformation. The luxury of hindsight and overview has permitted an analysis of political developments since 1968 which suggests a greater degree of coherence and intention than is often acknowledged. Similarly, the review of developments in the cultural approach has suggested that out of disparate beginnings an increasingly focused and directed strategy has been emerging. Far more centrally, however, the argument has been proffered that in practice both approaches validate and complement each other.

I write in the immediate aftermath of the IRA statement of 9 February 1996 announcing the breakdown of their ceasefire. None the less, whatever the current frustrations, these have been exciting times for Northern Ireland, as the ceasefires provided a respite from violence which few would have previously had the confidence to imagine. The momentum on the structural side has increased: progress towards an inclusive framework for political dialogue among all parties inches forward. It may all come to nothing, but there are grounds for at least a minimal optimism as we watch the politicians grapple with bewildering changes in their previously becalmed political landscape. The developments on the structural side will have implications for the cultural approach. Certainly, a long-term removal of violence would go some way to clear the atmosphere of much of the fear and protectionism that has characterised intercommunal dialogue and interaction for so long. The ongoing efforts to shift the cultural agenda to encompass the 'difficult issues' will become much easier if those issues no longer carry the potential to cause death. Community relations may find itself freed of some of the suspicion with which it has been treated. Dialogue, of all kinds and at all levels, suddenly becomes much more feasible when removed from the shadow of violence which has hovered behind every word for so long.

Specifically, the two case-studies presented here will take on an added significance if the current trends continue. The importance of the Brooke Initiative has a particular resonance. With hindsight, it is clear that Brooke's public overtures to Sinn Féin, although an apparently secondary strategy at the time, constituted only the visible element of Sinn Féin–British government dialogue in 1990–3, leading ultimately towards the 1994 ceasefire and to the potential involvement of Sinn Féin in the political process. Perhaps even more importantly, it is very clear that any future talks process will be based securely within the three-strand framework which Brooke developed in 1991. Indeed, both the Irish and British governments have publicly committed themselves to it as the blueprint for forthcoming negotiations. As future developments unfold in the political arena, closer study of the Brooke Initiative than was possible here will yield lessons for the resumption of political dialogue.

Should political dialogue bear fruit in terms of addressing possible structures for the governance of Northern Ireland, the cultural approach will become even more significant. There is a pleasing symmetry here: while recent events in the structural arena will enable easier progress in the cultural arena, those same events will increase the necessity of such progress. So the breakthrough on the structural side will not only produce renewed momentum for progress on the cultural side; the results of that momentum will in turn rebound positively in providing a healthier relationship and a more conducive atmosphere within which further structural movement can be achieved.

Protracted social conflict, like that in Northern Ireland, can often appear deadlocked and stagnant. That can breed a stasis of analysis, too, as the continuity of entrenched positions becomes comfortingly familiar. But when moments of drama occur, and the kaleidoscope of factors is shaken about, as has happened in Northern Ireland, they provide opportunities to look afresh at the situation, to develop new or more refined analyses, and to discard those which cannot assimilate the new situation. While it may involve the scholar in dispensing with some cherished notions, it is a situation to be positively embraced. Future events in Northern Ireland – for better or worse – will no doubt challenge the analysis presented here in healthy ways that can only improve that analysis.

In Northern Ireland, complementarity is not only possible, it is necessary. Indeed, complementarity is not only being attempted, it is working. The importance of the concept can be simply stated in practical terms. If all the involved politicians completely settled their dispute tomorrow, by developing a comprehensive settlement over agreed structures for the future political landscape of the entire region, the settlement would still stand or fall on the presence or absence of 'widespread acceptance'. For it to flourish in a sustained and durable form, it would depend on the existence of the atmosphere of trust, respect, cooperation and optimism within and between the Catholic and Protestant communities which the cultural approach aims to develop. Likewise, if those same communities suddenly managed to heal all their wounds and entered into a new relationship of complete trust and cooperation, they would still need the processes of the structural approach to provide a framework in which to operate their new society. Healthy and inclusive structures can support, even nurture, the different cultures and identities which they underpin; and healthy and inclusive relationships can sustain, even nurture, the structures within which they exist. That is the kind of functioning and transformative complementarity which Northern Ireland deserves, and which its people now may have an opportunity to achieve.

Appendix
Biographical Details of
Interviewees

All interviews were tape-recorded. Approval of the subsequent text was sought and obtained from all interviewees. In the text, interview quotations are the only ones to appear without full textual reference.

Joan Broder works for the Probation Board NI and the Extern Organisation in Belfast. Qualified as a probation officer, and with an MA in Social Policy, she trained as a mediator with Community Boards of San Francisco in 1986, and has since worked to develop the concept and practice of community mediation in Northern Ireland, and of mediation within services to criminal offenders and victims of crime. She has been Chair of the Conflict Mediation Network in Belfast since 1989, and was Chair of Victim Support NI 1989–94. She was a founder member of both organisations. She also works as a consultant trainer in mediation and conflict resolution skills for the Community Relations Council, Conflict Mediation Network and other agencies. She is a member of the Community Relations Council Sub-committee for Reconciliation.
   Interviewed at Magheraknock, Northern Ireland, 26 October 1993.

Peter Brooke is Conservative MP for the constituency of the City of London and Westminster South. He entered the British parliament in 1977, and has since held a variety of party and government positions, among them Conservative Party Chair 1987–9, and Secretary of State for National Heritage 1992–4. He served as Secretary of State for Northern Ireland from July 1989 to April 1992.
   Interviewed at the Department of National Heritage, Whitehall, London, 20 September 1993.

Mari Fitzduff is Director of the Community Relations Council

in Belfast. She has a PhD in Peace Studies from the University of Ulster. She is widely known throughout Northern Ireland and internationally as a trainer, writer and policy-maker on community relations work in Northern Ireland.
Interviewed at the CRC, Belfast, 20 October 1993.

Joe Hinds was Director of Northern Ireland Children's Holiday Schemes, a youth reconciliation agency, from 1986–91. Since 1991, he has been Development Officer for Peace and Reconciliation Groups with the Community Relations Council. He has an MA in psychology, and has carried out research for Queen's University Belfast into reconciliation work and the contact hypothesis. At the time of writing, he is currently seconded as Programme Coordinator of the Community Bridges Program of the International Fund for Ireland, in Belfast.
Interviewed at the CRC, Belfast, 21 October 1993.

David McKittrick has been Field Officer of Protestant And Catholic Encounter since 1988. Before that, he worked for the Ulster People's College, developing community education programmes in Northern Ireland.
Interviewed at PACE, Belfast, 27 October 1993.

Martin O'Brien has worked since 1987 for the Committee on the Administration of Justice, a monitoring and campaigning group concerned with issues of human rights and civil liberties in Northern Ireland. In 1992, he received the Reebok Human Rights Award for this work. He has been an involved member of the Peace People since its formation in 1976. He was co-founder of Youth For Peace and of the Irish Network for Nonviolent Action Training and Education (INNATE). He is chair of the Peace People's residential centre, and chair of the Peace People Charitable Trust.
Interviewed at the CAJ, Belfast, 28 October 1993.

Jerry Tyrrell was Director of Holiday Projects West, a youth reconciliation agency based in Derry, Northern Ireland, from 1973 to 1988. Since 1988 he has worked as Director of the Quaker Peace Education Project (QPEP) in Northern Ireland, developing mediation and conflict resolution training programmes for schools and youth groups. He is an affiliate of the

US National Coalition Building Institute, and a leading practitioner of prejudice reduction workshops in Northern Ireland. He has an MA in Peace Studies from the University of Ulster. He also works as a consultant trainer and practitioner in conflict resolution skills for a wide variety of agencies in Northern Ireland. Within Quaker circles, he has travelled widely to teach his skills and approach in a variety of international settings. In 1994, QPEP evolved into the EMU Promoting School Project.

Interviewed at the Centre for the Study of Conflict, University of Ulster, Coleraine, 29 October 1993.

Notes

1. Subsequent to developments on the broader scale, in particular the Anglo-Irish process which has produced not only the milestone of the Anglo-Irish Agreement of 1985, but more recently the Downing Street Joint Declaration of 1993 and the Framework Document of 1994, an argument could be made that the view of the conflict is once again opening out beyond the merely 'internal conflict' model to a more useful combination of elements of both a British–Irish conflict and an internal conflict.

2. Quoted directly by the Irish government in its proposals tabled at the Strand 2 negotiations in Autumn 1992 (*Irish Times*, 11 November 1992).

3. Ever since the decision by young nationalists in the mid-1960s to enter the political arena to claim their representational rights as citizens, rather than uphold the traditionally nationalist abstentionist stance, it was more clearly an internal conflict.

4. As political unionism began to fragment at this time, the Ulster Unionist Party (UUP) was beset by new unionist groupings: the DUP, the Ulster Popular Unionist Party (UPUP), the Unionist Party of Northern Ireland (UPNI), the Vanguard Unionist Party (VUP), the United Ulster Unionist Party (UUUP), and so on. For simplicity's sake during these years of fragmentation, the UUP became more frequently referred to as the Official Unionist Party (OUP). Apart from the DUP, few of these parties were long-lasting, but the habit still remains in some quarters of referring inaccurately to the OUP. For sake of clarity and consistency, and since the unionist fragmentation is not central to my argument, I use the term UUP throughout the book, even though for this brief mid-1970s period it might be temporarily inaccurate to do so.

5. The NICRC itself did not escape criticism of a middle-class bias. One NILP politician dismissed it as 'providing employment and amusement for academics who are in many cases remote from the people'. He wondered publicly if 'the working class [are] not good enough to serve on the commission. They certainly could not do a worse job than their supposed betters who dominate it at the moment.... Until the working class are actively involved ... the government is wasting time and money' (*Belfast Telegraph*, 6 December 1973). His opinion was not an isolated one at the time.

6. The necessary informality of the cultural approach also leads to a lack of documentation of its development. Consequently, this section is based on the modicum of written resources available on the subject, combined with my own experience as director (1982–7) of one of the holiday organisations/reconciliation groups mentioned, and on conversations and interviews with those directly involved in the development of the voluntary organisations in the field.

7. An earlier version of some of the arguments in this chapter appeared as an article in the Journal of Peace Research (Bloomfield 1995).

8. Of course, such a terminological choice is arbitrary to some extent, but in

its support I might quote Kenneth Boulding. Reflecting 21 years after founding the *Journal of Conflict Resolution*, he commented: 'In the light of hindsight I think perhaps we should have called the *Journal*, the Journal of Conflict Management, as I think frequently conflicts are not and perhaps should not be resolved, but should be managed' (Boulding 1978, p. 344).

9. 1. In common parlance these four parties comprise the main 'constitutional' parties in Northern Ireland. Sinn Fein, despite having at the time a Westminster MP (something Alliance has never achieved) was excluded by the common consent of all concerned because of its partnership with the Provisional IRA in the Republican movement.

    2. The Alliance Party figures little in what follows in this chapter, for two reasons. First, it has a smaller membership, a smaller constituency, no elected representatives higher than Local Council level and overall a considerably smaller power-base than most of the other parties. Secondly, being previously committed both to a dialogue process and to devolution, the Alliance view of the talks process rarely differed significantly from that of the British government. Thus, having declared its support for Brooke and for the talks process early on, its members had little further to contribute to the stalemate that followed subsequently, except to reiterate their position, and by and large support all that Brooke said.

10. Integrationism, at one time the guiding principle of Ulster Unionism but by Brooke's time entering decline due, at least in part, to repeated expressions of British antipathy to the whole idea, aspires to see Northern Ireland governed from Westminster on the very same principles and by the very same process as any region of Britain. It is, thus, the very antithesis of the local parliament at the heart of devolution.

11. Brooke's own comments on the question of the Strand 2 chair are informative: 'Now I always suspected we might have difficulties with this particular matter. But I had to make the decision in March 1991: do we add this to the mountains we've got to cross before we actually get everyone to the table, or do we get to the table and then seek to sort it out there? And I think I'd make exactly the same decision again.... It's arguable that if we'd added it to the things we had to do, given the limited window of time we had before the general election, I don't think we would have actually got to the table.'

12. The Protestant paramilitaries, whose resurgence began during Brooke's period in office and developed subsequently, must be accepted as a second source of antagonists for the security forces; but this recognition invalidates neither the Republican paramilitaries' view of Britain and its army as the primary enemy, nor this argument against seeing the British army as peacekeepers.

13. This marriage of convenience was at the insistence of Brian Mawhinney, then the British minister responsible for community relations, and against the wishes of some of those involved. As Hinds later commented: 'Since the formation of the CRC, the Cultural Traditions Group has remained quite distinctive and distant, and the existence of two groups with possibly two different approaches and means of emphasis has created continual tension within the Council in general' (written communication to the author, 18 August 1994).

14. Written communication to the author, 11 March 1994.
15. In 1994, the Quaker Peace Education Project was replaced by the EMU Promoting School Project, with Tyrrell still at the helm.
16. In terms redolent of the essence of the cultural approach, DENI has defined the aims of EMU as enabling pupils:
    – to learn to respect and value themselves and others;
    – to appreciate the interdependence of people within society;
    – to know about and understand what is shared as well as what is different about their cultural traditions;
    – to appreciate how conflict may be handled in non- violent ways. (Smith and Robinson 1992, p. 13)
17. For an excellent review of such public economic development policies, see Maeve Lankford (1994).
18. In this statement, Fitzduff paraphrases only slightly, but in an interesting and forthright way, the CRC's formal statement on the matter: 'The ultimate aim of the Community Relations Council must be to assist in the creation of just and sustainable solutions to the many issues that divide the communities in Northern Ireland' (CRC 1991, p. 5). Further, an interesting contrast can be made between her 1993 definition of her goal – a constitutional solution – and the argument she made with Fraser in 1986 for seeing community relations work in a supportive or enabling (and by implication to some degree subordinate) role to such a goal (Fraser and Fitzduff 1986, p. 19).
19. An example of such effect is the increasing popularity in several Local District Councils of exercising a kind of 'unofficial power-sharing' by an agreement to annually rotate the Chair of the Council among political parties, thus developing a degree of a cooperative, rather than simple majority–minority competitive, strategy.
20. The questions are presented in this form, beginning each time with 'Who?' simply for reasons of neatness, and no privileging of actors over elements or means should be inferred: the questions could be phrased just as effectively, but less elegantly, as, say, 'Which elements are being communicated over by whom and by what means?'

Bibliography

Allister, James, undated [1986?]. *Irish Unification: Anathema*. Belfast, Crown Publications.

Arthur, Paul, 1989. *Government & Politics of Northern Ireland* [third edition]. London, Longman.

Arthur, Paul, 1989a. 'Three Years of the Anglo-Irish Agreement', *Irish Political Studies*, no. 4, pp. 105–9.

Aughey, Arthur, 1989. *Under Siege: Ulster Unionism and the Anglo-Irish Agreement*. Belfast, Blackstaff.

Avruch, Kevin and Peter Black, 1987. 'A Generic Theory of Conflict Resolution: a Critique', *Negotiation Journal*, vol. 3, no. 1, pp. 87–96.

Azar, Edward, 1983. 'The Theory of Protracted Social Conflict and the Challenge of Transforming Conflict Situations', *Monograph Series on World Affairs* (University of Denver), vol. 20, no. 2, pp. 81–99.

Azar, Edward, 1985. 'Protracted International Conflicts: Ten Propositions', *International Interactions*, vol. 12, no. 1, pp. 59–70.

Azar, Edward, 1990. *The Management of Protracted Social Conflict: Theory and Cases*. Aldershot, Dartmouth.

Azar, Edward, and Chung-In Moon, 1986. 'Managing Protracted Social Conflicts in the Third World: Facilitation and Development Diplomacy', *Millenium*, vol. 15, no. 3, pp. 393–406.

Barritt, Denis and Charles Carter, 1972. *The Northern Ireland Problem: A Study in Group Relations* (2nd edition). Oxford, Oxford University Press.

Bercovitch, Jacob, 1984. *Social Conflicts and Third Parties: Strategies of Conflict Resolution*. Boulder, CO, Westview Press.

Bercovitch, Jacob, 1986. 'International Mediation: a Study of the Incidence, Strategies and Conditions of Successful Outcomes', *Co-operation and Conflict*, vol. 21, pp. 155–68.

Bew, Paul and Henry Patterson, 1987. 'The New Stalemate: Unionism and the Anglo-Irish Agreement', in P. Teague (ed.), *Beyond the Rhetoric: Politics, the Economy and Social Policy in Northern Ireland*. London, Lawrence & Wishart, pp. 41–57.

Blair, Brenda, 1991. 'Conflict Resolution Theory Examined in Light of the Brooke Initiative'. Paper presented to *Political Science Association of Ireland* conference, Belfast, 11–13 October.

Bleakley, David, 1972. *Peace In Ulster*. London, Mowbrays.

Bloomfield, David, 1991. 'Needs Theory in Conflict Resolution: a Review of Concepts in the Context of the Northern Ireland Conflict'. Unpublished MA dissertation, University of Bradford.

Bloomfield, David, 1995. 'Towards Complementarity in Conflict Management: Resolution and Settlement in Northern Ireland', *Journal of Peace Research*, vol. 32, no. 2, pp. 151–64.

Boal, Fred and David Livingstone, 1986. 'Protestants in Belfast: A View from the Inside', *Contemporary Review*, vol. 248, no. 1443, pp. 169–75.

Boulding, Kenneth, 1978. 'Future Directions in Conflict and Peace Studies', *Journal of Conflict Resolution*, vol. 22, no. 2, pp. 342–54.

Bruce, Steve, 1990. 'Protestant Resurgence and Fundamentalism', *Political Quarterly*, vol. 61, no. 2, pp. 161–8.

Burton, John W., 1979. *Deviance, Terrorism and War*. Oxford, Martin Robinson.

Burton, John W., 1987. *Resolving Deep-Rooted Conflict: A Handbook*. Lanham, MD, UPA.

Burton, John W., 1990a. *Conflict: Resolution and Provention*. London, Macmillan.

Burton, John W. (ed.), 1990b. *Conflict: Human Needs Theory*. London, Macmillan.

Burton, John W and Dennis D.J. Sandole, 1986. 'Generic Theory: The Basis of Conflict Resolution', *Negotiation Journal*, vol. 2, no. 4, pp. 333–44.

Central Community Relations Unit, 1991. *Community Relations Research Strategy*. Belfast, CCRU.

Central Community Relations Unit, 1993. *Community Relations in Northern Ireland*. Belfast, CCRU.

Channel 4 TV, 1992. 'The Big Picture Show: Northern Ireland'. Broadcast 18 July.

Cmnd. 5259, 1973. *Northern Ireland Constitutional Proposals*.

Cmnd. 5675, 1974. *The Northern Ireland Constitution*.

Cmnd. 7763, 1979. *The Government of Northern Ireland: A Working Paper for a Conference*.

Cmnd. 7950, 1980. *The Government of Northern Ireland: Proposals for Further Discussion*.

Cmnd. 8541, 1982. *Northern Ireland: A Framework for Devolution*.

Cohen, Stephen and Harriet Arnone, 1988. 'Conflict Resolution as the Alternative to Terrorism', *Journal of Social Issues*, vol. 44, no. 2, pp. 175–89.

Community Relations Council, 1990. *A Guide to Peace and Reconciliation Groups*. Belfast, CRC.

Community Relations Council, 1991. *Strategic Plan 1991–1994*. Belfast, CRC.

Community Relations Council, 1991a. *Annual Report*. Belfast, CRC.

Community Relations Council, 1992. *Annual Report*. Belfast, CRC.

Community Relations Council, 1993. *Annual Report*. Belfast, CRC.

Crozier, Maurna (ed.) 1989. *Cultural Traditions in Northern Ireland*. Belfast, Institute of Irish Studies, Queen's University.

Curle, Adam, 1986. *In the Middle: Non-official Mediation in Violent Situations*. Leamington Spa, Berg.

Daly, Cahal, 1991. *The Price of Peace*. Belfast, Blackstaff.

Dawn, 1978. *Dawn Magazine*, nos. 38–9. Dublin, Dawn Group.

Dawn, 1988. *Dawn Train Magazine*, no. 7. Belfast, Dawn Group.

Deutsch, Morton, 1991. 'Subjective Features of Conflict Resolution: Psychological, Social and Cultural Features', in Vayrynen (1991), pp. 26–56.

Fisher, Roger, 1964. 'Fractionating Conflict', in R. Fisher (ed.), *International Conflict and Behavioural Science*. New York, Basic Books, pp. 91–109.

Fisher, Ronald J., 1972. 'The Problem-Solving Workshop in Conflict Resolution', in R.L. Merritt (ed.), *Communication in International Politics*, Urbana, IL, University of Illinois Press, pp. 168–204.

Fisher, Ronald J., 1983. 'Third Party Consultation as a Method of Intergroup Conflict Resolution: A Review of Studies', *Journal of Conflict Resolution*, vol. 27, no. 2, June, pp. 301–34.

Fisher, Ronald J., 1990. 'Needs Theory, Social Identity and an Eclectic Model of Conflict', in Burton (ed.) (1990b), pp. 89–112.

Fisher, Ronald J. and Loraleigh Keashley, 1988. 'Third Party Interventions in Intergroup Conflict: Consultation is not Mediation', *Negotiation Journal*, vol. 4, no. 4, October, pp. 381–94.

Fisher, Ronald J. and Loraleigh Keashly, 1991. 'The Potential Complementarity of Mediation and Consultation within a Contingency Model of Third Party Intervention', *Journal of Peace Research*, vol. 28, no. 1, pp. 29–42.

Fitzduff, Mari, 1989. *A Typology of Community Relations Work and Contextual Necessities*. CRC Pamphlet No. 1. Belfast, Community Relations Council.

Fitzduff, Mari, 1991. 'The Plight and the Task of the Liberals . . .' Paper given to *Political Studies Association of Ireland* conference, Belfast, October.

Fitzduff, Mari, 1992. *Practising Conflict Resolution in Divided Societies. Northern Ireland – A Case Study*. Belfast, Community Relations Council, unpublished draft.

Fitzduff, Mari, 1993. *Uneasy Partners? Government, Community Relations, and the Voluntary Sector*. Belfast, Community Relations Council, unpublished draft.

FitzGerald, Garret, 1991. *All In a Life: An Autobiography*. Dublin, Gill & Macmillan.

Flackes, W.D. and Sydney Elliott, 1989. *Northern Ireland: A Political Directory 1968–1988*. Belfast, Blackstaff.

Foster, John Wilson, 1988. 'Who Are the Irish?' *Studies*, vol. 27 no. 308, pp. 403–21.

Frazer, Hugh and Mari Fitzduff, 1986. *Improving Community Relations: A Paper Prepared for the Standing Advisory Commission on Human Rights*. Belfast, Community Relations Council.

Galtung, Johan, 1993. *Peace Studies: Peace and Conflict: Development and Civilisation*. Unpublished compendium.

Gillwald, Katrin, 1990. 'Conflict and Needs Research', in Burton (1990b), pp. 115–24.

Griffiths, Hywel, 1974. *Community Development in Northern Ireland: A Case-Study in Agency Conflict*. Occasional Paper in Social Administration. Coleraine, New University of Ulster.

Hadden, Tom and Kevin Boyle, 1989. *The Anglo-Irish Agreement: Commentary, Text and Official Review*. Dublin, Higel.

Harding, Sandra, 1986. 'The Instability of the Analytic Categories of Feminist Theory', *Signs: Journal of Women in Culture and Society*, vol. 11, no. 4, pp. 645–64.

Hayes, Maurice 1972. *Community Relations and the Role of the Community Relations Commission in Northern Ireland*. Runnymede Trust.

Hewstone, Miles and Rupert Brown (eds.), 1986. *Contact and Conflict in Intergroup Encounters*. Oxford, Blackwell.

HMSO, 1972. *The Future of Northern Ireland: a Paper for Discussion*. Green Paper.

Hoffmann, Mark, 1992. 'Third-Party Mediation and Conflict-Resolution in the Post-Cold War World', in J. Baylis and N.R. Rennger (eds.), *Dilemmas of World Politics: International Issues in a Changing World*. Oxford, Clarendon, pp. 261–86.

Holst, Johan Jorgen, 1990. *Civilian-Based Defence in a New Era*. Monograph Series no. 2. Cambridge MA, Albert Einstein Institution.

Hunter, John, 1982. 'An Analysis of the Conflict in Northern Ireland', in Rea (1982), pp. 9–59.

Jackson, Alvin, 1989. 'Unionist History (1)', *The Irish Review*, no. 7, pp. 58–66.

Keashly, Loraleigh and Ronald J. Fisher, 1990. 'Towards a Contingency Approach to Third Party Intervention in Regional Conflict: A Cyprus illustration', *International Journal*, XLV, Spring, pp. 424–53.

Kelman, Herbert, 1991. 'Interactive Problem Solving: the Uses and Limits of a Therapeutic Model for the Resolution of International Conflicts', in Vamik Volkan et al. (eds.), *The Psychodynamics of International Relationships. Vol. 2: Unofficial Diplomacy at Work.* Lexington, MA, Lexington, pp. 145–60.

Kenny, Anthony, 1986. *The Road to Hillsborough: The Shaping of the Anglo-Irish Agreement.* Oxford, Pergamon.

Kressel, Kenneth and Dean Pruitt, 1985. 'Themes in the Mediation of Social Conflict', *Journal of Social Issues*, vol. 41, no. 2, pp. 179–98.

Lankford, Maeve, 1994. *Economic Inequality and the Northern Ireland Conflict: An Analysis of Public Policy and Resource Allocation in a Divided Community.* Unpublished PhD Thesis, University of Bradford.

Lederach, John Paul, 1995. *Preparing for Peace: Conflict Transformation across Cultures.* Syracuse, New York, Syracuse University Press.

Lee, Joseph J., 1989. *Ireland 1912–1985: Politics and Society.* Cambridge, Cambridge University Press.

Lijphart, Arendt, 1975. 'The Northern Ireland Problem: Cases, Theories and Solutions', *British Journal of Political Science*, vol. 5, pp. 83–106.

Mandel, Brian S. and Brian W. Tomlin, 1991. 'Mediation in the Development of Norms to Manage Conflict: Kissinger in the Middle East', *Journal of Peace Research*, vol. 28, no. 1, pp. 43–56.

McAllister, Brendan, 1993. *The Northern Ireland Conflict: A Mediation Response to Diverse Ideological, Theoretical and Strategic Approaches.* Briefing paper given to the National Conference on Peacemaking and Conflict Resolution, Portland, OR.

McAuley, James W, 1991. 'Cuchullain and an RPG-7: the Ideology and Politics of the Ulster Defence Association', in Eamonn Hughes (ed.), *Culture and Politics in Northern Ireland 1960–1990.* Milton Keynes, Open University Press, pp. 45–68.

McGarry, John, 1988. 'The Anglo-Irish Agreement and the Prospects for Power-sharing in Northern Ireland', *Political Quarterly*, vol. 59, no. 2, pp. 236–50.

McKeown, Ciaran, 1984. *The Passion of Peace.* Belfast, Blackstaff.

Mitchell, Christopher, 1981. *The Structure of International Conflict.* London, Macmillan.

Mitchell, Christopher, 1990. 'Necessitous Man and Conflict Resolution: More Basic Questions About Basic Human Needs Theory', in Burton (1990b), pp. 149–76.

New Ireland Forum, 1984. *Report.* Dublin, Government Stationery Office.

New Protestant Telegraph, September 1995. 'The Drumcree Victory'. Belfast, Protestant Telegraph Ltd, p. 4.

NICRC, 1971. *First Annual Report.* Belfast, NICRC.

NICRC, 1972. *Second Annual Report.* Belfast, NICRC.

O'Brien, Martin, 1993. 'The Justice of Peace', *Peace By Peace, Magazine of the Peace People.* October, p. 3.

O'Connell, James, 1985. 'Towards an Understanding of Concepts in the Study of Peace', in J. O'Connell and A. Curle, *Peace with Work to Do.* Leamington Spa, Berg, pp. 29–50.

O'Connell, James, 1990. 'Faith and Conflict in Northern Ireland', *The Month*, February, pp. 46–58.

O'Leary, Brendan, 1985. 'Explaining Northern Ireland: a Brief Study Guide', *Politics*, vol. 5, no. 1, pp. 35–41.

O'Leary, Brendan and John McGarry, 1993. *The Politics of Antagonism: Understanding Northern Ireland.* London, Athlone.

O'Leary, Cornelius, Sydney Elliott and R.A. Wilford, 1988. *The Northern Ireland Assembly 1982–1986: A Constitutional Experiment.* London, Hurst.

O'Malley, Padraig, 1990. *Northern Ireland: Questions of Nuance.* Belfast, Blackstaff.

O'Malley, Padraig, 1990a. 'The Anglo-Irish Agreement: Placebo or Paradigm?' in H. Giliomee and J. Gagiano (eds.), *The Elusive Search for Peace: South Africa, Israel and Northern Ireland.* Oxford, Oxford University Press, pp. 175–90.

Prein, Hugo, 1984. 'A Contingency Approach for Conflict Intervention', *Group and Organisation Studies*, vol. 9, no. 1, pp. 81–102.

Princen, Tom, 1991. 'Camp David: Problem-solving or Power Politics as Usual?' *Journal of Peace Research*, vol. 28, no. 1, pp. 57–69.

Prior, Jim, 1986. *A Balance of Power.* London, Hamish Hamilton.

Pruitt, Dean G. and Jerry Z. Rubin, 1986. *Social Conflict: Escalation, Stalemate and Settlement.* New York, Random House.

Rea, Desmond (ed.) 1982. *Political Co-operation in Divided Societies.* Dublin, Gill & Macmillan.

Rolston, Bill, 1987. 'Alienation or Political Awareness: The Battle for the Hearts and Minds of Northern Nationalists', in P. Teague (ed.), *Beyond the Rhetoric: Politics, the Economy and Social Policy in Northern Ireland.* London, Lawrence & Wishart, pp. 58–80.

Rose, Richard, 1971. *Governing Without Consensus: An Irish Perspective.* London, Faber & Faber.

Rothman, Jay, 1989. 'Developing Pre-Negotiation Theory & Practice', *Policy Studies*, no. 29. Jerusalem, Leonard Davis Institute.

Rothman, Jay, 1990. 'A Pre-negotiation Model: Theory and Training', *Policy Studies*, no. 40. Jerusalem, Leonard Davis Institute.

Ruane, Joseph and Jennifer Todd, 1990. ' "Why Can't You Get Along With Each Other?": Culture, Structure and the Northern Ireland Conflict', in Eamonn Hughes (ed.), *Culture and Politics in Northern Ireland 1960–1990.* Milton Keynes, Open University Press, pp. 27–43.

Smith, Alan and Alan Robinson, 1992. *Education for Mutual Understanding: Perceptions and Policy.* Coleraine, Centre for the Study of Conflict, University of Ulster.

Smith, James D.D., 1995. *Stopping Wars: Defining the Obstacles to Cease-Fire.* London, Westview Press.

Spencer, Dayle and William Spencer, 1991. *The International Negotiation Network: a New Method of Approaching Some Very Old Problems.* Atlanta, GA, Carter Center.

Spencer, Dayle, William Spencer and Honggang Yang, 1992. 'Closing the Mediation Gap: the Ethiopia/Eritrea Experience', *Security Dialogue*, vol. 23, no. 3, pp. 89–99.

Stephens, John B., 1988. 'Acceptance of Mediation Initiatives: a Preliminary Framework', in C.R. Mitchell and K. Webb (eds.), *New Approaches to International Mediation.* London, Greenwood Press, pp. 52–73.

Todd, Jennifer, 1987. 'Two Traditions in Unionist Political Culture', *Irish Political Studies*, vol. 2, pp. 1–26.

Todd, Jennifer, 1990. 'Northern Irish Nationalist Political Culture', *Irish Political Studies*, vol. 5, pp. 31–44.

Touval, Saadia, 1982. *The Peace Brokers: Mediators in the Arab–Israeli Conflict 1948–79*. Princeton, NJ, Princeton University Press.

Two Traditions Group, 1983. *The Two Traditions*. Belfast, Two Traditions Group.

Ulster Young Unionist Council, 1986: *Cuchulain the Lost Legend: Ulster the Lost Culture?* Discussion Paper No. 2. Belfast, UYUC.

Unionist Task Force, 1987. *The Task Force Report: An End to Drift*. Belfast.

Vayrynen, Raimo (ed.) 1991. *New Directions in Conflict Theory: Conflict Resolution and Conflict Transformation*. London, Sage/ISSC.

Wehr, Paul, 1986. 'Conflict Resolution Studies: What Do We Know?' *Dispute Resolution Forum* (Washington, DC, NIDR) April, pp. 3–4, 12–13.

Whyte, John, 1990. *Interpreting Northern Ireland*. Oxford, Clarendon.

Wilson, Harold, 1979. *Final Term: The Labour Government 1974–76*. London, Macmillan.

Wilson, Tom, 1989. *Ulster: Conflict & Consent*. Oxford, Blackwell.

Wright, Frank, 1973. 'Protestant Ideology and Politics in Ulster.' *European Journal of Sociology*, vol. 14, pp. 213–80.

Wright, Quincy, 1951. 'The Nature of Conflict', *Western Political Quarterly*, vol. 4 no. 2.

Zartman, William and Saadia Touval, 1985. *International Mediation in Theory and Practice*. Boulder, CO, Westview Press.

Index

Adamson, Ian, 18
Alliance Party of Northern Ireland, 27, 30, 36, 111, 125, 126, n. 9
Allister, Jim, 18
Anglo-Irish Agreement, 22, 180, n. 1
    as framework for Brooke talks, 46–7, 49, 98–100, 102, 105–8, 115–16, 123, 127, 129, n. 1
    development of, 38–9
    in Strand 1 discussion, 112
    paragraph 29 of, 121
    unionist reaction to, 17, 42–5, 99, 103
Anglo-Irish Intergovernmental
    Conference, 42, 102, 106–10, 112, 121, 123
Anglo-Irish Secretariat at Maryfield, 42, 44, 99, 106–8, 113, 117
Arab–Israeli conflict, 97
arbitration, 98, 116, 120–2, 129, 213–14
Areas of Common Agreement, discussion papers on, 112–13
Arthur, Paul, 35, 44
Assembly, the Northern Ireland
    (1973–4), 30, 49; (1982–6), 35, 37–9, 98
Atkins, Humphrey, 34–5, 172
Attwood, Alex, 188
Aughey, Arthur, 20, 44
Azar, Edward, 39, 71–4, 76, 80
    see also Azar and Moon
Azar, Edward and Chung-In Moon, 70, 72, 76

Bercovitch, Jacob, 69–71, 74–6, 77, 79, 80, 97
Bew, Paul and Henry Patterson, 40
Blair, Brenda, 118
Bleakley, David, 52, 55
Bloomfield, David, 72, n. 7
Boal, Fred and David Livingstone, 17
Bosnia, 217
Boulding, Kenneth, n. 8
British Social Attitudes Survey, 114, 184
Broder, Joan, 147, 163–4, 178, 180–3, 224
Brooke Initiative, 22, 46, 96–132, 168, 193, 222

events of, 105–15
Brooke, Peter, 46–7, 96–132, 172, 193, 222, 224, n. 9, n. 11
Bruce, Steve, 16
Burton, John W., 69, 71–2, 77
Burundi, 217

Campbell, Gregory, 16
Camp David, 97
Carrington, Peter, 111
Carter, Jimmy, 97
ceasefires (1994), 6, 48, 221
    see also IRA ceasefire
Central Community Relations Unit
    (CCRU), 190, 192
    and complementarity, 178–80
    and funding, 153, 155–6
    and Local District Councils, 163–4, 187, 189
    development of, 65, 135–8
    relationship with CRC, 140–1, 157, 162–3, 165, 169, 174, 191
Chichester-Clark, James, 26
Cohen, Stephen and Harriet Arnone, 78
Collins, Gerry, 99, 102, 106–10, 114, 117, 121, 130
Committee on the Administration of
    Justice (CAJ), 146, 225
Community Relations Council (CRC), 224, 225, n. 18
    and complementarity, 158–68, 174–5, 181–2, 191–2, 194, 197
    and Cultural Traditions Group, n. 13
    and funding, 152–8
    and structural approach, 185–8
    background, 133–8
    establishment and structures, 138–43, 169, 171
    relationship with CCRU, 179–80
    within cultural approach to conflict management, 50–1, 65–6
Community Relations Officers (CROs), 137, 163–4, 187
community relations work, typology of, 137, 142, 154, 173, 177, 182
conciliation, 97, 116, 118–19, 130, 213
Conflict Mediation Network (CMN), 147, 177–8, 224
Conservative Party, British, 104, 114

236

Constitutional Convention (1975 6), 32-3, 36, 49, 98, 171

consultation, 97, 116, 119-20, 130, 132, 213

contact hypothesis, 60, 64, 66, 134
  see also Hewstone and Browne

contingency model of intervention, 80-90, 94, 198, 203-4, 207, 210, 215

core funding programme, 153 4

Corrymeela, 51, 55, 59, 61-2, 150

Council of Ireland, 30

criteria for a model of conflict management, 94
  see also embedded criteria; generalised criteria

Cross-Community Contact Scheme, 137, 153

Crozier, Maurna, 135

Cruthin, the, 18

Cuchúlain, 18

cultural approach to conflict management
  and community relations, 139
  and complementarity, 169, 179, 191-3, 219
  and criteria, 91, 213 14
  and resolution, 84, 93 4, 196
  and structural approach to conflict management, 189, 194 5, 222 3
  definition of, 50
  development of, 59 65, 173 4, n. 6

cultural heritage curriculum, 137, 179

Cultural Traditions Group, 135, 137, n. 13

Curle, Adam, 69

Dáil Éireann, 30, 40

Daly, Cahal, 22

Darlington Conference, 27, 31

Dawn Magazine, 61 3

Democratic Unionist Party (DUP), 16, 18, 30, 33, 36, 45, 96, 102, 111, 188, n. 4

Department of Agriculture for Northern Ireland, 153

Department of Education for Northern Ireland (DENI), 58 61, 63, 135, 137, 143, 153, n. 16
  Community Relations Division, 58, 60
  Youth Service, 153, 163

Deutsch, Morton, 9, 77

devolution, 104
  see also power-sharing

direct rule, 27, 58, 122

Downing Street Declaration (1993), 22, 47, n. 1

Dublin, Irish government in
  and Anglo-Irish Agreement, 38, 42, 44 8, 98
  and Brooke Initiative, 96, 99, 105-10, 113-16, 121 6, 128 30
  and Irish dimension, 25, 29 30, 36
  and New Ireland Forum, 39, 41
  relationship with Brooke, 102 3
  see also Dáil Éireann

Education for Mutual Understanding (EMU), 137, 179, 189 90, n. 16

embedded criteria, 91 2, 203 4, 208, 211 15, 220

Ethiopia/Eritrea, 97

ethnic conflict, 217 18

Executive, the power-sharing (1973 4), 30, 58, 98, 171

Farrell, Michael, 9

Faulkner, Brian, 30 1, 33

Feeny, Brian, 21

Fianna Fáil, 41

Fine Gael, 41, 46

Fisher, Roger, 88

Fisher, Ronald J., 69, 80
  see also Fisher and Keashley

Fisher, Ronald J. and Loraleigh Keashly, 68, 77, 116, 118 23, 126, 196
  and contingency model, 80 3, 85 8, 93 4, 198 9, 203
  and criteria, 205, 207, 209 12
  typology of TPI, 97 8

Fitt, Gerry, 30 1

Fitzduff, Mari, 138 40, 144 5, 149, 152, 156, 158 60, 165, 176, 180, 183, 185 90, 212, 224 5, n. 18
  typology of community relations work, 137, 154, 173, 175, 177, 182, 193
  see also Frazer and Fitzduff

FitzGerald, Garret, 35, 38 43, 102

focused community relations work, 63 4, 66, 133 4

Foster, John Wilson, 19

Framework Document (1995), 22, 48, n. 1

Frazer, Hugh and Mari Fitzduff, 52-3, 63, 133 5, 142, 148, 157, 164, 173, n. 18

Gallagher, A.M., 18

Galtung, Johan, 75, 198 9

generalised criteria, 90–2, 204, 207–11, 220

Government of Ireland Act (1920), 25

Green Paper, *The Future of Northern Ireland* (1972), 27–9, 170

Griffiths, Hywel, 53–4, 56–7

Harding, Sandra, 199

Haughey, Charles, 35, 41, 107, 109, 113, 124

Hayes, Maurice, 52, 54–6, 137, 171

Heath, Edward, 30–1

Hewstone, Miles and Rupert Brown, 60, 134
see also contact hypothesis

Hinds, Joe, 146, 148–55, 159–62, 165, 167, 183–5, 188–90, 194, 225, n. 13

Hoffman, Mark, 5, 80–1

holiday organisations, 59–64

Holiday Organisations Group, 61–2

Holst, Johan Jorgen, 199

human needs, 72

Hume, John, 38–40, 42–3, 124

Hume–Adams dialogue, 47

Hunter, John, 10–14, 22

Hurd, Douglas, 37

integration (of Northern Ireland in the UK), 36–7, 104, 114, n. 10

International Body on Arms Decommissioning, 48

intervention, typology of, 81, 97–8
see also third party intervention

Ireland Act (1949), 26

Irish Constitution, its claim to Northern Ireland, 42, 110, 112, 115, 128

Irish dimension, 25, 28–31, 36, 41–9, 98, 100, 102, 121, 123

Irish government, *see* Dublin, Irish government in

Irish National Liberation Army (INLA), 34

Irish Republican Army (IRA), 18, 35, 40, 46, 114, 130, 177, 221, n. 9
IRA ceasefire (1994), 4, 221–2

Israel/Palestine, 71, 206–7

Jackson, Alvin, 9, 14

joint sovereignty/joint authority, 39–41

Keashly, Loraleigh, *see* Fisher and Keashly

Kelman, Herbert C., 69

Kenny, Anthony, 45

King, Tom, 46, 102, 105–6, 118, 127, 172

Kissinger, Henry, 97

Kressel, Kenneth and Dean C. Pruitt, 76

Labour Party, British, 114

Labour Party, Irish, 41

Lankford, Maeve, n. 17

Lebanon, 71

Lederach, John Paul, 200–3, 212

Lee, Joseph J., 40

Lijphart, Arendt, 10, 20

Local District Councils, 58, 137, 142, 144, 163–5, 179
Community Relations programmes, 187, 289, 192–3, n. 9, n. 19

Major, John, 111, 115, 126, 130

Mandell, Brian and Brian Tomlin, 97

Mason, Roy, 34

Mawhinney, Brian, 106, 113, n. 13

Mayhew, Patrick, 47, 115, 131

Mayhew Talks, 22, 105, 131, 193

mediation, 74
see also power mediation; pure mediation

Millar, Frank, 118, 125

Ministry for Community Relations, Stormont government, 51–8, 65, 136

Mitchell, Christopher, 75

Molyneaux, James, 43–4, 104, 108–9, 111, 114, 117–18, 123–5, 131–2
see also Unionist leaders

McAllister, Brendan, 177

McAuley, James, 18

McCusker, Harold, 43, 103

McGarry, John, 34, 39
see also O'Leary and McGarry

McKeown, Ciaran, 61

McKittrick, David, 146, 156, 164, 225

Neave, Airey, 34

needs theory, 72

New Ireland Forum, 19, 21, 37–42

New Protestant Telegraph, 15

Northern Ireland Community Relations Commission (NICRC), 51–8, 65–6, 133, 138–9, 156–7, 166, 171–2, 176, 179, n. 5

Northern Ireland Labour Party (NILP), 27, 33, n. 5

Northern Ireland Office (NIO), 65–6, 106, 135–6, 153

Northern Ireland Peace Forum (NIPF), 62, 134, 173

Northern Ireland (Temporary Provisions) Act (1972), 26
Northern Ireland Voluntary Trust (NIVT), 133, 142-3, 153

O'Brien, Martin, 146, 153, 155, 162-3, 173, 175-8, 181-3, 185-6, 225
O'Connell, James, 10, 78
O'Leary, Brendan, 10, 12
O'Leary, Brendan and John McGarry, 98-9, 102, 120-1
O'Leary, Cornelius *et al.*, 37-8
O'Malley, Padraig, 36, 40-3, 45, 100, 103
Orange Order, 52, 183

Paisley, Ian, 15, 45, 108-13, 117, 123, 125
see also Unionist leaders
Paisley, Ian Jr, 188
Palestine *see* Israel/Palestine
peace groups in Northern Ireland *see* reconciliation groups
peacekeeping, 98, 116, 126-7, 213-14
Peace People, 61-2, 146, 173, 175-6, 225
Powell, Enoch, 37
power mediation 98, 116-17, 119, 122-6, 128-30, 213-14
power-sharing 25, 28-9, 31, 36-7, 45, 47-9, 98, n. 19
Prein, Hugo, 78
Princen, Tom, 97
Prior, Jim, 35-7, 101, 121
problem solving, 74-5
problem-solving workshop, 71, 73-5
Progressive Unionist Party (PUP), 16
Protestant and Catholic Encounter (PACE), 55, 59, 61-2, 146, 176-7, 225
protracted social conflict (PSC), 71, 73, 220, 222
Pruitt, Dean G. and Jerry Z. Rubin, 70
see also Kressel and Pruitt
pure mediation, 97, 116-18, 128-9, 213
Pym, Francis, 30

Quaker Peace Education Project (QPEP), 147, 225-6, n. 15

Rea, Desmond, 13
reconciliation groups in Northern Ireland, 139, 142, 146, 148, 151, 158-9, 161, 183-4, 189, n. 6

Rees, Merlin, 31-3, 171-2
resolution approach, the, 1, 79, 200, 219
and complementarity, 93-4, 196-7, 204-6
and contingency model, 84-6, 88
and cultural approach to conflict management, 84-6, 167-8
and embedded criteria, 211-14
and settlement approach, 131-2
and typology of TPI, 116
definition, 67-9
Robinson, Peter, 102
Rolston, Bill, 39
Rose, Richard, 15
Rothman, Jay, 118
Royal Ulster Constabulary (RUC), 45
Ruane, Joseph and Jennifer Todd, 24
Rwanda, 217

settlement approach, the, 1, 67, 79, 97, 219
and Brooke Initiative, 131
and complementarity, 93-4, 196-7, 204-6
and contingency model, 84-8
and cultural approach to conflict management, 168
and embedded criteria, 211-14
and structural approach to conflict management, 84-6
and typology of TPI, 116
definition, 69-71
Sinn Féin, 35, 39-41, 46, 100, 180, 187, 193, 222, n. 9
British government dialogue with, 47, 222
Smith, James D. D., 128
Social Democratic and Labour Party (SDLP), 21, 27, 30-4, 36-41, 43, 46-7, 96, 100, 102, 104-15, 120, 124, 126, 188
Brooke's relationship with, 104-5
Spencer, Dayle and William Spencer, 97
Spencer, Dayle *et al.*, 97
Standing Advisory Commission on Human Rights (SACHR), 133, 135, 142, 154, 164
Stephens, George B., 118
Steven, Ninian, 111
Stewart, A.T.Q., 9
Stormont government/parliament, 24-7, 48, 51-3, 56-7, 120, 171
Strand 1 talks, 111-13, 123-4, 129-31
Strand 2

Strand 2 contd.
  dispute over independent chair,
    110–11, 117, 130
  dispute over venue, 110–11, 117, 123,
    130
strands *see* three-stranded talks formula
structural approach to conflict
  management
  and complementarity, 168–9, 173–4,
    179, 191–5
  and criteria, 91, 213–14
  and cultural approach to conflict
    management, 173–4, 221–3
  and settlement approach, 84, 93–4,
    131–2
Sunningdale conference (1973), 30–1,
  110, 119

'talks about talks', 106
Teebane Cross, killings at, 114–15
Thatcher, Margaret, 34–5, 37, 42–4,
  102, 106–7
third party intervention (TPI), 67, 70,
  73–5, 78, 80, 89, 121, 219
three-stranded talks formula, 46–7, 96,
  98, 103, 108, 110, 131
Todd, Jennifer, 14, 20
  see also Ruane and Todd
Touval, Saadia, 78
  see also Zartman and Touval
Tyrrell, Jerry, 147, 162–3, 184, 225–6,
  n. 15

Ulster British political culture, 15–17
Ulster Defence Association (UDA), 16,
  18, 176
Ulster Democratic Party (UDP), 16
Ulster loyalist political culture, 15–16
'Ulster Says No', 45, 99

Ulster Unionist Party (UUP), 16, 18, 27,
  30–1, 33, 36–7, 43, 45, 96, 102, 104,
  113–14, n. 4
Ulster Volunteer Force (UVF), 16, 176
Ulster Workers' Council (UWC), 31–2
Ulster Young Unionist Council (UYUC),
  18–19
Unionist leaders, 106–7, 110, 113,
  125–6, 130
  see also Molyneaux, James; Paisley, Ian
Unionist parties, Brooke's relationship
  with, 103–4
Unionist Party of Northern Ireland
  (UPNI), 33
unionist preconditions for talks, 106–8
United Nations (UN), 219–20
United Ulster Unionist Council (UUUC),
  31

Vayrynen, Raimo, 77
Victim Support NI, 224

Wehr, Paul, 76
Whitelaw, William, 27–30, 32, 170–1
White Paper, *Northern Ireland: A Framework
  for Devolution* (1981), 35–6
White Paper, *Northern Ireland Constitutional
  Proposals* (1973), 28–9, 32, 170–1
White Paper, *The Northern Ireland
  Constitution* (1974), 32–3
Whyte, John, 1, 3, 9–12, 18, 200, 216
Wilson, Harold, 26, 31–2
Wilson, Tom, 44
Women Together, 55, 59, 61–2
Wright, Frank, 15
Wright, Quincy, 88

Zartman, William and Saadia Touval,
  70, 78